Islamic Monetary Economics and Institutions

Muhamed Zulkhibri • Turkhan Ali Abdul Manap
Aishath Muneeza
Editors

Islamic Monetary Economics and Institutions

Theory and Practice

Springer

Editors
Muhamed Zulkhibri
Islamic Development Bank
Islamic Research and Training Institute
Jeddah, Saudi Arabia

Turkhan Ali Abdul Manap
Islamic Development Bank
Islamic Research and Training Institute
Jeddah, Saudi Arabia

Aishath Muneeza
Maldives Centre for Islamic Finance
Haveeree Hingu, Maldives

ISBN 978-3-030-24004-2 ISBN 978-3-030-24005-9 (eBook)
https://doi.org/10.1007/978-3-030-24005-9

This Springer imprint is published by the registered company Springer Nature Switzerland AG
The registered company address is: Gewerbestrasse 11, 6330 Cham, Switzerland

Foreword

In conventional monetary economics, monetary policy is often associated with the main function of the central bank. The central bank controls supply of money and monitors inflations through changes in interest rates, i.e., policy rates using monetary policy instruments such as open market operations, reserve requirement, and others. On the other hand, from an Islamic economics perspective, the monetary policy should be based on the real sectors (productive sector of the economy) with a minimum role of money and money market to perform economic exchanges and generate economic activities. Thus, the central bank in the Islamic monetary system should have determined the policy rate based on actual market transactions. However, contemporary Islamic monetary system, if there are any, is heavily influenced by conventional economic thoughts. This phenomenon has motivated Islamic economists to develop a comprehensive theoretical framework of Islamic monetary economics for the economic system.

On this occasion, this book addresses some of the critical issues such as the interest-free economy, financial system, and monetary policy framework from Islamic perspectives and discusses practical experiences of countries practicing both conventional and Islamic banking system. This book aims to answer questions related to the theoretical, empirical, and practical issues related to Islamic financial systems such as macroprudential policy and regulation by taking stock of recent academic and policy research on the topic. The major portion of this book is the outcome of the IRTI-MCIF Research Workshop on "Islamic Monetary Economics and Institutions: Theory and Practice" on November 2017, which was jointly organized by the Islamic Research and Training Institute, Islamic Development Bank, and Maldives Centre for Islamic Finance in Maldives.

I believe that money and monetary institutions could play an extremely important role in transforming an economy in ways good and bad. Hence, the discussion provided in this book is of great importance for policymakers, academics, and practitioners alike. In this respect, I would like to express my appreciation to authors who have penned down their thoughts which are scholarly well-grounded. The authors also provide important insights to readers around the world to undertake further research on Islamic monetary economics. I would like to take this opportunity to congratulate the editors for their tremendous efforts to publish this important book. Finally, I would also like to extend my deepest gratitude to those who have provided important contributions and rendered their support for making this publication a reality.

Islamic Research and Training Institute,
Islamic Development Bank,
Jeddah, Saudi Arabia
February 2019

Sami Ibrahim Al-Suwailem

Preface

Monetary economics has relatively more subtleties than other fields in economics, because monetary theory has been developed much later than the theory of value. The latter has acquired its neoclassical structure in a world of barter. Keynes' (1930, 1936) attempted revolution against neoclassical economics was frustrated by the fact that his ideas have falsely likened by Hicks (1937) as truly neoclassical ideas, taking the form of the IS-LM model. This has been admitted by Hicks himself (Hicks 1980), but the admission was generally ignored by mainstream economists. Keynes protested that the theory of value was devoid of money and expressed his strong objection to Says or Walras law. But the neoclassics have succeeded to drown his ideas first under their forced but false interpretation of his theory as an IS-LM model and later under the sad misrepresentation of Phillips curve as a tradeoff between inflation and unemployment and making it a part of Keynes' ideas. This way, the neoclassics succeeded in replacing their counterrevolution with the revolution of Keynes.

Similarly, Islamic monetary economics, like conventional monetary economics itself, whether according to the perspective of Keynes or the neoclassical perspectives under Lucas (2004) microfoundations or Friedman's (1969) monetarism, has a significant share of subtleties. Islamic monetary economics in particular brings forth numerous intellectual issues that require close scrutiny. Early writers in Islamic economics, because they were not specialists, were unaware of such subtleties. Similarly, those who focus on Islamic jurisprudence, or *fiqh*, and historical analysis do not reach deep enough into economic analysis. One of the ignored subtleties of Islamic economics is that it stands in the same line of revolution against neoclassical economics with Keynes. However, it does not accept Keynes' institutional structure of a market economy.

The prohibition of interest-based loan contract and its replacement with a multitude of finance contracts varying from partnership in product, partnership in profit, investment agency, and sale finance have confronted Islamic economics with numerous challenges. The first and utmost is the challenge of providing a monetary and financial structure that is capable of issuing and allocating money to different uses without relying on the classical loan contract and carrying out monetary policy without anchorage to the rate of interest. This has been done a long time ago (Al-Jarhi 1981, 1983). Al-Jarhi's model ignores the neoclassical fixation with microfoundations. It introduces an institutional structure that replaces interest-based finance and encompasses money creation and allocation and monetary and fiscal policies.

Money is issued in the form of central bank investment deposits (investment accounts) or central deposits (CDs) placed with banks on the basis of PLS. Banks here use a multitude of Islamic finance contracts. They are similar to universal banking in their ability to take equity in the firms they finance, while providing other types of financing without the use of the classical loan contract. In addition, and as a part of their financing modes, they trade in commodities, which they ultimately offer for sale to their customers seeking finance. Such banks have the advantage of mixing and matching between contracts to avoid information asymmetry and the related risks of adverse selection and moral hazard. This stands in contrast with commercial banks which have to cope with the weaknesses of the classical loan contract. Islamic banks are therefore similar in their use of such strategy to universal banks which use a combination of equity and loan finance to reduce information asymmetry.

The return on CDs flows back to the central bank as seigniorage and ends in the government budget. The government has to finance its non-income-earning activities through taxation. For income-earning activities, it must stand in line with the private sector to apply to banks for finance. In addition, a great deal of public services, like education and health care, would be provided through *awqaf* (private trusts or endowments). The government must therefore encourage the establishment of *awqaf* as a way to reduce the tax burden. In addition, a redistribution levy or *zakah* is collected by government and non-government organizations and used to finance microprojects whose titles are transferred to some of the poor each year as a way of self-employment.

Al-Jarhi's model replaces fractional reserves with total reserves, because the former redistributes wealth in favor of bank shareholders against the public. In addition, the money multiplier, which is the basis for fractional reserves, assumes that banks need excess reserves before they can make loans. At first primary deposits are made, creating excess reserves, which allow loans to be made, leading to the creation of derivative deposits. Each new loan uses up a part of excess reserves. Money creation by banks stops when excess reserves have fallen to zero. In reality, Holmes (1969) and Keen (2011) claimed a completely different process that runs in the opposite direction. Banks provide loans first, which produces derivative deposits. If banks ended with insufficient reserves, they would have a two-week period in which to get more reserves from the central bank. The central bank has to provide those reserves, unless it is willing to cause a bottleneck for production and commerce.

Empirical research initiated by Moore (2001) and later independently by several, including Kydland and Prescott (1990), confirmed this operational aspect of central banking, as observed early by the then senior vice-president of the New York Federal Reserve, Alan Holmes. Another disadvantage of fractional reserves is that it weakens central bank control over the money supply; besides, as a tool of monetary policy, it leads to instability. Naturally, when Al-Jarhi built his model in 1981, he abandoned the idea of fractional reserves.

In Al-Jarhi's model, the central bank in an Islamic monetary system issues central deposit certificates (CDCs), as a negotiable money-market instrument available to banks and the public. It is traded in an open market. Its proceeds supplement CDs. Meanwhile, CDCs are equity-based certificates, whose holders effectively own a proportional common share of the income-earning assets created by banks on the asset side of their balance sheets. They are placed by the central bank in all banks in the economy, based on its own criteria, that give efficiency the highest priority. The rate of return on CDCs is the average rate of return on the most diversified (least risky) PLS investment portfolio in the economy. It therefore represents the average profitability on assets in the economy. At the same time, it represents the rate of growth of the economy.

The central bank anchors monetary policy to its rate of return (RCDC). In contrast to the rate of interest, it is market determined and not just an administered price. The anchorage of monetary policy to the RCDC and the use of issuing more CDs and trading CDCs in the open market in order to fine-tune monetary growth would be the alternative policy tools in an Islamic monetary system. In such an economy, it would be easy for the central bank to achieve a degree of price stability that cannot be reached in a conventional economy, due to anchoring the policy to a good market measure of the rate of growth of the economy. Needless to say, Al-Jarhi's structure excludes the possibility of risk and debt trading, which are the operational tools through which speculation is carried out in financial markets.[1] This also eliminates the Ponzi scheme that is used to lend money to finance speculation (Keen 2011). In addition, Al-Jarhi's model assumes away the use of ruses to mimic conventional finance, as it is now common in the contemporary Islamic finance industry (Al-Jarhi 2016). Ruses are eliminated directly by central bank regulations and their effective enforcement.

Al-Jarhi's contribution has been ignored by some, as it has been published in the early 1980s with minimum exposure. However, it remains a viable alternative to the Friedman rule for bringing the *nominal* rate of interest to zero, while keeping the conventional institutional setup. The latter has been implicitly presumed by several Islamic economists, which rendered their analysis beyond logical and practical justifications. A particular example is the Chapra-Mirakhor pure profit-and-loss-sharing or *PLS* model[2] (Chapra 1996; Mirakhor and Zaidi 2007).

Monetary management according to this school would be conducted in a conventional fashion, while paying attention to the control of government deficits as well as banks borrowing from the central bank. Usually, conventional monetary policy tools are listed as Islamic tools, after excluding the discount rate, by keeping the required reserve ratio, which has been repeatedly discredited, as well as

[1] Obviously, risk and debt trading are prohibited by Islam.

[2] This school should also include many others, like M. N. Siddiqui, Khurshid Ahmad, Muhammad Uzair, and many others.

interest-free loans. Such loans would not be strictly interest-free unless the central bank implements a policy of absolute price stability. Naturally, this cannot be done without the institutional arrangement that generates the RCDC which is equal to the rate of economic growth. The pure PLS model takes for granted the way money supply is determined in the conventional system with the recognition that the government's and banks' appetite to borrow must be curtailed. Somehow, the average profit rate for the whole economy becomes common knowledge, is used as an anchor to monetary policy, and serves a benchmark for investment.

The failure of the Friedman rule to gain wide acceptance among intellectuals and policymakers is a good indicator that the problem of interest cannot be surmounted without an institutional change. The pure PLS model provides some of this but not enough to shake the system, except through switching completely to profit sharing, which is usually presented without spelling out specific institutional changes in the monetary and financial sector.

Al-Jarhi (1981) has a ready-made formula for rebuilding the blocks of an Islamic monetary and financial sector. However, the formula insists on continuing to provide finance through both partnership in profit and product and debt creating sale finance. Still this approach leaves the application of an acceptable formula for dividing finance between partnership and debt-creating means, to the monetary authority.

One of the variants of the pure PLS models is presented in this book by M. Fahim Khan. Like the neoclassics, Khan treats money as a medium of exchange without spelling out the underlying *raison d'être* of money. This does not appear at the outset as much of a problem. However, it may just happen that an explicit treatment of why money is being held in the model may provide a wider perspective of economic analysis. The explicit treatment of the *raison d'être* of money exposes some of the disadvantages of conventional finance (Al-Jarhi 2017b). Meanwhile, Khan's model stands out as an explicit formulation of his perception, within the pure PLS approach.

The model as expected from this approach narrows down monetary policy to setting the proper supply of money by the monetary authority under the rule of total reserves. The application of this rule has been rather cryptic in many writings. Al-Jarhi (1981, 1983) is more explicit about its rationale and mechanism. The application of total reserves needs more details regarding the types of deposits taken by banks in an Islamic monetary system and how they would be treated singly or across the board. However, the central bank application of total reserves, which would be unprecedented, would provide sufficient practical information to guide such details.

Ankara Social Sciences University
Ankara, Turkey

Mabid Ali Al-Jarhi

References

Al-Jarhi, M. (1981). *Towards an islamic monetary and financial system: Structure and implementation*, The Arabic Publications Series (5). Jeddah: King Abdulaziz University.

Al-Jarhi, M. (1983). A monetary and financial structure for an interest-free monetary economy: Institutions, mechanism and policy. In Z. Ahmad, M. Iqbal and M.F. Khan, (Eds.), *Money and banking in Islam*. Islamabad: Center for Research in Islamic Economics, Jeddah, and the Institute of Policy Studies.

Al-Jarhi, M. (2016). An economic theory of Islamic finance regulation. *Islamic Economic Studies. 24*(2), 1–44.

Al-Jarhi, M. (2017b). Inefficiencies in search models: the case for Islamic finance. *MPRA Paper No. 82064.*

Chapra, M. U. (1996). Monetary management in an Islamic economy, *Islamic Economic Studies. 4*(1), 1–35.

Friedman, M. (1969). The optimum quantity of money. In *The optimum quantity of money and other essays.* Chicago: Macmillan.

Hicks, J. R. (1937). Mr. Keynes and the "Classics": A suggested interpretation. *Econometrica. 5*(2), 147–159.

Hicks, J. R. (1980). IS–LM: An explanation. *Journal of Post Keynesian Economics. 3*(2), 139–154.

Holmes, A. R. (1969). Operational constraints on the stabilization of money supply growth. In F. E. Morris (Ed.), *Controlling monetary aggregates* (pp. 65–77). Boston: Federal Reserve Bank of Boston.

Keen, S. (2011). *Debunking economics: The Naked Emperor Dethroned.* London: Zed Books.

Keynes, J. M. (1930). *Treatise on money.* London: Macmillan.

Keynes, J. M. (1936). *The general theory of employment, interest and money.* London: Macmillan.

Kydland, F. E. & Prescott, E. C. (1990). Business cycles: Real facts and a monetary myth. *Federal Reserve Bank of Minneapolis Quarterly Review, 14*(2), 3–18.

Lucas, R. E. (2004). Keynote address to the 2003 HOPE Conference: My Keynesian education. *History of Political Economy, 36*(S1), 12–24.

Mirakhor, A. & Zaidi, I. (2007). Profit-and-loss sharing contracts in Islamic finance. Ch. 4, *Handbook of Islamic Banking* (pp. 49–63). Cheltenham: Edward Elgar Publishing.

Moore, B. J. (2001). Some reflections on endogenous money. In L.-P. Rochon and M. Vernengo (Eds.), *Credit, interest rates and the open economy: Essays on horizontalism* (pp. 11–30). Cheltenham: Edward Elgar.

Contents

About the Guest Editor

Mabid Ali Al-Jarhi is a Professor of Economics and Finance, ASBU, and Coordinator of the project of establishing the International Center for Islamic Economics and Finance, ASBU-ICIEF. He has also held the posts of Professor of Economics and Finance at INCEIF; Professor of Economics and Finance at Hamad Bin Khalifa University, Qatar; President of the International Association for Islamic Economics; and Member and Secretary of Shari'ah Board, Dubai Financial Market. He has taught economics at American and Egyptian universities and participated in establishing several Islamic banks and in introducing Islamic banking laws. He also has publications in economics and Islamic economics and is the former author of a yearly economic report on Islamic finance in the UAE and the Gulf. He holds an M.A. in economics from the University of Illinois and UCLA and a Ph.D. in economics from USC.

About the Editors

Muhamed Zulkhibri is a Senior Economist at the Islamic Research and Training Institute, Islamic Development Bank (IRTI-IsDB), Saudi Arabia. Prior to joining the IRTI-IsDB, he worked at the Central Bank of Malaysia and policy research institutions in various capacities. Previously, he lectured at the Universiti Putra Malaysia, Malaysia, and University of Nottingham, United Kingdom. His current research focuses on monetary economics, macroeconomics and economic development, and Islamic banking and finance. He published extensively in various publications in leading academic journals, industry reports, books, and the financial press. He is the co-editor of the *Islamic Economic Studies* journal. He earned a Ph.D. in economics from the University of Nottingham, United Kingdom.

Turkhan Ali Abdul Manap is a Senior Research Economist at the Islamic Research and Training Institute, Islamic Development Bank (IRTI-IsDB), Saudi Arabia. Prior to joining IRTI-IsDB, he was an Associate Professor of Economics in the Faculty of Economics and Management Sciences, International Islamic University Malaysia (IIUM), where he taught various courses for bachelor, master, and Ph.D. level. His research interests include macroeconomics, (Islamic) capital market, financial stability, and stress testing for Islamic financial institutions. He has spoken and attended various national and international conferences on economics and finance issues, while his research papers have appeared in numerous academic journals. He obtained his Ph.D. in economics from IIUM.

Aishath Muneeza of INCEIF is one of the key founders of Islamic finance in Maldives. She is the first female Deputy Minister of Ministry of Islamic Affairs and the first chairperson of the Hajj Pilgrimage Fund of Maldives. She was also the former Deputy Minister of Ministry of Finance and Treasury of Republic of Maldives. Currently, she is the chairperson of Maldives Centre for Islamic Finance. She has published books and numerous articles on Islamic finance, and her research areas include legal studies & corporate governance applicable to Islamic finance. She structured the first corporate sukuk, sovereign private sukuk, and Islamic Treasury instruments for the government of Maldives, and she has played the key role in offering Islamic finance products by more than 11 institutions. She also designed the first Islamic microfinance scheme offered in Maldives. She sits in Shariah advisory committees of financial institutions offering Islamic financial services such as Islamic hire purchase and takaful. She also holds the position of chairperson of three different in-house Shariah committees. She is the chairperson of Shariah Advisory Council of CMDA, the capital market regulatory authority of Maldives since 2011. She is the only registered Shariah Adviser for structuring capital market instruments in Maldives and she is a registered Shariah Advisor at the Securities Commission of Malaysia. The Islamic capital Market framework of Maldives was designed by her. She has won numerous national and international awards for her service in Islamic finance industry including the Rehendhi award, the highest award conferred to women by the government of Maldives. She is also a role model and a mentor for females who aspire to build their careers in Islamic finance industry and is the Vice President of Women on Boards, an NGO advocating women representation on boards of companies. She is an invited speaker in Islamic finance conferences and events held in different parts of the world. She is listed in 2017 as number 7 among the 50 Influential Women in Business and Finance by ISFIRE, which is an official publication of Islamic Bankers Association based in London, and she is among the most influential 500 in Islamic Economy. She is a member of the Association of Shariah Advisors in Islamic Finance Malaysia (ASAS), Malaysia. She obtained her Phd from the International University of Malaysia in law.

Contributors

Guest Editor

Mabid Ali Al-Jarhi Ankara Social Sciences University, Ankara, Turkey

Editors

Turkhan Ali Abdul Manap Islamic Research and Training Institute, Islamic Development Bank, Jeddah, Saudi Arabia

Aishath Muneeza Maldives Center for Islamic Finance, Male, Maldives

Muhamed Zulkhibri Islamic Research and Training Institute, Islamic Development Bank, Jeddah, Saudi Arabia

Contributors

Samir Alamad Aston University, Birmingham, Aston, UK

Azam Ali State Bank of Pakistan, Karachi, Pakistan

Atiq-ur-Rehman Department of Econometrics and Statistics, Pakistan Institute of Development Economics, QAU Campus, Islamabad, Pakistan

Muhammed Habib Dolgun INCEIF, Selangor, Malaysia, and Central Bank of the Republic of Turkey, Ankara, Turkey

Omar Javaid Institute of Business Management, Karachi, Pakistan

M. Fahim Khan Islamic Centre for Research in Islamic Economics, Minhaj University, Lahore, Pakistan

Tanveer Kishwar Jinnah University for Women, Karachi, Pakistan

Adam Ng Research Management Centre, INCEIF, Petaling Jaya, Selangor, Malaysia

Ibrahim A. Onour School of Management Studies, University of Khartoum, Khartoum, Sudan

Trisiladi Supriyanto Ibnu Khaldun University Bogor, Bogor, Indonesia

Md. Akther Uddin School of Business, University of Creative Technology, Chittagong, Bangladesh

Etsuaki Yoshida Kyoto University, Kyoto, Japan

List of Figures

List of Tables

Chapter 1
Introduction

Muhamed Zulkhibri and Turkhan Ali Abdul Manap

1.1 Overview

This book provides original works and provoking ideas covering the theoretical and empirical issues related to monetary economics and policy in an Islamic financial system. It highlights several options for authorities and regulatory bodies regarding monetary policy, regulation and instruments for Islamic financial institutions. This book also discusses Islamic monetary policy effects on economic growth, financial stability and resilience to shocks in practice. In a nutshell, this book addresses some critical issues such as the interest-free economy and financial system, monetary policy framework from Islamic perspectives, and country-specific experiences with Islamic monetary policy in a dual banking system. The book is organized into two parts: (i) theoretical foundation of monetary policy from Islamic perspectives and and (ii) monetary policy, policy instruments, and financial stability in Islamic economy.

In Part 1 of this book, M. Fahim Khan in Chap. 2 discusses a macroeconomic model that reflects economic features of an Islamic economy, implied in the Islamic system of property rights (elaborated in the literature on *Fiqh-al-Mal*) and in the Islamic system of exchange (elaborated in the literature on *Fiqh-al-Buyu'*). In Chap. 3, Md. Akther Uddin analyzes the re-emergence of Islamic economics and finance, especially Islamic banking in the middle of the last century, which has motivated economists to develop a comprehensive theoretical framework of modern Islamic banking. Chap. 4 by Atiq-ur-Rehman summarizes a number of logical flaws and socioeconomic consequences of the monetary policy, which shows that interest-based monetary policy would be harmful to the society. Chap. 5 by Omar Javaid uses the work of Greif (1994), Hollingsworth (2000), and Schumpeter (2006) to

M. Zulkhibri (✉) · T. A. A. Manap
Islamic Research and Training Institute, Islamic Development Bank, Jeddah, Saudi Arabia
e-mail: turkhanali@isdb.org

M. Zulkhibri et al. (eds.), *Islamic Monetary Economics and Institutions*,
https://doi.org/10.1007/978-3-030-24005-9_1

develop a criterion to understand the mainstream monetary framework of modern western economics as explained by the Austrian school of economic thought, which is then compared with the Islamic monetary perspective.

In Part 2, Azam Ali, Muhamed Zulkhibri, and Tanveer Kishwar in Chap. 6 examines the earlier efforts to revive and promote risk-sharing modes of financing (*Musharakah* and *Mudarabah*) with respect to the current international and local practices of Islamic banking industry. Chapter 7 by Ibrahim Onour determines the cost of deposit insurance premiums in a number of Islamic banks operating in GCC, Malaysia, and Bangladesh and assesses the relevance of insurance policy in each country with regard to risk-based versus flat-rate premium policy. Chapter 8 by Trisiladi Supriyanto provides a fundamental research to find a replacement of the Central Bank of Indonesia (BI) policy rate as a reference rate for the Islamic financial transactions. Chapter 9 by Samir Alamad provides an analysis of the real practices of stress testing as a risk management tool within an Islamic financial market that exists in a highly sophisticated and regulated financial center. Finally, Chap. 10 by Muhammed Habib Dolgun and Adam Ng examines the short-term and long-term determinants of Islamic banks' liquidity holdings. This chapter also provides the empirical analysis of liquidity risk management of Islamic banks in Malaysia.

Finally, in Chap. 11, Etsuaki Yoshida discusses recent trends of Islamic Fintech and sheds light on its potential effects on the stability of a financial system specifically in a dual banking system. The study argues that Fintech can provide practical solutions to criticisms relating to Islamic financial products, by focusing on the aspect of its networking capability. Given the rapid pace of development in this sector, the study argues that Islamic Fintech will contribute to mitigating financial instability, by promoting financial inclusion and involving the more diversified flow of funds.

1.2 Theoretical Foundation of Monetary Policy from Islamic Perspectives

In conventional monetary economics, monetary policy is often associated with the main function of the central bank. The central bank controls the supply of money and inflation through changes in interest rates, i.e., policy rates using monetary policy instruments such as open market operations, reserve requirement, and others. Although economists do not agree about how monetary policy affects the economy, under the most basic framework, the central bank is able to change the magnitude of the money supply. Monetary policy actions are usually done through open-market operations, in which short-term government debt is exchanged with the private sector. This policy-induced movement in the monetary base is to have any impact beyond their immediate effects on the central bank's balance sheet in a way that leaves the real value of the monetary base unchanged. Hence other agents must lack the ability to offset them by changing the quantity or composition of their own liabilities. The central bank will be able to modify the quantity of money in circulation only if it is able to influence the demand for money.

According to the theory of money demand, demand for money consists of three factors: (1) transaction demand, (2) precautionary demand, and (3) speculative demand. Increases in interest rate lead to an increase in the opportunity cost of money and in turn people prefer to hold less money. A shift in policy leads to a change in the money supply that, for a given money demand, leads to a change in money-market interest rates. This resulted in a negative relationship between the interest rate and the speculative demand for money. Furthermore, the demand for money is not only dependent on the interest rate. However, factors such as expectation of future inflation, income, and wealth in the economy, i.e., investment, have a large effect on demand for money. Consequently, in practice, monetary authorities should have precise information to be able to formulate appropriate monetary policy decisions.

In Islam, economic activities are carried out with the prescription of *Shari'ah*, i.e., the Islamic law, which is based on the *Quran* and the *Hadith*. In Islamic economics, the interest rate should not have any role in the economy. The general principles of Islamic finance could be summarized, but not limited, to the following: prohibition of interest, thus encouraging the profit and loss sharing mechanism; prohibition of contractual uncertainty; and prohibition of gambling, speculation, or excessive risk-taking in carrying out transactions, which makes the instruments and mechanism of monetary policy different from conventional economics. As argued by Chapra (1996), the absence of interest rate in Islamic economics and the existence of some institutions like *Zakat* minimize the speculative demand for money and make total demand for money in Islamic economics more stable. In this way, the demand for money in Islamic economics consists of only transaction demand and precautionary demand.

In the early era of Islamic economics, the functions of the monetary system were assigned to *Bayt al-Mal*, which has similar duties as the central bank today with government fiscal policy added. *Bayt al-Mal* was considered the central finance house for the Islamic empire, with many branches in all Islamic countries. Its main functions were issuing currency and maintaining the stability of its value. To conduct this function, *Bayt al-Mal* was established and formed with three different institutions (Mannan 1986): (1) *Bayt al-Mal al-Khaṣ*, (2) *Bayt al-Mal*, and (3) *Bayt al-Mal al-Muslimin*. *Bayt al-Mal al-Khas* is a treasury of a country that has a special function in managing government funds, such as the private expense of the caliphate, and some other special expenses. Since money at that period is composed of silver and gold coins (Dirham and Dinar), while fiat money and credit were not applicable, monetary expansion mechanism did not actually exist as it is in recent times.

As illustrated in this book, in the early Islamic state, there was no basis for changes in the money supply through discretionary measure as there was no banking system and commodity money was extensively used instead. Moreover, credit had no role to play in creating money because (i) credit was used only among few traders and (ii) the rules governing the use of promissory notes and negotiable instruments were in such a way that the credit was not capable of creating money (As-Sadr 1989). The above rules affected the equilibrium between the goods market and the money market based on cash transactions. Instead, he argues that profit-sharing ratio, refinance ratio, public share of demand deposits, value-oriented allocation of credit, and *qard al-hasan* ratio were distinctive Islamic monetary policy instruments.

The central bank in the Islamic monetary system can determine the profit rate based on actual market transactions as proposed in this book by Fahim Khan. The central bank can apply these rates as a policy tool on its own analysis of the economic conditions prevailing in the real sector and the macroeconomic objectives to be achieved in the economy. He further argues that the strategy to move gradually toward 100% reserve requirement and slowly reducing debt contents in the investments in the economy deserves immediate attention from the policy makers in Muslim countries that intend to transform their financial and monetary system to conform to *Shari'ah*. Hence, it is important for the monetary authority and the *Shari'ah* authority to jointly analyze the costs and benefits of monetary policy objectives and tools before a policy is implemented.

1.3 Monetary Policy, Policy Instruments, and Financial Stability in Islamic Economy

Contemporary Islamic monetary system is heavily influenced by conventional economic thoughts. In the real-world practice, only one of the components of the Islamic monetary system, the prohibition of *riba*, has been attempted through the limited use of Islamic finance products/contracts. A full-fledged Islamic banking system has yet to be implemented. The prevailing system is still dominated by the conventional model, which is the use of fiat money and fractional reserve banking system. Under this system, interest rates play an important role as an instrument and transmission process of monetary policy to ensure price and financial stability. The monetary authority also uses monetary policy in the form of monetary control to achieve the targeted rates of inflation.

Due to several logical flaws in the contemporary monetary policy, the policy may actually lead to the opposite of its desired goals, as indicated by the existence of a cost channel of the monetary transmission mechanism. It is suggested that the monetary authorities should broaden the spectrum of research and should abandon the blind faith in the so-called demand channel of the monetary transmission mechanism. Tight monetary policy that is exercised by increasing interest rates by many authors is shown to have negative implications for the employment and equity. In other words, lowering the interest rate can possibly enhance the employment and equity. In addition, a number of economies such as the USA and Japan have interest rate virtually close to zero. This could indicate that zero interest regimes are not necessarily an obstacle for higher growth and better employment. This provides support to Islamic economists who argue that a better economic system would be interest-free.

In the theory of Islamic economics, monetary policy is based on the real sectors (productive sector of the economy) with the minimum role of money and money market to perform economic exchanges and generate economic activities. Monetary policy in Islam does not only influence the money supply but also support the growth of the real sectors. In an Islamic economic setup, the dichotomy between the monetary sector and the real sector is absent as the monetary sector is always associated with the real sectors. Islamic economy requires the direct linking of financing with the underlying asset so that any financing activity is clearly and closely identified with the real economy (Iqbal and Mirakhor 2007). Hence, the prohibition of interest and the implementation of Islamic finance contracts, which are embedded in the Islamic economic system, connect these two sectors. Many scholars believe that Islamic finance is more stable in both long- and short-term, as opposed to the conventional interest-based system, which is very sensitive to any changes in interest rate. Moreover, to conduct Islamic monetary policy, innovative *Shari'ah* compliant financial instruments and products are inevitable.

In this context, it is suggested that the central bank's credit facilities, as lender of last resort, are important for the development of the Islamic money market. In certain countries, the credit facility is provided in the form of *Commodity Murabahah* arrangement or temporary accommodation of money on a free-of-charge basis. In others, central banks may provide credit with returns tied to *Mudarabah* deposit rates of banks receiving credit or may provide liquidity through buyback arrangements for specified *Sukuk* held by the banks. *Shari'ah*-compliant alternatives to repo, based on *Sukuk*, which can be priced in relation to market returns at an appropriate level, could be considered. Central banks in all jurisdictions impose reserve requirements on the deposit liabilities of the banks. Additionally, the central bank can offer *Wadiah* certificates as evidence of deposits placed with it, with returns tied to the average of the return on interbank *Mudarabah* investments.

On the other hand, this book argues that the use of participatory or profit loss sharing instruments like *Mudarabah* and *Musharakah* has been substantially absent, particularly on the asset side of the bank's balance sheet. When some Islamic banks execute *Musharakah* financings, it lacks true risk sharing as the return on *Musharakah* financing is based on the conventional pricing benchmark. These practices have attracted criticism on the current model of Islamic banking. Hence, efforts should be made to evolve participatory financing modes. For instance, in the case of Pakistan, the Steering Committee established by the Government of Pakistan has promoted the use of these instruments (*Mudarabah* and *Musharakah*) for Islamic banking. Moreover, all reports of high-level commissions and committees have recommended that participatory financing like *Musharakah* and *Mudarabah* is the spirit of Islamic finance and therefore may be promoted.

Liquidity risk is one of the important issues that need attention in terms of resilience of the Islamic banking sector. While there are several studies on the performance, growth, and efficiency of Islamic banks, empirical studies from the regulatory and supervisory perspectives are limited. In this line of research, this book contributes to the debate by providing a more recent evidence on Malaysian

Islamic banks' liquidity risk management perspectives. Their assessment shows that total assets, deposits, inflation, government bonds, capital adequacy, and interbank interest rate show positive significant relations with liquidity. On the other hand, the CDS rate of the country, statutory reserves, and *Sukuk* stocks show negative relations with the liquidity. The essence of the study indicates that market liquidity influences banks' liquidity, and banks' liquidity responds to the profitability of Islamic banks. Hence, by designing mitigating mechanisms both at the macro-level and micro-level is essential for the safety and profitability of Islamic banks.

A wave of development in information and communication technology (ICT) has completely reached the huge continent of the financial industry, and financial services highly enhanced by ICT are recently called Financial Technology or "Fintech." Fintech has been reshaping the financial services industry with the level and speed of innovation. In recent years, Islamic finance has also enjoyed the benefit of this growing Fintech. Originally, money is a conceptual existence, and theoretically, notes and coins contain no value by themselves under the current fiat money standard. As a result, financial services are well-harmonized with ICT that deals with data processing and can expect infinite varieties of forms of financial services even in the near future.

This book illustrates recent trends of Islamic Fintech and sheds light on its potential effects on the stability of a financial system. While growth of Islamic finance was evident not just in its market volume but in product development as well, the industry has often been criticized by academic scholars that the current practice of Islamic finance is not in the direction of pursuing its objectives, or *Maqasid al-Shari'ah.* Fintech can provide practical solutions to these criticisms, by focusing on the aspect of its networking capability. As a conclusion, increasing application of Fintech in Islamic financial system will contribute to mitigating financial instability, by promoting financial inclusion and involving the more diversified flow of funds.

1.4 Conclusion

The lack of understanding and confusion about Islamic economics in general, Islamic monetary economy in particular, can be attributed to the virtual absence of formal descriptions of the theory underlying the proposed system. It should be clear that "loan" and "equity" are not only of two different legal natures but also very different in economic consequences.[1] The monetary authority should gradually shift its mind-set from conventional monetary operation to dual monetary operation as a first step to approach an Islamic monetary system. However, under the current environment, optimum dual monetary policy can be achieved by adopting rate of profit as a benchmark policy rate, so that the goal of distributive social well-being and equity as well as minimizing inefficiency can be realized.

[1] In mainstream economic textbooks, money and capital markets are treated as loan and separated from one another by the length of the loan period.

The use of *Shari'ah* reference rate as a substitute for monetary policy rate and as a monetary operation tool is very important in determining the rate of profit for Islamic financial transactions. Theoretically, Islamic financial institutions should calculate the level of the profit and loss sharing itself based on the financing and market profit and company operational incomes. As proposed in this book, rate of profit should be used as a monetary policy tool to promote economic growth, and Islamic financial institutions should not benchmark their rate of return or margin to the market interest rate. Islamic financial institutions should establish their own market rate of return or margin based on the actual return in the real sector. In other words, Islamic financial institutions should gradually shift from interest rate benchmarking to profit and loss sharing return benchmarking.

Contemporary Islamic economic and financial systems have been developed under the dominance of capitalistic conventional economic and financial systems. The domination of capitalism has a significant impact on the development of the Islamic financial system. A full-fledged Islamic financial system is yet to be established to implement its operations purely and wholly (*kaffah*) according to Islamic law. In addition, many Muslim economists still believe that capitalist economic system is better than Islamic economic system, due to the fact that many developed and developing countries including some Muslim countries have improved their economic well-being under the conventional economic system. There is a long way to go to implement the Islamic financial system with many constraints and limitations.

References

As-Sadr, K. (1989). Money and monetary policies in early Islamic period. In B. Al-Hasani & A. Mirakhor (Eds.), *Easy on Iqtishad: The Islamic approach to economic problems* (pp. 199–217). Silver Spring: Nur Corp.

Chapra, M. U. (1996). Monetary management in an Islamic economic. *Islamic Economic Studies, 4*(1), 14–15.

Greif, A. (1994). Cultural beliefs and the organization of society: A historical and theoretical reflection on collectivist and individualist societies. *Journal of Political Economy, 102*(5), 912–950.

Hollingsworth, J. R. (2000). Doing institutional analysis: Implications for the study of innovations. *Review of International Political Economy, 7*(4), 595–644.

Iqbal, Z., & Mirakhor, A. (2007). *An introduction to Islamic finance*. Singapore: John Wiley & Sons (Asia).

Mannan, M. A. (1986). *Islamic economics, theory and practice*. Hodder and Stoughton: Cambridge.

Schumpeter, J. A. (2006). History of Economic Analysis (reprint). London: Routledge.

Part I
Theoretical Foundation of Monetary Policy from Islamic Perspectives

Chapter 2
Monetary Economics and Macroeconomic Model for an Islamic Economy

M. Fahim Khan

2.1 Introduction

Demand for and supply of liquid assets at an aggregate level can have different effects on the economy, which may be of concern to the managers of economy at macro level. Money market is currently considered in all economies as an important economic institution affecting aggregate demand in the economy. The economics of this institution is, therefore, needed to be understood to effectively manage the demand for and supply of money. In contemporary world, no economy can afford to leave the supply of and/or demand for money unregulated. Every economy has a monetary system supervised and regulated by a monetary authority. This requires a monetary policy. Muslim economies in contemporary world are no exception.

In a secular economic perspective, it is impossible for a market economy to think of regulating a monetary system without interest-based tool. The interest, which in Islamic terminology is equivalent to *riba*, is strictly prohibited to be used directly or indirectly in any transaction. With a growing interest in contemporary Muslim economies to conform their economic system to economic principles of Islam in all dimensions of the economy, the question arises how the monetary sector and monetary policy will be managed in such an economy where interest cannot exist in any form.

The Islamic economists[1] emphatically argue that market economy can never be void of alternative tools in the market, if interest is not allowed to exist in the market in any form. Most popular tool, alternative to interest, is the rate of return on capital in the market. Logically, it makes a lot of sense. Irrespective of religious prohibition of interest, the prevailing rate of return on investment in the economy is obviously a better alternative than the interest rate in the economy for monetary management.

[1] See Zarqa (2017).

M. F. Khan (✉)
Islamic Centre for Research in Islamic Economics, Minhaj University, Lahore, Pakistan

M. Zulkhibri et al. (eds.), *Islamic Monetary Economics and Institutions*,
https://doi.org/10.1007/978-3-030-24005-9_2

The argument is that a market economy cannot be short of policy tools to regulate monetary sector, even if interest does not exist in the economy.

Despite these theoretical claims, none of the contemporary Muslim economies are implementing monetary policy without interest or quasi-interest rates. The economies that intend to change their financial and monetary system still face the question, "how the monetary sector and monetary policy will be managed in the absence of interest." This study tries to answer this question in two scenarios:

1. In the scenario of an "Islamic" economy that would work, in contemporary economic and financial environment, in full conformity with Islamic law (*Shari'ah*) in all its economic dimensions
2. In the scenario of a contemporary Muslim economy that is not an "Islamic" economy in the above sense, but intends to eliminate interest from the economy, in a gradual process to ultimately make the economic system to conform to economic principles of Isla

Conventional economic theory that makes interest an inevitable and indispensable monetary policy tool and hence a core principal in the monetary economics is the Keynesian approach. Before attempting to answer the question "how the monetary sector and monetary policy will be managed in the absence of interest," we need to know what macroeconomic model we can assume within which we can answer this question. But there is no view available what macroeconomic model underlies in the "Islamic" economy that operates in full conformity of *Shari'ah* or in the contemporary Muslim economy that is looking forward to eliminating interest.

Currently, macroeconomics is understood under two distinct macroeconomic models; one is called Classical or Neo-classical approach and the other is referred to as Keynesian approach. In the absence of any knowledge of specific macroeconomic model underlying an Islamic economy in theory or any contemporary Muslim economy in practice, we may assume one of the two existing approaches that we may consider more relevant to describe a theoretical "Islamic" economy or a present-day Muslim economy.

We then try to determine the nature, dimensions, and significance of monetary economics and monetary policy for an Islamic economy in theory as well as for a Muslim economy in contemporary world. We first discuss below, which of the two existing approaches, Classical or Keynesian, can more closely be relevant for describing an Islamic economy (not contemporary Muslim economy) and what would be its monetary economics and monetary policy in the framework of the selected approach. The chapter will then discuss the same for a contemporary Muslim in economy.

2.2 Macroeconomic Model for an "Islamic" Economy

We can only assume the following features for an "Islamic" economy if it enforces and implements Islamic law of property rights (*Fiqh al-Mal*) and its laws for exchange (*Fiqh al-Buyu'*) in letter and spirit.

1. It is a market economy because the economy is based on a system of private property rights and enforces sanctity of property rights, which in turn creates markets in the economy.
2. The market structure in the economy is strictly based on Islamic laws for exchange as explained in the Islamic literature called *Fiqh al-Buyu'*.
3. The enforcement of Islamic laws of exchange as elaborately explained in *Fiqh al-Buyu'* will ensure the following features in the market:

    (a) Perfect information about products (the law minimizing the information asymmetry and moral hazard minimized).
    (b) Freedom of entry and exit in the market (even meeting the supplier outside the market, depriving the sellers an opportunity to face the entire set of potential buyers, is prohibited by law).
    (c) Prohibition of acquiring market power (prohibition of monopoly, monopolistic competition, hoarding, etc.), depriving the buyers to negotiate with the variety of sellers or suppliers.
    (d) Transaction cost is minimized by proper documentation and enforcement of all provision of Islamic laws of exchange

If Islamic law relating to property rights and their exchange is implemented in letter and spirit, we can safely claim that the markets in the economy will always be in equilibrium and that the economy will always be a balanced economy in terms of efficiency, equity, and other dimensions of the economy.[2] While Classical macroeconomic model only assumed this, Islamic system ensures this by the enforcement of the Islamic law of property rights and Islamic system of exchange. If enforced, Islamic system ensures that the equilibrium is achieved. We also assume that since the Islamic economy in theory will always be in equilibrium, the current real national income will be the income at the equilibrium level, and that this level is determinable. The equilibrium is determined by real variables only. This is more

[2] Though there is no proof for this statement, but it can be easily visualized that the Islamic system of property rights and rules of exchange in the market do not negate the proof of existence of general equilibrium in market economy as provided by Arrow and Debreu. However, in Islamic economic perspective, it does not make sense to use the term equilibrium for the economy because the term is relevant only for the market segment of an economy. Islamic economic system creates by law a segment beyond market, which is a substantial part of an Islamic economy meant to take care of equity considerations in the economy. The conventional economic theory ignores this segment by labeling it as philanthropy. In Islamic perspective, there is no reason to ignore it as an integral part of economy (for detailed discussion on this, see Khan 2017 on Economics of Philanthropy). Islamic economists have yet to prove a balance in the theory of "Islamic" economy, moving beyond general equilibrium in market segment in the economy.

or less the Classical macroeconomic model in conventional economic literature but without the presence of interest in the economy.

There are strong reasons that if an economy decides to be an Islamic economy, then Classical approach rather than Keynesian approach would be more relevant to describe macroeconomic model of an Islamic economy. The Classical macroeconomic model makes the following assumptions for an economy:

1. Markets are free and competitive. Markets are always clear and any surplus or deficit in any market is self-correcting.
2. Prices of goods and services are flexible including the rent/wage of factors of production, so that all, goods and factor, markets are in equilibrium.
3. Supply creates its own demand and demand in all markets equals demand. "Invisible" hand determines the prices.
4. Money only affects price and wage, and there is no money illusion that will require holding money only for the sake of enjoying its accumulation. All savings (income not consumed) are therefore invested rather than accumulating stockpiles of gold and silver.
5. Savings are equal to investment.

There will hardly be a dispute that any of these features will be missing if the economy is operating within *Shari'ah* framework in letter and spirit.

For Classical theory, the above features of an economy are a matter of assumption, but for Islamic economy, they are a matter of law that is required to be strictly enforced. There is nothing in *Shari'ah* or Islamic law governing Islamic economic dimensions to contradict any of the above features of an economy, in theory. *Fiqh al-Mal* that outlines the Islamic system of property rights and *Fiqh al-Buyu'* that elaborately explains Islamic rules and regulations for exchange will ensure above features in an Islamic economy. On the other hand, Keynesian model is simply a denial of the existence of the above features in an economy. In other words, Keynesian approach simply explains how an economy should be managed if it deviates from the assumptions of Classical macroeconomic model. In this scenario, we can safely say that monetary policy and monetary economic framework of Classical macroeconomic model will be relevant to discuss monetary economics and monetary policy of an "Islamic" economy. This will be only a theoretical perspective. It will not be valid for present-day Muslim economy.

This chapter, therefore, needs to explain monetary policy for contemporary Muslim economies that decide to eliminate interest from their economy in a gradual move toward making their economy completely Islamic economy[3] in a framework different from Neo-classical framework. Though the Classical approach was later changed to Neo-classical approach, the approach continues to be valid to describe "Islamic" macroeconomic model to a large extent in theory. The Neo-classical

[3] Elsewhere, I have argued that in converting a present-day Muslim economy into an Islamic economy, the starting point should be eliminating *Faqr* and *Maskanah* and developing institutions that will promote exchange beyond the market for the benefit of members of the society who cannot meet their survival needs from the market. A note in this respect is appended to this chapter.

approach that relaxes the assumptions of time and space to allow international trade and intertemporal choice, therefore, remains relevant for describing Islamic economy. The intertemporal choice though considers forward markets for goods on future dates; yet, it is under the assumption that "no market exists at any future date" and all market transactions are completed for the existing market and this is in line with the Islamic laws of exchange.[4]

Under Neo-classical assumption, if an inefficient equilibrium happens to exist, then either the system of property rights and rules of exchange will bring the equilibrium back to efficient equilibrium or the system of property rights and laws of exchange are not being precisely defined or their enforcement/implementation is not perfect to realize the assumptions of the model. Neo-classical approach also does not raise any issue about the conflict between efficiency and equity. The two issues can be separately dealt with and resolved within the general equilibrium conditions in Neo-classical framework. It only requires redistributing the initial endowment. Islamic economy is regulated by two sets of private property rights and sets of rules of exchange. There are private property rights that take care of the efficiency in the economy and there are property rights that relate to right of others in private property rights or the rights belong to public social interests that take care of equity and sharing of prosperity in the economy. There are rules for exchange in market that take care of efficiency in the economy, and there are rules for exchange beyond market that takes care of equity and sharing of prosperity in the equity.[5] Even if both sets of economic institutions (private property rights and rules for exchange in market) and other property rights and the rules for exchange beyond market) may not always produce optimum outcome with respect to either of the two goals (efficiency and equity), the objectives of *Shari'ah* will still be fulfilled because "the average of two equally good bundles is better than either of the two bundles" as classical approach implies.

On the other hand, the Keynesian model, which later on changed to Neo-Keynesian model and then to New Keynesian model, remains irrelevant to describe macroeconomic model for an "Islamic" economy. New Keynesians though made some reconciliation with Neo-classical approach and do not advocate any more use of expansive monetary policy for increasing output and employment in the short run and instead believe that it would be inflationary; yet, they advocate using monetary policy for stabilization. New Keynesian Dynamic Stochastic General Equilibrium (DSGE) models advocate the role of central bank in adjusting the nominal interest rate to stabilize inflation, which will in turn stabilize output. But these New Keynesian models too continue to remain invalid to provide a description of "Islamic" economy if such economies will apply economic principles of Islam in letter and spirit.

---

[4] *Fiqh al-Buyu'* though allow price to be paid for a delivery now and also allow a payment of price now for a future delivery but do not allow both price and delivery to be determined in the future.

[5] For further discussion on market and beyond market economics in Islamic perspective, see Khan (2017).

The conclusion of above discussion is that assuming Classical or Neo-classical macroeconomic model will be more relevant to draw lessons for the monetary sector and monetary policy in an "Islamic" economy. Keynesian approach even in its "New" perspective will not make sense for an "Islamic economy."

A bird's eye view of the present-day Muslim economies would reveal that these economies hardly conform to the features of the Classical macroeconomic model. Keynesian model therefore becomes relevant for a Muslim economy, by default. This chapter, therefore, discusses monetary economics and monetary policy in two scenarios. In the first scenario, we discuss it in the framework of Classical theory and draw lessons for monetary economics and monetary policy for an "Islamic" economy in theory. Section 2.3 covers this scenario. In the second scenario, we discuss monetary economics and monetary policy for the present-day Muslim economies by taking into account Keynesian approach by default. Section 2.4 covers this scenario. It will be a futile exercise to develop monetary economics and monetary policy in Islamic perspective for the present-day Muslim economies, taking Classical approach.

2.3 Monetary Economics in an "Islamic" Economy

As concluded in the previous section, Islamic approach to property rights and exchange in the economy and Islamic norms about money and money demand can safely allow us to analyze monetary economics and monetary policy in the framework of Classical macroeconomic model. In Islamic economy, real money balances held by the households are not expected to create any utility (i.e., money illusion does not exist). Let us have an overview of how the monetary system of an Islamic economy may look under the assumption of Classical macroeconomic model. Money in an Islamic economy will only be a medium of exchange. Money in the hand of households is the asset that is readily available either for routine household transaction needs or for investment needs. This definition is directly visible in the Islamic system of property rights and Islamic rules of exchange. Apparently, neither in early history of Islam nor in current practice in Muslim economies, money is assumed to have a demand for its own sake (no one feels psychological happiness from just feeling the touch or sight of money).

In this scenario, the money therefore will not have any influence on real economy. To start with, let us assume that money stock is determined only by the monetary base and there is no credit created by the banking as counterpart of money stock to determine money supply in the economy. The only instrument for controlling money supply in an "Islamic" economy therefore will be the monetary base. Money supply, hence, will be exogenous in an "Islamic" economy. The government will decide the money supply. Money supply is exogenously given. Nothing precludes in Islamic perspective, to let the central bank or monetary authority determine exogenously the size and growth rate of money for the economy.

We can visualize that money demand will emerge out of household savings that are meant to be invested as soon as suitable investment opportunity arise except for that proportion that is needed for transaction and precautionary purposes. Households saving, thus, will have two components. One part will be held for meeting routine daily transactions and meeting such contingency needs that may arise unexpectedly. The other part will be meant for investment in a suitable opportunity to make their savings grow. There may be a time lag between savings created for the purpose of investment and savings actually deployed in investment opportunities. The households may find some beneficial use, in this interim period, for these savings while waiting for the opportunities to deploy them in long-term investment opportunities that would ensure them an expected rate of return matching with their time value of money.[6] Islamic economy may develop certain institutional framework to utilize these idle funds for whatever short term they are available (while searching opportunity for deploying them in suitable investment). For a temporary utilization of money in hand, they may get attracted only by such opportunity that it may or may not earn any significant income but will be liquidated as soon as households see proper investment opportunity to deploy them. The central bank may determine from nationwide data real short-run rate of return in the commodity market or in stock in market. These rates can be the basis for issuing government securities as well as for issuing short-run financial instruments in the private sector. Such deployment in short-term investment opportunities without using interest rate in any form can be possible only in the government sector or in the segment of an Islamic economy that is referred to as Third Sector in the contemporary Islamic economic literature. Details on such institutional possibilities in an Islamic economy have been discussed in Khan (2015, 2017). Modeling an Islamic economy with such monetary sector is left to the next generation of economists that will see Islamic economy in the making.

If Islamic laws of exchange in market (*Fiqh al-Buyu'*) are implemented in letter and spirit, we can safely assume that the markets will always be in equilibrium. Islamic economic system creates, by law, a segment beyond market that takes care of social welfare and equity considerations in the economy. The conventional economic theory ignores this segment by labeling it as philanthropy, but in Islamic perspective, there is no reason to ignore it. It is indeed an integral part of economy.[7] We also assume current real national income will always be at its full potential equilibrium level and that this level is determinable by real variables.[8] In this theoretical framework, let us then understand the following dimensions of monetary economics.

---

[6] See Zarqa (2017) and Khan (2017) for Islamic perspective on investment decision and time value of money.

[7] See Khan (2017) for detailed discussion on this, particularly in the macroeconomic perspective of Islam.

[8] Basically, the assumption of classical macroeconomic model, but deliberately avoiding full employment equilibrium (see Appendix I).

Monetary sector in Islamic economy will have money supply (MS) and money demand (MD), both determined exogenously and there will be no money market. MS will be determined by monetary authority (in consultation with a board of economists and *Shari'ah* scholars). MD will be determined by households based on several exogenous factors. There will be no question of determining equilibrium or equilibrium conditions for monetary sector in this economy. The monetary sector will require a balance. Households will need to maintain a balance in holding money for meeting pure timely needs and money waiting for investment purposes. And monetary authorities need to maintain a balance in growth and inflation in the economy to decide level of money supply.

2.3.1 Demand for Money in "Islamic" Economy

Currently, demand for money in textbooks is dominated by Keynes' theory about motives behind holding money. Classical as well as Neo-classical economists and new Neo-classical economists reject Keynes' theories for demand for money. The demand for money for the love of it is a matter of mind-set. The mind-set that Islamic system of life creates is not in line with the mind-set implicit in the Keynesian approach. Classical approach on money demand is more in line with the Islamic teachings about money holdings. This approach is rational and realistic for majority of humanity.

We, therefore, assume that in Islamic perspective, money is demanded only as medium of exchange and it has no value in itself. There is no money illusion in the mind-set of a Muslim. On the contrary, the admonition in the *Quran*, "And those who hoard gold and silver and spend it not in the way of Allah – give them tidings of a painful punishment" (9:34), serves as deterrent to hold or accumulate money in hand for its own sake. Economic teachings of Islam provide motivation to spend, invest, or give away rather than hold it.

Textbook definition says, "*Money* is the set of assets in the economy that people regularly use to buy goods and services from other people."[9] We, therefore define demand for money as the set of (so-called liquid) assets that the households want to keep in hand either as readily available resources to buy goods and services or as resources waiting to avail an investment opportunity or to give away to seek divine pleasure.

Money demand affects aggregate demand and hence becomes relevant to give it a role in monetary policy. We now need to argue that there will be demand for money in an Islamic economy and this demand will be a stable function of such variables as income, price level, and rate of return on investment. If this is established, then this will make the case for developing monetary economics in Islamic perspective.

---

[9] Mankiw (2014)

2.3.2 Money Demand Function in "Islamic" Economy

Money in the hands of a Muslim has two components:

(a) *For pure time preference*. Households just want to have some money in hand to meet the needs for various routine transactions, to meet some precautionary needs, or to meet the demand for help from friends and relatives (a consideration particularly in Islamic framework). This demand may depend on several factors, all exogenous.
(b) *For investment purposes*. Households want to make more money from it to increase their wealth.

Let the money demand be represented by the following equation.

$$M_{\mathrm{d}} = M_0 + M_{\mathrm{i}} \tag{2.1}$$

where M_0 is money demand for pure time preference and M_{i} is the money available for investment. This is in fact one side of a coin. The other side of the coin is household savings, which are the base of monetary assets. Household savings also have two components:

(a) Savings to be kept in liquid form for current use
(b) Fixed savings to be kept in the form of income-generating assets

Let the savings be represented by the following equation:

$$S = S_0 + S_{\mathrm{i}}, \tag{2.2}$$

where S_0 is household savings to keep them liquid. This will be savings kept in hand as current resource to be used for meeting current needs and for unforeseen needs. S_{i} is meant to be invested to make it grow.[10]

The savings function in the economy would be like[11]

$$S = S(Y,R) \text{or } S = S_0 + aY + bR, \tag{2.3}$$

[10] In this discussion, we will avoid discussing specific macroeconomic variables and equations for an Islamic economy. We just keep in mind that the macroeconomic variables will be aggregate values of income (Y), consumption (C), savings (S), and investment (I), and there will be no interest rate, but market will not be short of some benchmark rate of return for making investment decision (R).

[11] We cannot go into the discussion of savings function, investment function, and equilibrium conditions in the real sector. This will require a whole macro model to be specified and discussed. In economics with Islamic perspective, I do not like to talk in terms of equilibrium and equilibrium conditions, because equilibrium refers to only economics in the market. But in Islamic economy, there is a lot of economics that happens beyond market where equilibrium makes no sense and we can only try to ensure balance.

where Y is the national income and R is the rate of return on investment. The investment function would be would be like

$$I = I(Y,R) \text{ or } I = I_0 + cY - d\mathrm{R} \tag{2.4}$$

In an Islamic economy, money demand, therefore, will be a part of the real sector of the economy. This will be determined endogenously, since an Islamic economy cannot theoretically assume that there will be opportunities of such investment whether, in the short or long run, which

(a) Can keep the principal amount intact
(b) Can be liquidated immediately on demand
(c) Still yield some return

Therefore, there will be no market in an "Islamic" economy.

The existence of interest-based lending and borrowing makes the above possible, but currently we cannot envisage that there can be any such possibility to investment money in short run with above features, in an Islamic economy where Islamic laws relating to property rights and exchange are enforced in letter and spirit. There will be, thus, no money demand for the sake of keeping liquidity in the form of investment in money market. The households will only hold an exogenously determined amount in hand to meet household's own contingencies and contingencies of others (neighbor, relative, and friends) *fisabilillah*. This will be M_0 as explained above and will not be a part of money market.[12] The other part of money demand will be only for purpose of availing available investment opportunities. This money demand will be part of the real sector and not of money market.

It is here that Islamic macro model will differ from Classical model. Classical model assumes savings are equal to investment ($S = I$). They have to assume this because the savings decisions taken by households may not all go to meet the investment demands from firms. The theory has to assume that nothing is leaked out of savings and all goes to investment. On the other hand, Islamic macroeconomic model will assume that part of the savings will be held in hand in liquid or quasi-liquid form called S_0 and S_i will be part of the real sector and will be equal to investment. Thus, the assumption (Eq. 2.4) mentioned in the beginning of this paper will be

$$M_i = S_i = I, \tag{2.5}$$

where I = investment, and Eq. (5) $M_i = S_i = I$ is a deviation from the classical macroeconomic model, which assumes that $S = I$ implying that there is no leakage from the economy. The difference $S\text{-}S_i = S_0$ does not go to the real sector but stays in the monetary sector representing money demand. S_0 *is the money demand.*

[12] There may exist lending from S_0, but it will be in the form of *Qard Hasan*, requiring no return from lending. Hence, this lending will not be part of money market.

The above deviation of Islamic economy from the perspective of classical model may apparently be regarded as a leakage of S_0 from the economy. But in the perspective of Islamic economy, S_0 is not leakage from the economy; it is leakage from the market segment of the economy only. Islamic economy has another formal economic segment operating beyond the market and S_0 becomes part of that segment. The economic implications of this leakage from the market segment into beyond market segment for the economy are not the subject for discussion here. This discussion will come when we discuss a complete macroeconomic model for an Islamic economy where equilibrium will not be the focus and instead some other terms will be needed to refer to balance rather than equilibrium in the economy. The term homeostasis from biology probably may be a more relevant term for describing balance rather than equilibrium in an Islamic economy.[13]

This is in theory. The actual proposition of demand for money in an Islamic economy, however, will be a matter of empirical testing when an "Islamic" economy comes into existence. It is possible that empirical evidence may show money demand to be endogenously existing, and if it happens then absolutely a new macroeconomic theory and model will need to be developed. Until this happens, we will assume that the theoretical scenario mentioned above for discussing monetary economics and drawing lessons for monetary policy will be valid in an Islamic economy.

2.3.3 Monetary Policy in "Islamic" Economy

Since money is simply a medium of exchange, a change in money supply will only change the price level, but the real income, the real wage and real rate of return on capital and level of real output in the economy will remain unchanged. According to the classical quantity theory of money, the price level has the following relationship with the money supply

$$MV = PT, \tag{2.6}$$

where M = money supply, V = velocity of money, P = price level, and T = real total output. In simple words, it means that a change in money supply (M) causes a proportional change in the price level (P).

Monetary policy in Islamic framework will only be a matter of deciding an optimal level of money supply to meet desirable inflation rate and growth target for the economy. The exercise to determine the level of money supply should therefore be a matter of central bank or monetary authority's decision that will be taken in consultation with an advisory board consisting of economists and *Shari'ah* scholars who will advise size of money supply, keeping in view economic and *Shari'ah*

[13] See Khan (2013) who discusses the relevance of methodology and jargon of biology which are more relevant for Islamic economics.

objectives for the economy based on ground realities. If need arises to expand output level and other *Shari'ah*-based macroeconomic objectives in the economy, an expansionary monetary policy may be considered to be formulated. The increase in the money supply will increase the money in the hands of households. Households would simply spend, invest, or give away the increased liquidity and hence increase the aggregate demand for goods and services. This will raise the price level. Real wages and real rental on capital goods will go down hence providing incentive to employ more labor and capital to produce more goods and services. The empirical test of this theory will be possible only when Islamic laws on property rights and exchange are adequately enforced in an economy.

So far, we excluded the credit created in the component of money supply and considered money stock (currency issued by the monetary authority) as the only source of money supply. In modern world, the financial system and monetary system are intertwined. Financial system provides credit to expand investment and consumption creates credit. Interest-based financial system then allows the credit to circulate in the market irrespective of the potential capacity of growth in the economy. The financial sector often lets the monetary sector grow way beyond the growth of real economy. This creates inflation and creates business cycles and hence instability in the economy and gives monetary policy a bigger role.

Can this happen in Islamic economy in the above-mentioned scenario? Financial system may exist in Islamic economy allowing credit-creating financing for investment as well as for consumption. But can this credit create money and money market? *Shari'ah* scholars, in principle, agree that this is not allowed in Islamic law. Banks can finance an economic activity on credit in Islamic way ensuring their *Shari'ah* permissible profit, but the credit created by the banks cannot be traded in the money market. Though *Shari'ah* scholars advising current practice of Islamic banking and finance in contemporary Muslim economies have found ways to create secondary market for the credit created in the process of financing investment and consumption, yet there are serious reservations from some *Shari'ah* schools as well as from Islamic economists on the permissibility to sell credit in the secondary market.

2.4 Islamic Perspective on Monetary Policy for Present-Day Muslim Economies

Financial system, monetary economics, and monetary policy in these economies are basically interest-based. Though popular preference in several of these countries is to have an interest-free financial system, very few of these more than 50 economies are trying to transform their financial system to conform to Islamic law. About a dozen Muslim countries claim to have substantial Islamic banking and finance in their economy. Two countries Sudan and Iran claim they have made Islamic financial and monetary system totally Islamic. Excluding these two countries, there is no

Table 2.1 Unemployment rates in major Muslim countries in current decade

Malaysia	3%
Bangladesh	5%
Pakistan	6%
Saudi Arabia	6%
Indonesia	6%
Turkey	8%

Source: World Development Indicator

other country where any substantial Islamic financial/monetary policies can be claimed to be taking place. Only three of the countries where Islamic banking exists are reported to be holding 10–33% of their banking in the form of Islamic banking, while the rest is hard-core interest-based banking.[14] This paper does not aim at evaluating Islamic banking and finance in any present-day Muslim economies. This study only refers to theory and application of monetary economics and monetary policy in a present-day Muslim economy that likes to convert its financial and monetary system in a gradual process.

The central banks of all Muslim countries continue to depend on interest rate as a kingpin of financial system and monetary policy. Let us first see if we can continue to assume classical macroeconomic model to analyze monetary economics of the present-day Muslim economies. The official statistics in the present-day Muslim economies show very low unemployment rates (which according to the standards of developed economies is equivalent to full employment) (Table 2.1).

On the other hand, there is also evidence that all Muslim economies have un-utilized or underutilized capacity, which continues to exist in the long run as well, and hence have output far below so-called full employment level. The Classical model, therefore, will not be a good representation of a present-day Muslim economy.

The most important reason why Classical framework is not valid for present-day Muslim economies, however, is that these countries have a vibrant money market dealing on interest-based products. Money demand functions have been estimated in several Muslim countries and have been found to be a significant function of interest. This empirical evidence cannot allow to assume a Classical or Neo-classical model for the present-day Muslim economies.

Even the Muslim countries, where Islamic finance holds a substantial share in the financial market, heavily depend on money market and the monetary policy is formulated by their central banks based on interest. The question is what approach we should take toward monetary economics in Muslim country which is not really "Islamic" in the sense explained earlier but picks up "elimination of interest" as the starting point in the process of transforming its economy into "Islamic" economy.

The Keynesian approach dominates in the economies of all Muslim countries' fiscal and monetary policies. And Keynesian models are in the background of

[14] World Economic Forum Report (2015).

economic planning and forecasting models in the present-day Muslim economies. It is implicitly assumed that people have liquidity preference and demand for money is a function of interest rate in the economy.

2.4.1 Cost of Holding Money in Islamic Perspective

What would represent the cost of holding money in a Muslim economy for the households that do not like to receive interest income on their money holdings? The problem arises when a Muslim country is gradually moving toward transforming the financial system and for some time, the economy will run a dual system, partly Islamic and partly interest-based. The maximum share of Islamic financial system is reported to be 30% in Saudi Arabia, and the rest of the financial system continues to be interest-based. In such an economy, there are households that have opportunities to earn income on their short-run investments in interest-based money market, but there is no such opportunity for those who do not want to avail interest-based investment opportunities to make income on their money holdings. As the proportion of such households increases in the economy, the open market operations to control money demand will become less and less effective. The market definitely would have alternatives to earn almost risk-free return in short-run investments on liquid assets, but no empirical evidence is available on such alternatives and hence no basis available to define an Islamic tool for monetary policy that will manage demand of both types of households.

The issue is to develop a market for short-run investment in products that can be quickly liquidated when needed and can yield an almost risk-free return. Central bank needs to allow development of financial instruments and products with following features:

1. They yield *Shari'ah* compatible rate of return for short-term investment.
2. The rate of return is almost risk-free.
3. They are easily and conveniently negotiable in the secondary market.

These instruments/products will serve as alternative options for such households to invest their liquidity in the short run for almost risk-free return for which interest-based instruments are not acceptable. We cannot assume that the believers are not aware of the cost of holding money. If the absence of alternative to interest rate is not allowed in the money market, the population that abhors interest is forced to bear the cost of holding money. The system therefore would be inefficient, and monetary policy will lose its efficacy as proportion of households not investing in interest-based securities, treasury bills, etc. increases. There is evidence that people are moving in increasing proportions from interest-based finance toward Islamic finance if the options are available in the Muslim country. The Muslim countries running dual financial system has to find a solution that would not put the population that abhors interest at disadvantage compared to the rest of the population.

Markets in Muslim world are not short of opportunities of short-term investment in real sector to develop almost no risk products that could become a basis of Islamic money market to absorb money demand of those who do not want to deal in the interest-based money market. It is only a matter of institutional arrangement to develop financial instrument for Islamic money market that will offer opportunities for short-run investment, with almost no risk. Two types of financial products can be developed for this market:

(a) The debt-creating instruments carrying fixed markup or profit rate which can be traded in secondary market, but this will not be *Shari'ah* permissible.
(b) The profit-sharing instruments which can be traded in the secondary market and this will be *Shari'ah* permissible too.

The short-term debt-creating instruments can easily be generated from the commodity market. These instruments will carry a fixed markup rate. But these will not be negotiated in the secondary market because of *Shari'ah* restrictions on negotiating debt-based instruments on discount basis. However, some institutional arrangements can allow the holder to liquidate the instruments readily at least at face value in case the holder is forced to meet emergency need. The short-term profit-sharing instruments can be generated in commodity market as well as in equity market. The profit-sharing-based instruments from the commodity market may be preferable because the equity market is often manipulated by those who have market power.

It should not be difficult to develop institutional setup where commodity market will reveal short-term profit rates in trade contracts involving deferred payments (1 month, 3 months, 6 months, etc.) and government securities can be developed based on these profit rates to finance its various purchases. Thus, commodity market can yield a markup rate or *Murabahah* rate if government seeks to issue *Murabahah*-based purchases with deferred payment. The commodity market can also yield profit rates on short-run investments in commodity trade, and this would provide government to issue instruments profit rate-based financing of government purchases rather than borrowing money through sale of treasury bill or interest-based securities. The profit-sharing-based instruments will be negotiable in the secondary market, hence providing opportunity to provide for short-term investments of households who do not consider interest-based securities. They will be able to negotiate it in the secondary market as well. Markup-based securities will also be available for both types of households: those who like to invest only in *Shari'ah* compatible instruments and those who do not mind investing in interest-based instruments. The former households, however, will not be able to negotiate these debt-based *Murabahah* instruments, but the other households will not mind selling and purchasing them.

Central bank or monetary authority will need to plan to ensure the above. The *Murabahah* rates and profit rates will be based on the trading contracts of commodities whose prices remain stable over time. The central bank will announce a profit rate as benchmark as it announces the interest rate and discount rate. This profit rate will replace the rate that is called interest rate or benchmark rate or discount rate currently existing in Muslim economies.

Let this rate be called *R*. It should be possible for the government to make all its purchases against the issuance real trade and investment-based government securities with profit rate *R* determined in the real market. These instruments will be negotiable in the secondary market. For those who do not consider the debt-based securities permissible to be negotiated in the second market may have the option to invest only on those instruments that are *Shari'ah* compatible for negotiation in the secondary market. It should not be difficult for the government's purchase department to issue such certificates carrying real market-based financial instruments. Government can also issue *Qard Hasan* securities and *Sukuk* redeemable on demand to absorb the money demand in the Islamic money market. Muslim economy may have substantial demand even for such zero rate government securities. With such institutional development, the management of money demand in the economy can be managed keeping in view the needs of the dual financial system where Islamic financial system and interest-based financial system are operating side by side.

2.4.2 Money Demand Management in Present-Day Muslim Economies

We can assume that the present-day Muslim economies are Keynesian economies because people do prefer liquidity. Money demand does exist in the economy and there is no evidence to reject this hypothesis. This money demand will be a function of some rate of return that exists in the economy on short-term investment. Since present-day Muslim economies have an active money market, the money demand happens to be the function of interest rate announced by central bank for those who do not mind earning interest income. The Muslim economies that are running a dual system on their way to converting the entire system in a gradual process face several issues in the context of their monetary system which prove to be serious hurdle in the way of transforming their entire system.

First, those households who do not want to manage their financial matters on interest basis, no formal opportunities exist in the economy to help them manage their liquidity. They keep large liquidity in informal channels. They may be using it in short-term investment but only through informal channels or may simply be holding excessive liquidity beyond their liquidity preference. The first issue, therefore, is how to bring this liquidity into money market so that people reveal their true liquidity preference. Second, there is large majority of financial institutions in these countries that operate on the basis of interest and there are households who do not mind investing their liquidity in money market or keeping their savings in interest-based financial institutions for convenience reason or otherwise. The presence of interest and interest-based financial institutions in the economy does not allow pricing of Islamic products in the Islamic financial market to be determined in the real market. Interest rate in the economy becomes the benchmark for pricing the products of Islamic financial and money market. If this continues, the wish of the countries to change the entire system to Islamic norms will never be achieved, and the benefits of Islamic finance in the economy will never be able to show its benefits because interest-based products will keep leading the Islamic products to tread the path of interest-based products. Third, the central bank has to use interest rate for managing interbank lending and borrowing or to serve as lender of resort because neither the central bank nor commercial banks have Islamic financial products to accommodate each other's short-term financial needs. The lending and borrowing from banking system is an important monetary tool to regulate money supply, and this lending/borrowing is currently done only on interest basis. Interest rate therefore is a necessity for the monetary policy even for the present-day Muslim economies that have substantial component of Islamic finance in their economy. And if it remains a necessity, then money demand will continue to depend on the interest rate, and substantial part of the money demand of those who abhor interest will remain in the informal channels. The dilemma of these present-day Muslim economies is that if the central bank eliminates interest from the financial and monetary system, it will lose an important tool of monetary policy, and if it keeps interest rate, then a substantial amount of liquidity and money demand remain outside the formal money market and the entire system may never be able to convert fully to Islamic system.

A starting point for a Muslim country that has a dual system of interest-based financing and Islamic financing is to change its terminology and jargon in its financial and monetary market. Central bank and government treasury should use the term profit rate (instead of interest rate) for its financial and monetary instruments and financial and monetary operations. A country that has intention to make the system Islamic has no reason to continue the use of the term interest in the economy. Changing the terminology will be helpful creating appropriate mind-set and environment in the economy to move to the Islamic system. The change will in terminology will not be required every time a change is introduced in the financial and monetary system. Central bank or monetary authority should announce the profit rate based on information from the real economy, such as commodity market and therefore can determine a profit rate (as explained above). The central bank and monetary authority can gradually replace the base of its from securities simple interest-bearing debt to trading-based debt securities fulfilling *Shari'ah* requirement or financing-based profit-sharing securities fulfilling *Shari'ah* requirement for negotiation in secondary market.

2.4.3 Money Supply in Present-Day Muslim Economies

Money supply is generated by the two sources in present-day Muslim economies. Central bank prints currency and the banking system creates credit. The banking system has the ability to create credit because banks can issue loans several times of the deposits they hold. Islamic scholars have raised no specific objection on this process of credit creation. No practical suggestion has yet come from the scholars with respect to any restriction in, Islamic perspective, on conventional banking systems' or Islamic banking system's ability to create credit. Credit creation puts the money supply in the economy at the discretion of banking system. The decisions of banks to increase or not to increase credit creation has impact on the real economy leading to short-run fluctuations in the growth of economy, often creating instability in the economy. The credit creation ability of banking system does not affect the real economy in a Classical model. But the present-day Muslim economies are not believed to be money-neutral. A monetary policy is, therefore, needed to regulate money supply to adjust to money demand in a balanced way. The central banks, though, currently can curtail the creating powers of banking system through reserve requirements, but banking system still has ways to bypass the central bank monetary objectives. If central bank puts 100% reserve requirement, the banking system will not be able to create any credit or increase money supply at its discretion. The money supply will be totally at the discretion of central banks. But present-day Muslim economies do not want to do this. Currently, Muslim economies follow global pattern of keeping low reserve requirement, hence, allowing banking system to create credit. The banks create credit almost as much as they want despite central bank's controls.

The first issue for the present-day Muslim economies, with respect to money supply, is why to leave the economy at the mercy of banking system by allowing them to benefit from marginal reserve requirements and allow them to earn unlimited profits by credit creation. This issue was discussed in late 1970s and early 1980s by the Islamic economists, but the policy makers did not pay attention to them. The repeated crash of financial system at the global level (the last one in 2008) that shook the entire world should motivate the Islamic economic scholars to raise this issue again in the context of the transforming the present-day Muslim economies to conform to Islamic law.

The conventional economic thinking is sold to the idea that promoting debt in the economy is an easy way of accelerating investment and hence growth in the economy, despite its adverse consequences on efficiency, equity, and stability in the economy. The economies have now become so much accustomed to having an easy access to debt-creating banking system that thinking of stopping it is impossible. This has made banks to have gained so much market power, through credit creation that it is now impossible to think of 100% reserve requirement. The economists understand this problem and have raised their voice. The policy makers, however, believe that since the monetary system is totally interest-based, the governments' monetary authorities can use interest rate as an effective tool to control and regulate money supply. The interest-based government securities and central banks' discount rates are considered sufficient to have full control on debt expansion to go beyond the limit where it will become damaging for the economy. But there is now sufficient evidence that this assumption is wrong. Despite the central banks' power to determine the interest rates and discount rates, banking system has sufficient leeway to expand credit in the economy beyond limits and hence become a source of financial crisis.

Islamic economic principles do not favor the concept of promoting debt-creating investment and consumption in the economy. The absolute prohibition of interest rate is sufficient indicator of this economic principle, and if present-day Muslim economies intend to transform their financial system to conform to Islamic financial laws, then, the first step should have been to curtail the powers of banking system to create credit at their discretion in a gradual process. The money supply needs of the economy should gradually be taken over by central bank through printing currency. This will be the first issue that should be the concern of monetary economics in Islamic perspective.

The second issue for the monetary policy of the present-day Muslim economies is what would replace the interest rate as a policy tool to control the credit-creating powers of banking system until this power has been completely been erased. The presence of interest in the economy serves several purposes with respect to the monetary economics. One, it allows to issue interest-bearing government securities, which carry no risk and can be liquidated easily on demand. Central bank can sell and purchase these securities in the money market to expand or contract money circulating in the economy. Two, it allows the central bank to fix a rate for interbank borrowing and lending. Third, it serves as a discount rate for the sale and purchase of short-run investment instruments. What policy tool a Muslim economy will have that would play the same role that interest rate plays in the present-day economies? For the time being, let us assume that *R* discussed earlier is the answer to this question.

2.4.4 Equilibrium in Money Market

Since money demand is negatively related to cost of holding money (*R*), money demand becomes a downward sloping function with respect to *R*, which reflects cost of holding money in hand. With supply of money fixed by government, there will be a money market that will determine an equilibrium amount of money held by the household and *R*. The equilibrium in money market, therefore, can be represented by the following Fig. 2.1.

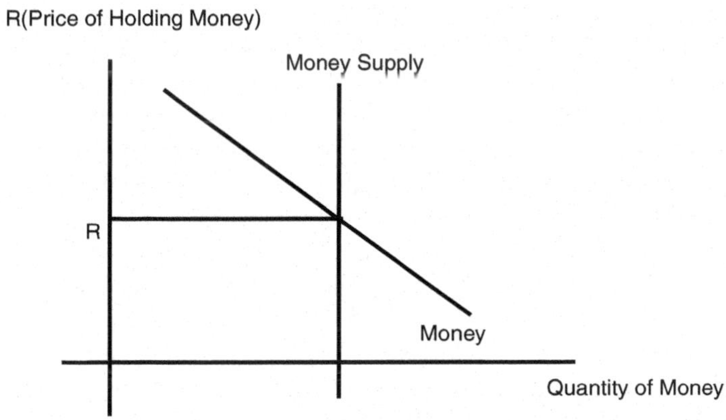

Fig. 2.1 Equilibrium in money market. (Source: author's own illustration)

The *R* will increase whenever the money demand from households shifts up or money supply is reduced by the central bank. When *R* goes down, investment goes up as discussed earlier. This increase in investment will increase aggregate demand and hence increase output. The higher the rate of return *R* on investment, the lower the demand for money and vice versa. This negative relationship between the demand for money and the rate of return on investment provides a link between the monetary sector with the real sector.

The *R* will increase whenever the money demand from households shifts up or Money supply is reduced by the central bank. When *R* goes down, investment goes up as discussed earlier. This increase in investment will increase aggregate demand and hence increase output. The higher the rate of return *R* on investment, the lower the demand for money and vice versa. This negative relationship between the demand for money and the rate of return on investment provides a link between monetary sector with the real sector.

2.4.5 Need for Monetary Policy in Present-Day Muslim Economies

Though the Keynesian original view that money supply can affect the output went through several transformations, it is no more favored by new Keynesians and they do not believe that monetary policy can affect employment and output, but still the new Keynesians advocate using monetary policy for other macroeconomic objectives such as stability, if not for employment or output. The need for monetary policy is now being emphasized also to offset the effects of unexpected external shocks to the economy. Do the present-day Muslim economies need monetary policy for any meaningful macroeconomic objective?

In the monetary framework described above for a present-day Muslim economy, let us recapitulate the need of monetary policy that underlies in the above-mentioned framework. *R* will be determined by the money market. If either the demand for money or the supply of money changes, the equilibrium rate of return on investment (*R*) would change. Changing the supply of money can effectively change real variables like output by influencing the aggregate demand. The effect on output will depend on the elasticity of the supply of aggregate output. As long as there is excess capacity in the economy, the increase in supply of money will increase investment by raising the return on investment *R* which will raise effective demand through the multiplier effect, thereby increasing income, output, and employment.

Unless the rate of return is too low in a Muslim economy, the money demand curve will remain downward sloping if Keynesian hypothesis of liquidity preference is valid for the present-day Muslim economies and there will remain the need for monetary policy. None of the Muslim countries, particularly those introducing Islamic finance, have a rate of return on investment too low to imply an infinitely elastic demand for money so that monetary policy will become redundant. If the hypothesis that households do have liquidity preference even without any love for money for its own sake is true in present-day Muslim economies, then the monetary policy will continue to be needed.

The issue for Muslim countries that was discussed was that while being in the process to transform their entire financial system to conform to *Shari'ah*, what monetary policy tools they need for the interim period until transformation is completed. Continuing with interest rate as a policy tool will be counterproductive in any effort to move toward bringing Islamic financial and monetary system in the economy. The primary question is why Muslim countries need monetary policy? What macroeconomic objectives do Muslim countries need to achieve monetary policy? The answer requires pointing out the macroeconomic objectives of a Muslim economy, if the objective is to convert to "Islamic" economy. This requires identifying macroeconomic model. Will Keynesian macroeconomic objectives remain valid for an objective for such Muslim economies that want to convert to "Islamic" economy? This paper would briefly mention that the present-day Muslim economies need to review the objective that they want to achieve from the monetary policy. Discussion into the macroeconomic objectives of an Islamic economy is outside the scope of this paper.[15]

2.5 Outline of Monetary Policy for Present-Day Muslim Economy

In the background of the above discussion, if we are sold to the Keynesian idea that present-day Muslim economies need monetary policy to increase output employment (and for stability purposes according to New Keynesians) and that central bank needs adequate monetary tools to regulate money supply for this purpose, then let us see what will be a suitable monetary policy for the present-day Muslim economies to help them move toward transforming their financial and monetary systems to conform to *Shari'ah*. The following policy directions are suggested:

(a) Gradually increasing reserve requirements to meet the money supply needs for investment and growth by printing currency. The Keynesians' devotion to consider discount rate as a better tool than controlling money supply directly through reserve requirement has no sanctity in Islamic perspective.
(b) Gradually eliminating the secondary market of debt-based instruments. *Shari'ah* compatible profit-sharing instruments for negotiation in the secondary market to be rapidly promoted for until it completely replaces the secondary market of debt-based instruments and the secondary market exists only for *Shari'ah* compatible profit-sharing-based financial instruments.

[15] Appendix II of this paper gives a brief perspective on the macroeconomic objective that present-day Muslim economy should aim at in the process of converting to an "Islamic" economy.

(c) Introducing an alternative to current benchmark and discount rate right away and call it profit rate. The almost risk-free profit for short-term investment should be found from the real commodity market which can yield profit-sharing-based benchmark and discount rates.
(d) Commodity market rather than equity market is suitable to derive profit-sharing-based benchmark and discount rate because commodity market is unlikely to yield losses on deferred payment transactions while equity market will yield profit and loss sharing-based benchmark and discount rates which money market cannot sustain.

2.5.1 Strategy for Gradually Reducing the Trading of Debt-Based Financial Instruments in Secondary Market

Thanks to efforts of *Shari'ah* scholars of contemporary Muslim world who have engineered a variety of financial instruments to suit every need of every person, there are *Shari'ah* compatible instruments that are debt-creating instruments, profit-sharing instruments, and profit and loss-sharing instruments, which can meet the risk-return profile of every person in the economy. These instruments are asset-based and are not merely monetary instruments, and the rate of return on these instruments relates to the real market and not money market.

The first step that Muslim countries may like to consider in introducing Islamic financial system is to replace the terminology of interest rate with profit rate. This may be initially a change in name only, but it will prepare people mentally at home and abroad to accept the modalities when profit rate will refer to the rate determined from real market, not from money market. This will also make people conscious to look into the details of their financial contracts and deals when making a profit rate-based financial dealing.

Second, profit rate determined by the central bank from real market should be applicable as the benchmark rate to all financial institutions whether interest-based financial institutions or Islamic financial institutions while dual system is in operation in the economy. All banks whether interest-based or Islamic will use the same rate in their banking and financing operations whether as a benchmark rate or an interbank rate or a discount rate.

2.5.2 Shari'ah Supervision of Monetary Policy

Monetary policy intervenes in the market and in the economy. Several questions may arise from *Shari'ah* point of view. Can government intervene in the market? Many scholars deny that government can intervene in the market and economy. But there are other scholars that give government substantial authority to intervene in the economy in public interest or in the interest of society. Still another view is that government intervention would be subject to certain conditions and certain limits.

The first question is: what is *Shari'ah* argument for monetary policy in an Islamic economy? The Western economists argue that monetary policy may not necessarily create stability (currently, the only objective) through monetary policy. While growth and stability are both valid objectives, stability loses its significance when macroeconomic models assume money neutrality. Even if monetary policy can smooth out short-run economic fluctuations, does that mean that we should use it for that purpose? The *Shari'ah* question "why monetary policy" is a valid question for an Islamic economy. The monetary authority and *Shari'ah* authorities should analyze together costs and benefits of monetary policy objectives and tools before a policy is implemented. The Keynesian economic objectives to be pursued need to be weighed against the macroeconomic objectives of *Shari'ah* for the economy. I have elsewhere discussed that the macroeconomic model of an Islamic economy implies that the economy moves in the long run to "Poverty Free Output" level (poverty in Islamic terminology referring to *Maskanah*), instead of the full employment level as envisaged in both Classical and Keynesian approach.[16]

Second, can absolute discretion be given to the government for the use of monetary policies? What is the safeguard against abuse of this discretion by the government? Monetary authorities need to be given *Shari'ah* guidelines to ensure judicious use of monetary policy and its tools. Monetary policy will generate inflation. How much inflation would be feasible is not only an economic issue but also a *Shari'ah* issue. Some *Shari'ah* rules will have to be laid down along with economic rules for the monetary authority with respect to monetary policy.

2.6 Conclusion

Ideally speaking, if a Muslim economy is implementing Islamic system of property rights (*Fiqh al-Mal*) and Islamic laws of exchange in market (*Fiqh al-Buyu'*), then monetary policy does not pose a big challenge for an Islamic economy. It will be similar to the conventional monetary policy under the assumptions of classical macroeconomic model where monetary sector does not affect real sector. But this is only a theoretical scenario.

Present-day Muslim economies are far from the scenario of a Classical macroeconomic model. Influenced by Keynesian thought, these economies have assigned interest rate a central role in the economic management. Several major Muslim economies are in the process of introducing Islamic finance and monetary system, probably as a part of a policy to gradually convert the entire financial system to confirm to *Shari'ah*. These economies face the issue how to manage the monetary sector of such an economy in a process of gradually eliminating interest from the

[16] See Khan 2017. A summary is given in Appendix II.

economic, while effectively achieving desired macroeconomic desired objectives. The following strategy is proposed.

Gradually reduce the private sector's dependence on debt-creating investment and let economy grow not on debt but on profit/loss sharing-based financing. Secondary market of debt-based financial instruments should be gradually eliminated whether the debt is interest-based or it is profit-based. Secondary market should exist only for profit and loss sharing-based financing contracts in the real market or profit-sharing-based financing contracts in the real commodity market. If all government purchases and projects are financed using profit-sharing-based securities and *Sukuk* based on the central bank profit rate, there will be no shortage of *Shari'ah* compatible government securities and bonds for monetary sector.

The central bank-determined profit rate for financing will also serve as a benchmark for determining profit-sharing ratio in financing and investment contracts as well as in government security bonds. The central bank can determine the profit rate based on actual market transactions, and it can determine these rates as a policy tool on its own analysis of the economic conditions prevailing in the real sector and the macroeconomic objectives to be achieved in the economy. In a nutshell, the strategy to move gradually toward 100% reserve requirement and slowly reducing debt contents in the investments in the economy deserves immediate attention from the policy makers in Muslim countries that intend to transform their financial and monetary system to conform to *Shari'ah*.

Appendix I: Beyond Market Economics in an Islamic Economy

Islamic economy is usually distinguished from capitalist economy because of the absence of interest. The fact is that this is not as important a distinction as the exchange "beyond market" is in the economic system of Islam. It will not be oversimplification to say that Islamic economic system has been comprehensively outlined in the *Quran* in the verses 261–281 of Chap. 2 (*al-Baqarah*). These verses say:

1. Allah has permitted Trade (2:275)
2. Allah has prohibited interest on loans (2:275); Allah destroys interest (2:276)
3. Allah gives increase for *Sadaqat* (charities) (2:276)

Read other 12 verses (2:262–274) before the above two verses. They all relate to *Sadaqat*. The verses 277–281 are about financial accommodation which is required to be beyond market (loans to carry no interest, recovery of loans to be postponed if debtor is in distress) and *infaq* (help to those who cannot benefit from market) emphasized. Besides above references, the two obligations repeatedly mentioned in the *Quran* are *Salah* (five times prayers) and *Zakah*. This shows two components of economic system in Islamic framework:

1. Market segment where people trade or exchange in the market what they own. The tool for this exchange will be price that will be determined by market in a fairly competitive environment. There is elaborate guidance from *Sunnah* about how to exchange conduct in the market and about rules to be followed for the exchange (explained in volumes of on *Fiqh al-Buyu'* – understanding the trade in Islam). These principles, in jargon of conventional economics, boil down to nothing but that markets should be "free" and "competitive." The only restriction on the market is that it will be free of *riba*. It is clear that Islamic economic system allows a market segment in the economy. Self-interest is recognized in Islam, and system of property rights elaborated in the literature on *Fiqh al-Maal* explains the sanctity of property rights, and the rules for the protection of this sanctity and how to exchange these rights are sufficient to create a strong market segment in the economy in the Islamic system. Gains implicit in exchange create market. The leading Islamic principle for market segment of the economy is "O you who have believed, do not consume one another's wealth unjustly but only [in lawful] business by mutual consent. And do not kill yourselves or one another" (The Quran 4:29).
2. Beyond market segment where people exchange *Sadaqat* for divine pleasure. This is also trade or exchange and there is gain in this exchange also, but not in the market environment. It is an exchange of value for a counter value that does not come from the market but from beyond the market. This exchange is also created by divine command market and is approved by divine command. This exchange is an obligatory part of life of a Muslim.

In Islamic framework, this component is part of economics, and there is no objective reason for conventional economics to exclude this part from the definition of economics. Including it in economics will make economics relevant to address problems like poverty, development, environment, etc. which currently stay excluded from economics despite that their roots lie in economic behavior. Its inclusion into economics distinguishes the economics in Islam from conventional economics and hence the need to call economics in Islam as Islamic economics.

To understand economics in Islamic perspective, it is therefore important to understand how beyond market segment of an Islamic economy works and what is economics rather than to understand how to introduce the futile exercise of conducting Islamic banking and finance within interest-based financial system. Economies, like Pakistan, that made serious efforts in making its economy Islamic would have gained considerable mileage if it had started the process by including the beyond market segment as defined above in its macroeconomic framework. Incorporating beyond market segment of the economy in its macroeconomic framework can help the economy achieve its targets of growth and equity simultaneously.

The repeated failures of macroeconomic policies based on conventional framework of macroeconomic model, the latest one being 2008 crises, have finally made conventional economics realize that neglecting the economics beyond market is not good economics.[17]

Appendix II: Macroeconomic Objectives of an Islamic Economy

Full employment is one of the key macroeconomic objectives in conventional economics. The current unemployment rates in some major Muslim countries and in some developed countries do not qualify them as meaningful macroeconomic objective even for so-called "developed" economies. Unemployment rate is believed to indicate the health of an economy. The current unemployment rates ranging between 5% and 8% in almost all major Muslim economies do not really indicate the health of the economy. Full employment is considered a solution for the improvement of health in the economy problem but in what sense? Full employment does not even mean eradication of poverty. Instead, it often forces people to remain in poverty.

We do not find any reference in the *Quran* and *Sunnah* about unemployment or the objective of ensuring full employment in the economy. What we find are the injunctions for feeding the *Masakeen* and giving support to economically less privileged members of the society.[18] Conventional economics would consider such injunctions outside the realm of economics and would consider injunctions for feeding or supporting poor as free lunch, creating beggars and free riders. Conventional economics would rather suggest creating jobs for poor in an economy. This is what Professor Yunus, a Nobel Prize Laureate from Bangladesh and a founder of Grameen Bank, hinted at in a lecture delivered in Islamic Development Bank while referring to *Zakah* and *Sadaqat* injunctions in Islam. According to conventional economics, the focus of the economy at macro level is "output growth with full employment." What would be the focus of Islamic economy at macro level? "Growth with 'what', if not full employment?"

There is no direct reference in the *Quran* and *Hadith* with respect to growth and full employment in the economy, which are considered two topmost macroeconomic goals in conventional economics. Growth did not need a reference. Once instinct of self-interest has been recognized, the sanctity of private property rights has been secured, rules for exploitation-free market laid down, and then it goes without saying that the system would make "growth" to take care of itself. However, it is very much evident that the *Quran* and *Hadith* require taking care of *Maskanah* (an Islamic term for poverty) of *Masakeen* (the Islamic term for poor). *Masakeen* can be

---

[17] Extracted from my Facebook Page Islamic Society of Islamic Economics. This can also be seen in my article, "Beyond Market Segment of an Islamic Economy: A Key Element of Islamic Economy" to be published soon in Journal of Philanthropy.

[18] See the *Quran* (69:34), (74:39–48), (76:5–9), (89:18) and (107: 1–3).

interpreted as the people who are unable to meet their minimum living needs from the market and look toward help from beyond market.

Islam makes it the responsibility of every individual in the society to take care of the *Masakeen* around beyond market. Twenty-two verses (261–282) toward the end of Chap. 2 and many other verses in the *Quran* emphasize giving away to needy, deprived, and less privileged members of the society. Feeding the *Masakeen* is a top priority item in giving away as is evident from the *Quranic* references mentioned above.

The macroeconomic objective in an Islamic economy, therefore, needs to be specified about poor and poverty (*Faqr* and *Maskanah*, in Islamic terminology) and not in reference to full employment or unemployment. "Growth free of *Maskanah*" instead of "Growth with Full Employment" will be a more relevant macroeconomic objective from the Islamic perspective. No doubt, it may be hard to visualize that there would be zero *Maskanah* or there will be no *Masakeen* at any point of time in any society, but we can objectively fix a natural rate of *Maskanah* in the society for declaring the society free of *Maskanah*. We may assume, for example, that the incidence of up to 5% *Maskanah* may be considered as if there is no *Maskanah* in the society. This 5% of incidence of *Maskanah* may be reflecting the number of people suffering from various permanent physical and mental disabilities, making it impossible for them to make their livelihood from the market.

In view of this reality, we can therefore declare an economy as free of *Maskanah* if the incidence of *Maskanah* is below a natural rate of *Maskanah*. This is like saying "An economy is at full employment when the unemployment rate is below a certain level of natural unemployment rate." The natural rate of *Maskanah* can be determined objectively, through household surveys, labor force surveys, and censuses. This makes the macroeconomic model of the economy similar to Classical macroeconomic model with the exception that while Classical macroeconomic model looks at "Output at Full Employment Level," the Islamic economy looks at "Poverty-Free Output level" (poverty in Islamic terminology referring to *Maskanah*).

References

Khan, M. F. (2013). Theorizing Islamic economics: Search for a framework for Islamic economic analysis. *JKAU: Islamic Economics, 26*(1), 209–242.

Khan, M. F. (2015). Islamic social finance: Inclusive financial development and elimination of extreme poverty through Awqaf, *Proceedings of International Conference on Islamic Banking and Finance*, organized by Ummul Qura University, Makkah, Feb 2015.

Khan, M. F. (2017). Economics and philanthropy in Islamic economic framework. *Journal of Philanthropy, 1*(1), 1–15.

Mankiw, N. G. (2014). *Principles of economics* (7th ed.). Stamford: South-Western College Publishing.

World Economic Forum. (2015). *Top 9 Countries for Islamic Finance*. Geneva: World Economic Forum.

Zarqa, M. A. (2017). Allocation of investment in an Islamic zero-interest economy. *JKAU: Islamic Economics, 30*(1), 63–72.

Chapter 3
Islamic Monetary Economics: Insights from the Literature

Md. Akther Uddin

3.1 Introduction

Monetary economics is the economics of the money supply, demand, prices, and interest rates and their impacts on the economy. It focuses on the monetary and other financial markets, the determination of interest rate, the extent to which these affect the behavior of the economic units, and the implications of that influence in the macroeconomic context (Handa 2009). The literature of monetary economics is perhaps the oldest part of literature of economics as a whole, with contribution stretching back to the Greek era (O'Brien 2007). Monetary system has been evolving since the beginning of human civilization. However, managed money is a new phenomenon, which has gained prominence after the collapse of the Bretton Woods system in August 1971. There is no possibility of finding precedence for managed money in the days of the Prophet (peace be upon him) or in early Islamic history. Monetary management is neither existent nor needed under the gold standard, which was predominant during that time. A number of questions are, therefore, continually raised about the monetary system that a Muslim country may adopt (Chapra 1996).

The re-emergence of Islamic economics and finance, especially Islamic banking in the middle of the last century, has motivated economists to develop a comprehensive theoretical framework of modern Islamic monetary economics. As *riba*,[1] literally interest rate, is prohibited in Islam, a viable alternative is required. The early writings of Maududi[2] on *Sud* (interest) have motivated many economists to rethink about

[1] The Quran (Al-Rum, 30:39; Al-Nisa, 4:161; Ali-Imran, 3:130 and Al-Baqarah, 2:275–9).

[2] Al-Maududi, A.A. (1961). *Sud* (interest).

An earlier version of this paper was published as a working paper in Munich Personal RePEc Archive MPRA Paper No. 72081.

Md. A. Uddin (✉)
School of Business, University of Creative Technology, Chittagong, Bangladesh

M. Zulkhibri et al. (eds.), *Islamic Monetary Economics and Institutions*,
https://doi.org/10.1007/978-3-030-24005-9_3

interest-free economic system and many renowned Muslim economists have come up with different *Shari'ah*-compliant instruments to solve this problem.[3] Two international seminars on monetary and fiscal economics of Islam were held at Jeddah and Islamabad in 1978 and 1980, respectively. Since then, the discourse on these themes coincides with the development of Islamic economics in general (Tahir 2013).

Early literature on Islamic monetary economics argues that money demand function in Islamic economics system would be stable as there is no interest rate and no room for speculative demand for money (Chapra 1985, 1996). However, some researchers argue that speculative demand would exist, as return on equity-based instrument is unstable, so demand for money would be also unstable (Khan 1996).

Although interest rate is not acceptable as a monetary instrument in Islamic economic system, a number of conventional monetary instruments are still available: changes in reserve requirements, overall and selective controls on credit flows, changes in the monetary base through management of currency issue, and moral suasion. Anwar (1987), Khan and Mirakhor (1989), and Khan (1996) attempted to develop interest-free economic model with the help of conventional IS-LM framework. The argument is that equity-based profit and loss-sharing instruments would work in interest-free economy and monetary policy would be effective. In addition, profit-sharing ratio, refinance ratio, public share of demand deposits, value-oriented allocation of credit, and *Qard Hasan* ratio have been recommended as distinctive Islamic monetary policy instruments in the literature. The field has lost its motivation since mid-1990s and no significant contributions have been made on theoretical development of monetary economics from Islamic perspectives since then.

Islamic banking has emerged as a viable counterpart of conventional banking system; especially in a crisis period, Islamic banks have performed better than conventional banks as the former enjoys higher capitalization and higher liquidity reserves (Beck et al. 2013; Hussain et al. 2015). Consequently, monetary transmission mechanism through Islamic banks has gained significant attention. While some economists argue that monetary policy will be less potent under Islamic banking system, others argue that if Islamic banks truly operate under profit and loss-sharing arrangement, monetary policy through bank credit channel would be effective.

The number of empirical studies on monetary policy from Islamic economics perspective is still very few, but recent attention from IMF has motivated few insightful publications (Cevik and Charap 2011; Kammer et al. 2015; Khatat 2016). Earlier empirical works confirm the stability of money demand function in interest-free economy (Darrat 1988), but the results are still not convincing and need further research in this field. On the one hand, some findings suggest that monetary policy works through Islamic bank channel (Sukmana and Kassim 2010; Basu et al. 2015; Zulkhibri and Sukmana 2017; Zulkhibri 2018), while others argue monetary transmission channel does not pass through Islamic banks (Zaheer et al. 2012). The mix results are not surprising as in most Muslim countries Islamic banks operate under dual banking system and financial developments are heterogeneous.

[3] Kurshid Ahmed, Nejatullah Siddiqi, Mohammad Uzair, Umer Chapra, Al-Jahri, Mohsin Khan, Muhammad Anwar, Fahim Khan, Abbas Mirakhor, and others have contributed in providing a foundational framework of Islamic economic system.

The remainder of the chapter is structured as follows. Section 3.2 discusses monetary evolution and early Islamic monetary policy. Section 3.3 analyzes empirical studies. Section 3.4 provides implications of the findings and Section 3.5 concludes.

3.2 Literature Review

3.2.1 A Brief History of Monetary Evolution and Early Islamic Monetary Policy

The monetary system that prevails in the world now has come into existence after passing through several stages of evolution. The monetary system that prevailed during the Prophet's (pbuh) days was essentially a bimetallic standard with gold and silver coins (dinar and dirham) circulating simultaneously. The ratio that prevailed between the two coins at that time was 1:10. This ratio seems to have remained generally stable throughout the period of the first four caliphs. However, such stability did not persist continually. The two metals faced different supply and demand conditions, which tended to destabilize their relative prices. During half of the Umayyad period (41/662–132/750), the ratio reached 1:12, while in the Abbasid period (132/750–656/1258), it reached 1:15 or less. In addition to this continued long-term decline in the ratio, the rate of exchange between the dinar and the dirham fluctuated widely at different times and in different parts of the then Muslim world (Chapra 1996). A structure of the brief evolution of money is given in Fig. 3.1.

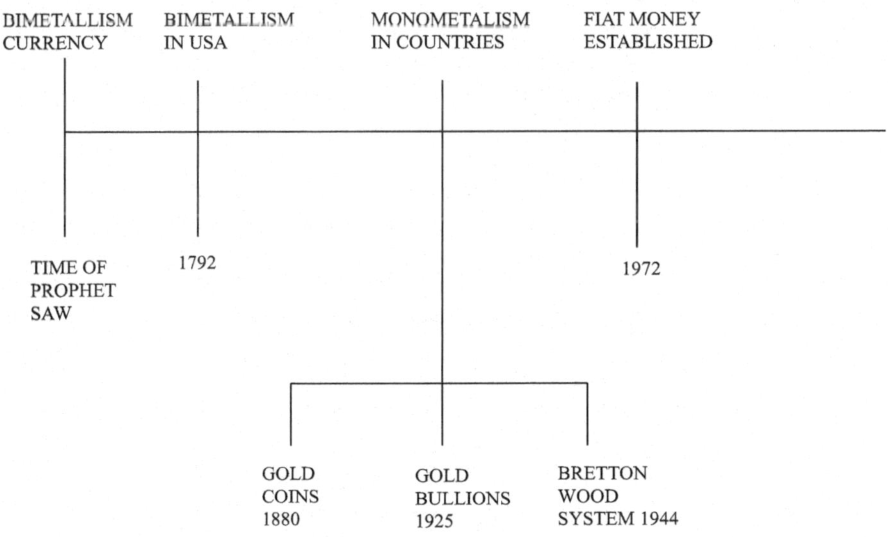

Fig. 3.1 Evolution of money over time (Source: Chapra 1996)

Is monetary policy a new phenomenon in Islam? To answer this question, we have to go back to the first Islamic state established by our beloved Prophet (pbuh) in Medina. In the early Islamic state, there was no basis for changes in the money supply through discretionary measure as there was no banking system and commodity money was extensively used instead. Moreover, credit had no role to play in creating money because i) credit was used only among few traders and ii) regulations governing the use of promissory notes and negotiable instruments were in such a way that the credit was not capable of creating money. Promissory notes or bills of exchange (draft) were issued for purchase of a real commodity or receiving an amount of money. These documents could not be issued merely for purposes of credit. After issuances of these documents, the creditor could sell the note but the debtor was not allowed to sell the money or commodity before receiving it (As-Sadr 1989). Therefore, there was no market for buying and selling of negotiable instruments, speculation, or use of money market fund. Thus, credit could not create money.

The above rule affects the equilibrium between the goods market and the money market based on cash transactions. In *Nasiah* or other Islamic legal transactions where a commodity is bought now but payment is made later, money is paid or received for commodity or an economic service. In other words, money is exchanged only in a trade, which creates real value added in economy, that falls under the framework of Islamic legal criteria. Other transactions such as gambling and usury were prohibited by Islam. As a result, the equilibrium between money and goods circulation in the economy was always maintained. Considering the relative stability of velocity of money in any given period, we can conclude that the volume of money in the economy was always equal to the value of goods produced.

Like current monetary policy instrument, open market operation, buying and selling of the negotiable instrument by the *Bayt al-Mal* (the central bank) was not used in the early Islamic period (As-Sadr 1989). Interest rate regulation, increasing or decreasing the rate of interest on loans made by banks, was not available because of prohibition of *riba* in Islam. Legal system governing, savings, investments, and trade have provided mandatory devices for the execution of monetary policies, which guaranteed an equilibrium between money and goods and prevented the diversion of savings away from real investment and creation of real wealth in the society. Giving spiritual and religious rewards for work and all other types of legitimate economic activities and participation of the companions of the Prophet(pbuh) themselves in trading and agricultural activities had increased the worth of these activities in the eyes of Muslims (As-Sadr 1989).

3.3 Islamic Monetary Economics: Equity vs. Interest Rate

The re-emergence of Islamic economics, especially Islamic banking in the middle of the last century, has motivated economists to develop a comprehensive theoretical framework of modern Islamic monetary policy. Considerable amount of literature on the subject matter has emerged. Ariff (1982) conducted some preliminary observations on the working of monetary policy in an interest-based economy and the possibilities in an interest-free economy. The three main goals of Islamic monetary policy are (i) economic well-being with full employment and optimum rate of economic growth, (ii) socioeconomic justice and equitable distribution of income and wealth, and (iii) stability in the value of money (Chapra 1985). First and third goals are covered in conventional monetary policy, but the second goal has added new dimension in the theory of Islamic monetary policy.

Stream of literature has flowed and economists proposed different Islamic monetary policy theories but two views were dominant: on the one hand, use of conventional tools available for conducting monetary policy only rejecting interest rate-based instruments and, on the other hand, use of equity-based profit and loss-sharing securities to conduct monetary policy in addition to other *Shari'ah*-compliant available tools.

Naqvi (1981) argues that an equity-based economic system is unstable. This is because equity financing, in contrast to interest financing, makes the return on investment unstable. Hence, an element of uncertainty is introduced into the investor's expectations. Therefore, to hedge against the probability of a loss, ways and means must be found, through some kind of deposit insurance scheme, to guarantee the normal value of deposits. Otherwise, not only the banking system but also the entire economy will become highly unstable (Naqvi 1981). Moreover, in an interest-free economy, people would save and invest optimally only if forced to do so by the state.

By supporting the argument provided by Naqvi (1981), Kuran (1986) argues that prohibition of interest is unenforceable in a large heterogeneous society. Equity-based profit and loss-sharing contracts constitute a beneficial instrument in the absence of a well-functioning stock market; they do not prevent relatively risk-averse individuals' need to lend for interest. He further argues that not all banks would be content with lending to firms on a profit-sharing basis or that firms would necessarily desire to borrow on this basis.

On the other hand, Zarqa (1983) argues that the uncertainties facing any real investment (whether common to all business or specific to the given enterprise) are there, regardless of how it is financed. Equity financing does not change the level of uncertainty; it only redistributes the consequences of uncertainty over all parties to a business. Debt financing, in contrast, relieves the financier from uncertainty by shifting it on to the real investor (equity holder) who then alone bears the entire risk of the enterprise. He also argued that, equity financing, by spreading the same risk over more heads, would promote stability. Each party can absorb its modest share of a loss without significantly upsetting its normal activities or defaulting on its obligations, hence no panic reactions are generated among other business units. Regarding deposit insurance, it has little to do with interest vs. equity financing. Rather, it has to do with fractional reserve banking system, which always faces the risk of a panicky run on the banks – with many depositors asking to exchange their deposits for cash on short notice. The author argues that elimination of interest, especially when coupled with other institutional features of an Islamic economy, tends to enhance stability.

Islamic financial system can adjust relatively faster to shocks than would the traditional system (Khan 1986). Henry Simons (as cited in Khan 1986) argued that interest-based banking system is unstable and leads to financial crisis and proposed 100 percent reserve banking and equity-based financial system. Khan (1986) proposed a theoretical model of interest-free banking and concluded that in equity-based banking system that excludes predetermined interest rates and does not guarantee the nominal value of deposits, shocks to asset positions are immediately absorbed by changes in the values of shares (deposits) held by the public in the bank. Therefore, the real values of assets and liabilities of banks in such a system would be equal at all points in time.

The debate on stability of interest-free economic system has been going on. A group of researchers have tried to develop a tentative framework of Islamic monetary policy starting from money demand and supply, Islamic financial system, and IS-LM framework to explain interaction of monetary policy and real sector.

3.4 Demand and Supply of Money in Islamic Monetary System

A well-behaving and stable money demand function is required by almost all theories of macroeconomic activities and particularly for the smooth operation of an effective monetary policy. An unstable function undermines the monetary policy, which becomes a source of economic disturbance.

Demand for real money balances depends on the level of real income and the expected return, conventionally interest rate, on financial assets. First, this is so because individuals hold on to money to finance their expenditures, which, in turn, depend on their income. The demand for money depends also on the expected return on the financial assets. The higher the expected return on the financial assets, the less worthwhile it is to just hold on to money. Khan (1996) argued that this part of demand for money might not be directly speculative demand. There is a demand for meeting the short-term borrowing needs of others. With the importance attached to *Qard Hasan* and with the embarrassment attached to not helping in a brother in need, the Islamic environment would motivate everyone to keep some cash to meet the short-term borrowing needs of others.

Khan (1996) also states that the speculative demand for money would also exist in interest-free economy, as the expected rate of return will be more volatile than the fixed interest rate and hence give rise to a greater urge to speculate. Though speculation will always be on expected rate of return, it can always be translated into the profit-sharing ratio prevailing in the market. Thus, the higher the profit-sharing ratio, the lower the speculative demand for money and vice versa. Moreover, there is some institutional control on speculative demand for money in the form of *Zakah*. Finally, he argued that speculative demand for money would be overshadowed by altruistic demand for money.

Chapra (1992) argues that Islamic economic system tries to regulate money demand by a strategy that relies on a number of instruments: (a) a socially agreed filter mechanism, (b) a strong motivating system to induce the individual to render his/her best in his/her own interest as well as in the interest of society, (c) restructuring of the whole economy with the objective of realizing the *Maqasid* (aim) in spite of scarce resources, and (d) a positive and strong goal-oriented role for the government.

The above given elements of the Islamic economic system may not only help minimize the instability in the aggregate demand for money but also influence the different components of money demand in a way that would promote greater efficiency and equity in the use of money. The relatively greater stability in the demand for money in an Islamic economy may also introduce greater stability in the velocity of circulation of money. The demand for money in an Islamic economy may thus be represented by the following equation (Chapra 1996):

$$M_{\mathrm{d}} = f\left(Y_{\mathrm{s}}, S, \pi\right)(1) \tag{3.1}$$

where Y_{s} represents goods and services that are related to need fulfillment and productive investment and are in conformity with the values of Islam; S represents all those moral and social values and institutions (including *Zakah*) that influence the allocation and distribution of resources and that can help minimize M_{d} not only for conspicuous consumption and unproductive investment but also for precautionary and speculative purposes; and π represents the rate of profit or loss in a system, which does not permit the use of the rate of interest for financial intermediation.

It can be argued (normative in nature) that the profit rate alone is the determining factor in the performance of a portfolio in interest-free economic system. Investors do not need to rebalance their portfolios as there is no ex ante interest rate change. Chapra (1992, 1996) argues that there would be no speculative demand for money in interest-free system.

After successfully stabilizing money demand and maintaining general well-being and development of common people, the most important questions of, firstly, how to bring aggregate money supply into equilibrium with such money demand and, secondly, how to bring the allocation of this money supply in conformity with the needs of goal realization without using coercion arise. The first question attains further significance as the two most important instruments of monetary management in the capitalist economy, discount rate and open market operations in interest-bearing government securities, would not be available in an Islamic economy (Chapra 1996).

However, Khan and Mirakhor (1989) argue that open market operations could be conducted with securities that do not bear a fixed rate of return. In line with that, Kia and Darrat (2007) restated that even though under the profit-risk-sharing banking system, the central bank will lose one of its monetary policy tools, i.e., interest rate, but can rely on a more powerful tool, i.e., to control money supply. In other words, the central bank can target monetary aggregate. The central bank can keep the money supply at its optimal level. At this level, the stable money demand allows the central bank to always operate at the optimum money supply where the consumer surplus is maximized. Assuming demand for money is stable, Friedman (1969) shows that the optimum level of money supply can be achieved when the interest rate is zero.

3.5 Framework of Interest-Free Monetary Policy

Khan and Mirakhor (1989), in their seminal paper on Islamic monetary policy, developed a theoretical model of an Islamic financial system by generalizing the standard IS-LM model to study the effects of monetary policy on the macroeconomic variables of an Islamic economy. They argue that monetary change in money supply and using the flow of *Mudarabah* financing as an intermediate objective would work equally and affect economic variables. For example, an expansionary monetary policy would reduce rates of return and increase output.

Islamic economy rejects the concept of a predetermined interest rate and permits an uncertain rate of return based on trade and profits, and banks in an Islamic economy can strictly operate only on some type of profit and loss-sharing basis. There are a number of alternatives proposed by Islamic scholars that satisfy such requirements. Most importantly, there is a question of how monetary policy would be expected to operate in an interest-free economy as interest rate-based monetary instruments are unavailable, and therefore, suitable substitutes would have to be found if monetary policy is to continue to play a role in Islamic economies.

In addition open market operations could be conducted with securities that do not bear a fixed rate of return. They also pointed out that the monetary authorities also have the possibility of directly changing the rates of return on both deposits and loans by altering the ratios in which the banks and the public are expected to share in the profits and losses that are associated with the transactions, i.e., the profit-sharing ratios. Through performance of its regulatory, supervisory, and control functions, as well as its lender-of-last-resort role, the central bank can continue to exert substantial influence on the financial system.

This is still a somewhat controversial issue as there are certain scholars who believe that it would be inappropriate for the central bank to unilaterally change a contractually determined ratio (Chapra 1992, 1996). Other writers have argued in favor of regulating profit-sharing ratios to achieve the goal of monetary stability, provided such actions affect only new deposits and not existing ones (Khan 1986). Hasan (1991) raised a number of questions against certain aspects of Khan and Mirakhor's model and the conclusions drawn from the same. The rate of return (r) the banks receive on loans must in some way be related, as Khan and Mirakhor hold, to the rate (rb) the banks pay on their liabilities. But even with the simplifying assumptions of operational and other costs of bank being zero, r and rb could not be equal. If one can show that $rb < r$, the conclusions of the models could be questionable as the whole exercise was hinged on the equality of these two rates. The equality of the two rates was just not possible under a "two-*tier Mudarabah*"-based banking system.

Another important theoretical contribution was made by Khan (1996) in which he developed a model of income determination, growth, and economic development in an interest-free economy. It was emphasized that growth in the Islamic economy can be manipulated on the supply side by mobilizing human resources through peculiar nature of Islamic financial system. With the help of the model, the author shows that Islamic financial system generates an implicit macro framework that leads the economy toward full employment and then sustains it to further growth and development.

The conventional IS-LM framework was used to link a simple income determination model to growth in the economy, but the framework was developed under the assumptions of an Islamic economy. The author particularly highlighted the investment and money demand functions in an interest-free economy to link this to the process of economic development. According to this model, investment is the function of profit-sharing ratio in an interest-free economy and relationship between profit-sharing ratio and investment is negative; moreover, mathematical model shows the profit-sharing ratio is negatively correlated with output.

The summary of other notable contributions in early Islamic monetary policy is as follows. Khan (1986, 1992) focused on the financial side and presented a macroeconomic model in order to establish that monetary policy would work in an interest-free economy in the same way as in interest-based economy but with better speed of adjustment economy in disequilibrium situations. Non-guarantee of the deposits provides the main ground for his argument.

Khan and Mirakhor (1994) highlight the *Mudarabah*-mode deposit mobilization and lease financing instruments that might be available in the Islamic financial system. They point out that apart from the Islamic banking system, there would also be primary, secondary, and money markets. There are great similarities between their thinking and what is available in conventional economics. The instruments like *Mudarabah* and *Musharakah* certificates are expected to have *Shari'ah* legitimacy. They regard macroeconomic stability, characterized by price stability, and viable balance of payment position as the chief goals for monetary policy. As for monetary policy, their conclusion is as follows: monetary policy of an Islamic state takes place in a framework in which all conventional tools normally available in a modern economy are at the disposal of the monetary authorities with the exception of the discount rate and other policy tools that involve interest rate. All other tools, namely, open market operations (where equity shares rather than bonds are traded) and credit policies, can be as effective in an Islamic system as they are in the conventional system. Additionally, the authorities in an Islamic system can utilize reserve requirements and profit-sharing ratios to achieve changes in the stocks of money and credit (Khan and Mirakhor 1994).

A good deal has been written on goals of Islamic monetary policy and conventional instruments suitable for Islamic economic system, and unique Islamic monetary instruments have also been proposed since the developments in the Islamic finance from the late 1970s and onward. By analyzing the literature, we show the key Islamic monetary policy instruments in Fig. 3.2.

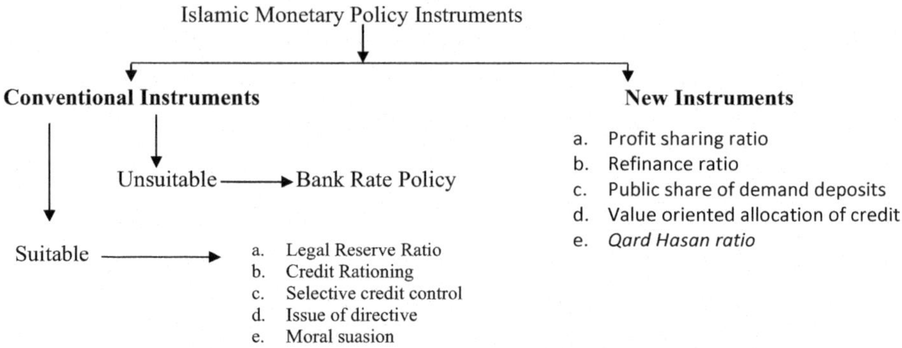

Fig. 3.2 Islamic monetary instruments (Source: author's own illustration)

3.6 Empirical Literature on Islamic Monetary Economics

Although Islamic banking and finance have progressed significantly in the last four decades, we have not seen much Islamic monetary policy theories after a remarkable work was done in the 1980s and 1990s. In the following section, some empirical evidence supporting the earlier Islamic monetary policy theories, interest-free money demand, and role of Islamic banks in monetary transmission mechanism will be discussed briefly.

Kia and Darrat (2007) have studied profit-sharing banking systems by modeling money demand behavior in Iran. They have estimated demand for M1 and profit-sharing deposits over the period 1966–2001. It is found that the demand equation for profit-sharing deposits is particularly stable and policy invariant in Iran despite numerous policy and non-policy shocks.[4] They argue for profit-sharing banking system and suggest that profit-sharing monetary aggregates are credible instruments for monetary policy-making. Their findings support well with theoretical evidence (Chapra 1992, 1996; Khan 1986) indicating that the profit-loss-sharing banking scheme insulates the monetary system from interest-rate exposure risk and minimizes financial instability.

In one of the few earlier empirical works, Darrat (1988) examines empirically whether the absence of interest-bearing financial assets from the Tunisian economy would enhance (or hamper) the stability of her financial system. Non-interest money supply is defined as currency in the hands of the public plus their demand deposits at commercial banks. As is typically the case in most developing countries, all demand deposits in Tunisia are non-interest bearing. On the other hand, interest-bearing money supply is defined as the public's time and savings deposits at commercial banks. He uses time series data from 1960 to 1984 for Tunisia as the case study as he argued cross-sectional data from several Islamic countries would lead to biases due to heterogeneity. The results suggest that non-interest monetary assets

[4] In Iran, the rate of profit on partnership and the markup on sale finance are administered.

exhibit better stability than interest-bearing. Interest-free monetary system has a structurally stable public demand for financial assets. The growth of non-interest-bearing aggregate adheres more closely to movements in the monetary base than does the growth of interest-bearing aggregate.

Many economists have looked into the effectiveness of monetary transmission mechanism under Islamic banking system. Sukmana and Kassim (2010), by using the co-integration test, impulse response functions, and variance decomposition analysis for Malaysia during the period from January 1994 to May 2007, find that both Islamic banks' financing and deposit play important roles in the monetary transmission process in the Malaysian economy. In particular, both Islamic deposit and financing are shown to be statistically significant in linking the monetary policy indicator to the real output. The results also imply that ensuring the stability of the Islamic financial institutions is just as important as that of the conventional counterpart to achieve an effective transmission of monetary policy in the economy. They also find that Islamic deposit is a very important source of financing and a heavy reliance on deposit to some extent is not healthy for the Islamic banks. They recommend the Islamic banks to raise fund other than deposit. One of the solutions would be to develop the Islamic money market which could provide the Islamic banks with an alternative source of funding.

Cevik and Charap (2011) study the empirical behavior of conventional bank deposit rates and the rate of return on retail Islamic profit and loss-sharing (PLS) investment accounts in Malaysia and Turkey. They found them co-integrated and a significant positive correlation, and that conventional bank deposit rates Granger-cause returns on PLS accounts. There could be many plausible explanations, but they argue mainly on moral hazard and ex post information asymmetry in PLS instruments; lengthy due diligence, not appropriate or cost-effective for short-term financing needs; lack of secondary markets for PLS-based financial products that complicate liquidity and credit risk management at Islamic banks; and intense competition. They conclude that participatory financing requires the development of Islamic money markets and the modernization of regulatory frameworks. It is also important for assessing the impact on monetary policy transmission.

Cevik and Teksoz (2013) examine the effectiveness of monetary policy transmission in the Gulf Cooperation Council (GCC) countries. They find the interest rate and bank lending channels appear to be effective in transmission, while exchange rates do not play an important role due to the pegged exchange rate regimes. They argue that bank lending tends to increase with monetary expansion and that the impact of monetary policy shocks typically depends on the propagation mechanism. Moreover, the effectiveness of interest rate and bank lending channels depends largely on the bank balance sheets. They further argue that the issuance of *Shari'ah*-compliant securities, *sukuk*, in local currency in recent years helped to sterilize surplus liquidity from the interbank money markets. They conclude that strengthening financial intermediation and facilitating the development of liquid domestic capital markets would advance the effectiveness of monetary transmission mechanisms in the GCC countries.

Zaheer et al. (2012) find that Islamic banks in Pakistan, even though similar in size like conventional small banks, behave like large banks during contractionary monetary policy and continue lending irrespective of their liquidity positions. Therefore, they argue that monetary policy would be less potent if Islamic banks grow in size and their current asset-liability structure remains intact. Basu et al. (2015) argue that Islamic and conventional banks in the Gulf Cooperation Council (GCC) are segmented and Islamic banks have excess liquidity, which deters their growth. They ask for concerted efforts to build Islamic liquid interbank and money markets, which are crucial for monetary policy transmission through the Islamic financial system. They argue that it can be achieved by deepening Islamic government securities and developing *Shari'ah*-compliant money market instruments.

With the rapid development of Islamic banking, the importance of Islamic monetary policy framework has gained importance but still not enough empirical literatures to support the distinctiveness and effectiveness of it. The non-availability of data hinders the process but current review shows that Islamic monetary policy could work effectively with comprehensive Islamic economic framework and Islamic banks can play vital role in monetary transmission mechanism. In addition to other legal and regulatory issues, the lack of financial intermediation and non-existence of *Shari'ah*-complaint financial instruments hold back the development of Islamic banking system.

3.7 Implications

At the advent of global financial crisis, conventional monetary policy has failed to regulate the money market and the consequence of which has been observed in the global financial market. Even though there are only two countries, Iran and Sudan, that operate under interest-free economic system, emergence of Islamic banking and finance in many Muslim and non-Muslim countries compels us to develop interest-free monetary policy framework. Most importantly, many Muslim-majority countries have been suffering from higher inflation and unemployment, which create output instability and hinder the equitable economic growth. To overcome this, sustainable monetary policy is required.

Comparative analysis shows that Islamic monetary policy can adopt many conventional instruments, which are in line with the *Shari'ah* guidance such as legal reserve ratio, credit rationing, selective credit control, issue of directive, and moral suasion. As interest rate, the key tool of conventional monetary policy regulation, is prohibited in Islamic economic system, the need for sustainable alternative is the order of the day. However, Khan (1995) argued against complete elimination of interest by a legal decree and favored free market forces to bring the interest rates down to zero. Khan further stresses on providing incentives for the use of equity over debt financing. He proposes the following policy measures: (i) reducing reserve requirements to increase supply of loanable funds; (ii) enforcing unlimited liability; (iii) gradual decline in interest to make investments in debt-based instruments less lucrative and shift loanable funds toward equity-based instruments; (iv) allowing dividend as a tax-deductible expense; and (v) providing fiscal incentives to non-leveraged firms and disincentives to leveraged firms. At the same time, some researchers argue to eliminate fractional reserve banking and impose 100% reserve requirements for demand deposits (Khan and Mirakhor 1989, 1994). In post-crisis scenario, there is an interesting development in many developed countries where nominal interest rates hit almost zero or close to zero, the so-called Zero Lower Bound. Consequently, many central banks have started experimenting with unconventional monetary policy instruments, and some countries even go beyond zero and impose negative interest rates. It clearly shows that interest rate has lost its importance as a major monetary policy instrument and it is high time to seek for viable alternative instrument.

From theoretical analysis, we have observed many economists propose equity-based profit-sharing instruments for conducting open market operations and control deposit level of Islamic banks. However, conducting monetary operations through *Shari'ah*-compliant instruments is challenging; for example, Iran and Sudan are facing the same problem (Kammer et al. 2015). To this end, it is necessary to adapt monetary policy instruments and spur the development of Islamic interbank markets. In addition to weakening the transmission channel for monetary policy, the scarcity of instruments also forces Islamic banks to hold higher unremunerated reserves, affecting their ability to compete with conventional banks. *Sukuk* issued by governments appear to be suitable collateral for monetary operations in the context of Islamic banks as currently practiced in Sudan and Iran (Hussain et al. 2015).

3.8 Conclusion

Islamic monetary economics have been evolving for the last four decades or so. While an Islamic economics system appears viable in theory, as well as to some extent in practice, significant obstacles and problems remain. Some of these include the following: lack of or non-existence of floating rate assets for Islamic banks, interbank market, *Shari'ah*-compliant short-term financial instruments, fiscal dominance, foreign relationship banking, and others.

Monetary policy of an Islamic state takes place in a framework in which all conventional tools normally available in a modern economy are at the disposal of the monetary authorities with the exception of the discount rate and other policy tools that involve an interest rate. All other tools, namely, open market operations (where equity shares rather than bonds are traded) and credit policies, can be as effective in an Islamic system as they are in the conventional system. Additionally, the authorities in Islamic system can utilize reserve requirements and profit-sharing ratios to achieve changes in the stocks of money and credit, although there is still some dispute among Muslim scholars on the appropriateness of these particular measures.

The role of Islamic banks in monetary policy transmission mechanism is still somewhat controversial, but empirical investigations have been going on. To restate one of the principal goals of Islamic monetary policy is to ensure macroeconomic stability, characterized mainly by price-level stability. The establishment of a stable macroeconomic environment is a prerequisite for increased savings, investment, and foreign capital inflows, all of which are central to the growth process. Without macroeconomic stability, economic growth can falter and cannot be sustained. The other objectives of the Islamic society, such as a more equitable distribution of resources and income, providing useful employment, improving living standards and the quality of life, and the alleviation of poverty, are unlikely to be met.

References

Anwar, M. (1987). *Modelling interest-free economy: A study in macroeconomics and development (No. 4)*. International Institute of Islamic Thought (IIIT).

Ariff, M. (1982). Monetary policy in an interest-free Islamic economy – nature and scope. In *Monetary and fiscal economics of Islam* (pp. 287–302). Jeddah: International Center for Research in Islamic Economics, King Abdulaziz University.

As-Sadr, K. (1989). Money and monetary policies in early Islamic period. In Al-Hasani B and Mirakhor A. *Easy on Iqtishad: The Islamic approach to economic problems*, Silver Spring: Nur Corp, 199–217.

Basu, R., Prasad, A., & Rodriguez, S. L. (2015). *Monetary operations and Islamic banking in the gcc; challenges and options (No. 15/234)*. International Monetary Fund.

Beck, T., Demirgüç-Kunt, A., & Merrouche, O. (2013). Islamic vs. conventional banking: Business model, efficiency and stability. *Journal of Banking & Finance, 37*(2), 433–447.

Cevik, S., & Charap, J. (2011). The behavior of conventional and Islamic bank deposit returns in Malaysia and Turkey. In *IMF Working Papers No. 11/156*. Washington, DC: International Monetary Fund.

Cevik, S., & Teksoz, K. (2013). Lost in transmission? The effectiveness of monetary policy transmission channels in the GCC countries. *Middle East Development Journal, 5*(3), 1350018–1-1350018-21.

Chapra, M. U. (1985). *Towards a just monetary system*. Leicester: The Islamic Foundation.

Chapra, M. U. (1992). *Islam and economic challenge*. Leicester: The Islamic Foundation.

Chapra, M. U. (1996). Monetary management in an Islamic economy. *Islamic Economic Studies, 4*(1), 1–34.

Darrat, A. F. (1988). The Islamic interest-free banking system: Some empirical evidence. *Applied Economics, 20*, 417–425.

Friedman, M. (1969). The optimum quantity of money. In *The optimum quantity of money and other essays*. Chicago: Aldine.

Handa, J. (2009). *Monetary economics*. London: Routledge.

Hasan, Z. (1991). Comments on The Financial System and Monetary Policy in an Islamic Economy. By Mohsin S. Khan and Abbas Mirakhor. *Journal of King Abdulaziz University: Islamic Economics, 3*, 85–93.

Hussain, M. M., Shahmoradi, A., & Turk, R. (2015). An overview of Islamic finance. In *IMF Working Paper No.WP/15/120*. Washington, DC: International Monetary Fund.

Kammer, M. A., Norat, M. M., Pinon, M. M., Prasad, A., Towe, M. C. M., & Zeidane, M. Z. (2015). *Islamic finance: Opportunities, challenges, and policy options, IMF staff discussion note SDN/15/05*. Washington, DC: International Monetary Fund.

Khan, M. S. (1986). Islamic interest-free banking. *IMF Staff Papers, 33*(1), 1–27.

Khan, M. S. (1992). *Principles of monetary theory and policy in an Islamic framework. Lectures on Islamic economics, Jeddah: IRTI*. Islamic Development Bank.

Khan, M. S. (1995). *Elimination of interest: A proposed strategy*. New Horizon/London: Institute of Islamic Banking and Insurance.

Khan, M. F. (1996). A simple model of income determination, growth and economic development in the perspective of an interest-free economy. In M. A. Mannan (Ed.), *Financing development in Islam* (pp. 79–108). Jeddah: IRTI, Islamic Development Bank.

Khan, M. S., & Mirakhor, A. (1989). The financial system and monetary policy in an Islamic economy. *Journal of King Abdulaziz University: Islamic Economics, 1*(1), 39–57.

Khan, M. S., & Mirakhor, A. (1994). Monetary management in an Islamic economy. *Islamic Economics, 6*(1), 3–22.

Khatat, M. H. (2016). Monetary policy in the presence of Islamic banking. In *IMF Working Papers No. 16/72*. Washington, DC: International Monetary Fund.

Kia, A., & Darrat, A. F. (2007). Modeling money demand under the profit-sharing banking scheme: Some evidence on policy invariance and long-run stability. *Global Finance Journal, 18*(1), 104–123.

Kuran, T. (1986). The economic system in contemporary Islamic thought: Interpretation and assessment. *International Journal of Middle East Studies, 18*(02), 135–164.

Naqvi, S. N. H. (1981). *Ethics and economics: An Islamic synthesis*. Leicester: The Islamic Foundation.

O'Brien, D. P. (2007). *The development of monetary economics: A modern perspective on monetary controversies*. Cheltenham: Edward Elgar Publishing.

Sukmana, R., & Kassim, S. H. (2010). Roles of the Islamic banks in the monetary transmission process in Malaysia. *International Journal of Islamic and Middle Eastern Finance and Management, 3*(1), 7–19.

Tahir, S. (2013). Fiscal and monetary policies in Islamic economics: Contours of an institutional framework. *Islamic Economic Studies, 21*(2), 1–22.

Zaheer, S., Ongena, S., & Van Wijnbergen, S. (2012). The transmission of monetary policy through conventional and Islamic banks. *International Journal of Central Banking, 9*(4), 175–224.

Zarqa, M. A. (1983). Stability in an interest-free Islamic economy: A note. *Pakistan Journal of Applied Economics, 11*(2), 181–188.

Zulkhibri, M. (2018). The impact of monetary policy on Islamic bank financing: Bank-level evidence from Malaysia. *Journal of Finance and Administrative Science, 23*(46), 306–322.

Zulkhibri, M., & Sukmana, R. (2017). Financing channels and monetary policy: Evidence from Islamic banks in Indonesia. *Economic Notes, 46*(1), 117–143.

Chapter 4
On Normative and Logical Foundations of Monetary Policy

Atiq-ur-Rehman

4.1 Introduction

It can be easily shown that every monetary policy action is associated with serious socioeconomic consequences. Despite this, the monetary policy around the globe is conducted without any care or consideration of the ethical, moral, or socioeconomic implications consequences of its use. Today, the primary mandate of many central banks is to control inflation, and sometimes they are mandated to look for unemployment and economic growth. Recently, many studies have shown that inflation has serious implications for distribution of income in the society (Coibion et al. 2012; Al-Marhubi 1997; Albanesi 2007; etc.). This is also clarified from the fact that the inflation is one of the major correlates of income inequality and the inflation is being controlled by monetary policy. This implies that the monetary policy is indirectly linked to the distribution of income through the channel of inflation. On the other hand, the distribution of income is a serious concern of humanity today. The Millennium Development Goals and Sustainable Development Goals both require to work for increased equality in the distribution of income. Therefore, the central banks need to analyze the distributional implications of their monetary policies before the policies are implemented. However, the practice of monetary policy is badly silent about any socioeconomic implication associated with the monetary policy.

Indeed, the *value implications* of monetary theory is not a new concept and Gunnar Myrdal (1889–1987), a famous economist and the winner of 1974 Nobel Prize in Economic Sciences, introduced the concept of strict non-neutrality thesis. His most famous stance was that social scientists (with no exclusion of economists) cannot make their judgments without *value implications*. It was not only a general statement by Myrdal, but he also explicitly wrote a separate article on the value

Atiq-ur-Rehman (✉)
Department of Econometrics and Statistics, Pakistan Institute of Development Economics, QAU Campus, Islamabad, Pakistan
e-mail: atiq@pide.org.pk

M. Zulkhibri et al. (eds.), *Islamic Monetary Economics and Institutions*,
https://doi.org/10.1007/978-3-030-24005-9_4

judgments in monetary policy (Myrdal 1939). Despite this, the monetary policy doesn't give any weightage to the value judgements involved and to the socioeconomic and normative implication. The fact is that the monetary policy until today is somewhat related to *quantity theory of money* which assumes the monetary policy to be independent of any real implication except the price changes. Therefore, central banks don't consider any value-related or socioeconomic implications while analyzing their monetary policies.

Beside the ignorance about value and socioeconomic implications, the monetary policy has many logical flaws. It frequently adapts the route which leads to what is opposite to its target. For example, central banks use to increase the interest rate in a hope to reduce inflation, but many economists have shown that increased interest rate adds to inflation, owing to the cost side channels of monetary transmission mechanism (Gibson 1923; Barth and Ramey 2001; Rehman 2015). The strong evidences on existence of cost side effects of monetary policy imply that at least these effects must be part of monetary policy modeling, but the econometric models used by central banks rarely pay any attention to the cost side effects. The so-called Taylor rule which is currently used by majority of central banks to design their monetary policies has no place for the cost side effects in it. Conduct of monetary policy without any care of cost channel of monetary transmission mechanism is just one example of big logical flaw of the contemporary monetary policy, with many more blunders frequently repeated.

The aim of this review is to discuss the socioeconomic implications of monetary policy and the loopholes in its logical foundations. The rest of this chapter is organized as follows: Section 4.2 discusses why do monetary authorities use inflation targeting framework. Section 4.3 discusses how sensible it is to target inflation, and Sect. 4.4 discusses the moral implications of trade-off between unemployment and inflation. Section 4.5 is about moral implications of inflation targeting, Section 4.6 is about cost channel of monetary transmission mechanism, and Sect. 4.7 discusses how cost and demand channels affect employment. Section 4.8 discusses the impact of monetary policy on income inequality, and finally Sect. 4.9 concludes the discussion.

4.2 Why Monetary Authorities Target Inflation?

The monetary policy now has become inflation centered. The inflation targeting was started by New Zealand in 1990, and now most of the central banks have opted inflation targeting as their major framework for designing monetary policy. The literature suggests the following reasons for the popularity of inflation rule over the monetary targeting (Mishkin 2001):

(a) Inflation targeting can promote growth and does not lead to increased output fluctuations.
(b) Inflation targeting has greater stress on transparency and communication with the public.
(c) Inflation targeting increases accountability which helps improve the time-inconsistency problem.

(d) Increased transparency and accountability under inflation targeting help promote central bank independence.
(e) Accountability to the general public seems to work as well as direct accountability to the government.
(f) Inflation targeting is consistent with democratic principles.

Inflation is also a serious public and political concern and whole society takes interest in it. Shiller (1997) reports that the term inflation was the most commonly used economic term by the newspaper in the United States and Germany with no other economic terms coming even close to it. Until now, inflation is one of the decisive factors in elections of governments and in building political environment. Why do people are concerned about inflation; the answer to this question is also given by Shiller (1997) as "it increases cost of living and decreases the real income." Unfortunately, these reasons which are considered most important by public are not even considered by the monetary authorities while making their monetary decisions.

4.3 Monetary Authorities Don't Care About Socioeconomic Implications

It is pertinent to note that the welfare costs of inflation which is a very important concern for many social policymakers are not among the reasons for adapting the inflation targeting. Inequality is very important social concern having strong theoretical linkage with inflation. The targets decided to be achieved by the nations around the globe, i.e., Millennium Development Goals and Sustainable Development Goals, both agree on reduction of income inequality. In addition, monetary economists think that they can control inflation by monetary policy. This automatically implies that the monetary policy is indirectly linked to inequality. Moreover, many researchers including Nordhaus (1973), Rothbard (1994), Romer and Romer (1999), Fowler (2005), and Easterly and Fischer (2001) have indicated strong direct linkages between monetary policy and income inequality. Therefore, the monetary policy might be effecting progress toward Sustainable Development Goals. Owing to the significance of income inequality in the global development agenda and the linkages between monetary policy and inequality, the monetary policy modeling should never ignore its effects on inequality. However, it seems as if the costs of inflation and the progress toward Sustainable Development Goals are a subject of academics only with no familiarity among the monetary authorities. To the monetary economists, the inflation targeting seems to be quite neutral to socioeconomic implication. This is why Yves Mersch, a member of executive board of European Central Bank, while addressing to a Corporate Credit Conference in Zurich, admitted that:

> As I noted at the start, the ECB has a clear mandate to deliver price stability – and that mandate does not involve policies aimed at the distribution of wealth, income or consumption. Nevertheless, we need to be aware that there are distributional consequences of our actions. (Mersch 2014)

4.4 Is It Sensible to Control Inflation?

The classical economists believed in neutrality of inflation which means that the change in inflation is just change of measuring unit (Serletis and Krause 1996). They believe that inflation does not change any of the real variables. This can happen only when price of all commodities and services grows simultaneously and in equal proportion. The famous invisible hand theory, which assumes that free markets automatically adjust prices to equilibrium, provides the basis of neutrality hypothesis. However, later it was realized that inflation is much more than just change of scale and it can have serious implications for several real variables. After Keynesian revolution, the effects of inflation were also being viewed through the lenses of long run and short run. In fact, the classical economists believe that inflation does not change the real variables, neither in the short run nor in the long run. On contrary, many economists, e.g., Faria and Carneiro (2001), believe that inflation can affect the real variables in the short run; however, in the long run, the real variables depend only on real variables. Another group of economists thinks that inflation is capable of bringing permanent change in the real variables.

In fact, the debate on relating aggregate inflation with real variables stands on the false grounds. It is not the aggregate inflation which affects the real variables; instead, it is the relative movement of the components of consumer price index which can affect the real variables. If all the components of consumer price index grow in same proportion simultaneously, there must be no real effect as it is believed by classical school of thought. However, if there is difference in the growth rates for various components of consumer price index, it must bring real effect. The socio-economic consequences of inflation also depend on the relative movement of disaggregate price indices.

Consider the famous Phillips curve effect. The Phillips curve postulates negative relation between inflation and unemployment. The underlying assumption is that the prices of consumer commodities are flexible, but the wages, i.e., the prices of labor services, are sticky. Because the commodity prices have gone up, the firms have incentive to produce more, and they will hire extra labor to produce, which leads to a reduction in unemployment. This argument implies that the Phillips curve effect appears because of change in the relative movement of commodity prices and labor prices. If this relative movement was not there, there would be no Phillips curve effect.

Now consider the situation when there is an abrupt hike in the fuel prices. The increase in fuel prices would increase the cost of production which will push the aggregate price level upward. However, the resultant inflation would not have any Phillips curve effect because the firms have no incentive to produce more even if the aggregate inflation has gone up. This phenomenon happened during the 1970s as a result of oil price shock which was termed as stagflation (Hunt 2006). The stagflation also implies that the real effects of inflation depend on the relative movement of disaggregate price indices. This analysis implies that it does not make sense to discuss the effect of aggregate inflation on any real variable, and it also implies that welfare cost inflation would depend the relative price movements. Thus the debate of real effects of inflation should be transformed into the debate of relative movement of disaggregate price indices. However, it seems as if there is no attention of the academics and the policymakers toward the relative price movements and a wrong debate of costs of inflation is going on. Therefore, the monetary policy is targeting an irrelevant variable and is necessarily misguided. Inflation targeting framework must be reanalyzed with a clear focus on the co-movement of disaggregate price indices instead of aggregate inflation.

4.5 Unemployment and Inflation Trade-Off and Its Moral Implications

Economists assume that there is a trade-off between unemployment and inflation. They think that if inflation goes up, the unemployment is going down and vice versa. Therefore, some economists hypothesize a welfare function with two components, i.e., inflation and unemployment (Di Tella et al. 2001; Taylor 1993). They assume that this society's welfare function is like utility function which is convex to origin, so that one can find the elasticity of substitution of inflation with unemployment and vice versa. There are several research studies which calculate this elasticity of substitution. Some people name this substitution elasticity as sacrifice ratio (Fuhrer and Moore 1995; Fuhrer 1994).

Unlike the individual utility curve, the so-called society welfare function involves many individuals. The trade-off in the society welfare function is in fact a conflict of interest of two different individuals, and the so-called sacrifice is imposed sacrifice of one individual for the welfare of another individual. The economists who believe in Pareto optimality should never opt any such action which makes some individuals better off by making some other individual worse off.

The advocate of economic liberty who claims to believe in so-called Pareto optimality theory assumes that one cannot say whether or not the social good is served by taking away land from the rich to give to landless peasants. This is because the utility loss to the rich landlord with refined tastes who loses an extra cup of wine may be far greater than the utility gain to the peasant with coarse tastes who is given an additional loaf of bread (Zaman 2010). However, there is a grieve concern when the poor is made to loose for the welfare of someone who is already better off. The monetary decision which seems quite innocent at the first look is a source of creating this disorder.

4.6 Inflation Targeting and Its Moral Implication

As mentioned above, inflation targeting has become a dominant monetary policy framework today. Inflation could be targeted for the two reasons:

(a) To stabilize the business activities whose primary beneficiaries would be the businessmen

(b) To maintain the purchasing power of the consumers who more probably belong to the lower-middle and low-income groups

As I have discussed, the literature on monetary policy has no or negligible mention of the any consideration of consumer protection. I have cited above the advantages of inflation targeting from monetary literature, which make it quite clear that business stability is the primary objective of the monetary policy. Thus the primary beneficiary of monetary policy is the businessmen belonging to high-income cohort of society. It is also worth noting that most popular view about effect of monetary policy which is referred as demand channel of monetary transmission mechanism says that by adapting a contractionary monetary policy, the aggregate demand would decrease which will decrease the aggregate output and employment. The victims of this pressure on unemployment would be those with very small resources and not having their own businesses. This indicates an important normative and moral implication; is it legitimate to protect the interest of business community by victimizing the poorest cohort of society?

Suppose for a moment that the focus of monetary policy is consumer protection and the central banks wants to maintain the purchasing power of the lower-income cohort of the society and for that purpose the central bank wants to reduce inflation by using contractionary monetary policy. If this is the case, it is well known to every economist that the demand of necessities could not be reduced significantly by small changes in prices. The reform(s) by central bank can only reduce the demand for luxuries. Therefore, if the prices are reduced, it shall be so because the price of luxuries. The advantage of such reform(s) will go to the people having higher proportion of luxuries in their consumption portfolio, i.e., higher-income cohort of the society. The discussion implies that the use of tight monetary policy redistributes income in a manner which favors the high-income cohort.

4.7 The Cost Channel of Monetary Transmission Mechanism

The central banks assume that using the contractionary monetary policy by increasing interest rate or by reducing money supply, the people will postpone spending decisions especially consumption on durables, so that the aggregate demand decreases. This reduction in aggregate demand shall reduce aggregate inflation.

On contrary, many economists believe in cost channel transmission mechanism. The cost channel says that since firms produce by borrowing from banks and pay interest on borrowing, therefore, the interest is part of cost of production. Therefore, if there is increase in interest rate, the cost of production will increase which will result in higher price level.

Thomas Tooke (1774–1858), the author of *History of Prices and of the State of the Circulation during the Years 1793–1856* who is considered as the forefather of monetary economics was the pioneer of the idea of cost channel of monetary transmission mechanism, and he predicted that inflation shall increase by increase in interest rate. His opinion found empirical support from Gibson (1923) in the early twentieth century who found positive correlation between interest rate and prices in the United Kingdom for a data of over 200 years. Keynes referred to the observation of Gibson as "One of most established fact in the whole field of Quantitative economics." After the 1970s, very large number of people including Barth and Ramey (2001) Chowdhury et al. (2006), Ravenna and Walsh (2006), etc. found evidences favoring cost channel of monetary transmission mechanism. Rehman (2015) take a very large data set for a large number of countries and explore the nature of relationship between the interest rate and inflation. He reports to find supports for the cost channel. The author reports that the results are robust to sample size, sample period, and various definitions of interest rate and inflation.

Regardless of the strength of evidences in favor of cost channel, the channel deserves serious attention because if the cost channel was functioning, the use of monetary policy could be counterproductive. Because of this, Wright Patman, a former American congressman and chair of the United States House Committee on Banking and Currency (1963–1975), commented on such a monetary policy by saying that "using interest rate to control inflation is like throwing gasoline on fire." However, despite such a strict warning, the monetary policy practices are continuing without paying any heed to the cost channel, and the monetary policy until today is based on the assumption of demand channel of monetary transmission mechanism.

4.8 Cost Versus Demand Channels and Employment

Employment is one of the most important concerns because in the economies with no social securities for unemployed people, nothing could be more frustrating for an educated youth than the unemployment. The tight monetary policy, whether it is working through demand channel of monetary transmission mechanism or whether it is working through the cost channel, has negative impact on employment. The popular demand channel of monetary transmission mechanism indicates that by a contractionary monetary policy, the equilibrium price level shall go down and the employment shall also go down. On contrary if the cost channel is effective, the tight monetary policy will result in higher equilibrium price level and lower employment. This means contractionary monetary policy, whether it is effecting through cost channel or through demand channel, would result in a reduction in the employment (Ghaffari et al. 2014; Rehman 2015). Rehman (2015) discusses that it could also happen that the demand channel and the cost channel are working simultaneously so that effect of monetary intervention on price level is insignificant. Rehman (2015) shows that in such a case, the reduction in unemployment and output would be twofold. The reduction in employment would be larger if the cost and demand channels are working simultaneously. Therefore, a contractionary monetary policy would always victimize the temporary job holders, regardless of the exact transmission channel.

4.9 Monetary Policy and Income Inequality

Niggle (1989) and Gali (2001) discuss number of channels through which the monetary policy can affect the income distribution. These include income composition channel, financial segmentation channel, interest rate channel, and inflation channel. For example, it is well known that if the inflation turns out to be different from expectation, this has distributional consequences. This is because the real interest rate changes from expectation which changes real gains of lender and borrower. Similarly, the financial segmentation channel says that the regular agents in market make better use of change in monetary policy and the occasional agents get less advantage of the policy, which makes regular agents better off.

The empirical literature on inequality rarely considers monetary policy as a determinant of inflation. However, the few studies exploring relationship between two variables found strong relationship between two. These include Romer and Romer (1999), Fowler (2005), Easterly and Fischer (2001), etc. Most of these researchers argue that a tight monetary policy hurts both in terms of employment and inequality.

The evidences for and against the distributional consequences of monetary policy could be debatable. However, the growing literature on distributional impacts of monetary policy and the world commitment to reduce income inequality as agreed upon in Sustainable Development goals necessitate to have proper research on the issue. However, there is serious deficiency of any such research which is both logical and moral deficiency of the contemporary monetary policy.

4.10 Conclusion

The discussion above makes it clear that the monetary policy is not "innocent bystander" and has serious implication for the employment, income, and income inequality. By signing the Sustainable Development Goals and previously the Millennium Development Goals declarations, the world has shown commitment to reduce inequality. The existence of socioeconomic consequences of monetary policy implies the monetary policy may hurt the progress toward these goals. Therefore, it is necessary to properly investigate the socioeconomic consequences for the conduct of monetary policy.

The chapter also shows that there are numerous logical flaws in the contemporary monetary policy and the policy may actual be leading to opposite of its desired goals, as indicated by the existence of cost channel of monetary transmission mechanism. So the monetary authorities should broaden the spectrum of research and should abandon the blind faith in the so-called demand channel of monetary transmission mechanism.

Tight monetary policy which is exercised by increasing interest rate is shown by many authors to have negative implications for employment and inequality. This means lowering the interest rate can enhance the employment and equality. Therefore, a number of economies have interest rate virtually close to zero. This indicates that zero-interest regime is probably better regime for higher growth and better employment. This provides support to Islamic economists who argue that better economic system is interest-free system.

References

Albanesi, S. (2007). Inflation and inequality. *Journal of Monetary Economics, 54*(4), 1088–1114.

Al-Marhubi, F. (1997). A note on the link between income inequality and inflation. *Economics Letters, 55*(3), 317–319.

Barth, M. J., III, & Ramey, V. A. (2001). The cost channel of monetary transmission. *NBER Macroeconomics Annual, 16*, 199–240.

Chowdhury, I., Hoffmann, M., & Schabert, A. (2006). Inflation dynamics and the cost channel of monetary transmission. *European Economic Review, 50*, 995–1016.

Coibion, O., Gorodnichenko, Y., Kueng, L., & Silvia, J. (2012). *Innocent bystanders? Monetary policy and inequality in the US (No. w18170)*. National Bureau of Economic Research.

Di Tella, R., MacCulloch, R. J., & Oswald, A. J. (2001). Preferences over inflation and unemployment: Evidence from surveys of happiness. *The American Economic Review, 91*(1), 335–341.

Easterly, W., & Fischer, S. (2001). Inflation and the poor. *Journal of Money, Credit and Banking, 33*(2), 160–178.

Faria, J. R., & Carneiro, F. G. (2001). Does high inflation affect growth in the long and short run? *Journal of Applied Economics, 4*(1), 89–105.

Fowler, S. J. (2005). *Income inequality, monetary policy, and the business cycle (No. 184)*. Society for Computational Economics.

Fuhrer, J. (1994). Optimal monetary policy and the sacrifice ratio. In *Conference series; [proceedings]* (Vol. 38, pp. 43–84). Federal Reserve Bank of Boston.

Fuhrer, J. C., & Moore, G. R. (1995). Monetary policy trade-offs and the correlation between nominal interest rates and real output. *The American Economic Review, 85*(1), 219–239.

Gali J. (2001). *Monetary policy in early years of EMU*. Pompeu Fabra University, unpublished manuscript.

Ghaffari, A. B., Rehman, A., & Muhammad, M. (2014). Interest rate and inflation: A case study of Pakistan. *Pakistan Business Review, 16*(3), 451–515.

Gibson, A. (1923). The future course of high class investment values. *Banker's Magazine, 115*(946), 15–34.

Hunt, B. (2006). Oil price shocks and the US stagflation of the 1970s: Some insights from GEM. *The Energy Journal, 27*(4), 61–80.

Mersch, Y. (2014, October 17). Monetary policy and economic inequality. In *Keynote speech, corporate credit conference*, Zurich.

Mishkin, F. S. (2001). *From monetary targeting to inflation targeting (No. 2684)*. World Bank Publications.

Myrdal, G. (1939). *Monetary equilibrium*. London: William Hodge.

Niggle, C. J. (1989). Monetary policy and changes in income distribution. *Journal of Economic Issues, 23*(3), 809–822.

Nordhaus, W. D. (1973). The effects of inflation on the distribution of economic welfare. *Journal of Money, Credit and Banking, 5*(1), 465–504.

Ravenna, F., & Walsh, C. E. (2006). Optimal monetary policy with the cost channel. *Journal of Monetary Economics, 53*, 199–216.

Rehman, A. U. (2015). Revival of legacy of Tooke and Gibson: Implications for monetary policy. *Journal of Central Banking Theory and Practice, 4*(2), 37–58.

Romer, C. D., & Romer, D. (1999). Monetary policy and the well-being of the poor. *Economic Review, Federal Reserve Bank of Kansas City, 84*(1), 21–49.
Rothbard, M. N. (1994). Austrian economics: Tensions and new directions. *Southern Economic Journal, 61*(2), 559–561.
Serletis, A., & Krause, D. (1996). Empirical evidence on the long-run neutrality hypothesis using low-frequency international data. *Economics Letters, 50*(3), 323–327.
Shiller, R. (1997). Why do people dislike inflation. In C. H. Romer & D. H. Romer (Eds), *Reducing inflation*. The University of Chicago Press.
Taylor, J. B. (1993, December). Discretion versus policy rules in practice. In *Carnegie-Rochester conference series on public policy* (Vol. 39, pp. 195–214). North-Holland.
Zaman, A. (2010). Anti-poverty policies and anti-poor philosophies, unpublished paper SSRN.

Chapter 5
Historical and Ideological Peculiarity of the Monetary Institutions: Islamic and Austrian School's Perspectives

Omar Javaid

5.1 Introduction

Classical Muslim scholars till the sixteenth century have discussed the factors behind the deterioration of value of money. These factors include debasement of currency by political authorities and flight of money supply to other regions (Islahi 2008). Scholars in Islamic history do not seem to be concerned about the growth of their respective economies as economic growth never appears as a parameter to gauge the health of the economy in classical literature. The primary concern of these scholars, it seems, has been on the social impact of the fluctuation in the purchasing power of money. Some examples of social impact are as follows: increase in prices may deplete the savings of ordinary individuals; or decrease in purchasing power of money may cause monetary loss to a creditor who is accepting payments from the borrowers. These losses would perhaps lead to social disruptions and chaos, particularly when money loses a significant amount of its value in a short period of time (Allouche 1994; Pamuk 2000).

The focus of concern of these scholars perhaps reflects their value system, which was perhaps grounded in the teachings of Islam. For that reason, they do not seem to approve debasement of currency by the political authorities no matter what the cause of debasement may be (Islahi 2008). If these classical scholars were prehaps present in contemporary times, would they have approved the contemporary monetary establishment, which allows governments to print and borrow money to finance its expenses? Would they have allowed the elite to manipulate the money supply for their own gains while adversely affecting the economic well-being of the population? Would they have approved those designs of monetary institutions, which by default cause these problems as externalities? The answer would perhaps be no.

O. Javaid (✉)
Institute of Business Management, Karachi, Pakistan
e-mail: omar.javaid@iobm.edu.pk

M. Zulkhibri et al. (eds.), *Islamic Monetary Economics and Institutions*,
https://doi.org/10.1007/978-3-030-24005-9_5

From the perspective of Austrian School of Economics (ASE), the banking system is primarily responsible for aforementioned problems, which include: multiplying many times the money supply issued by the central bank (which is believed to cause inflation or debasement of money), economic cycles (high growth period followed by recession) and bank runs. The banking system is allowed to run on a fractional reserve system, which creates new unit of money with every unit of credit issued to a borrower. The elite can borrow a lot more than the ordinary individuals; therefore, their borrowing creates most of the amount of money in circulation. The government likewise borrows and further leads to creation of money supply. In any economy, using a fractional reserve model of banking, the deposits exceed by many times than the physical stock of money contributing to aforementioned problems from the perspective ASE (de Soto 2009; Reisman 1998).

The mainstream economic thinkers consider it as legitimate form of banking, which can be effectively managed through the monetary policy of the central bank of the country. ASE, however, assumes fractional reserve banking (FRB) system to be at the heart of the aforementioned economic problems. ASE believes that any form of government regulation cannot restrain the banks to issue more credit than the economy can handle, subsequently leading to economic cycles. These cycles either hurt the ordinary individual through inflation or by taking away employment opportunities, respectively.

The academia of Islamic banking and finance (IBF) also seems to be either neutral or concur with the views of mainstream economists on the subject of FRB or the ability of the commercial banks to create money supply. There seems to be negligible debate in the scholarly literature of IBF to establish the theoretical legitimacy of FRB in the light of its historical significance in the modern western economic system. The academic discussion is rather focused more on improving the efficiency of the system and *Shari'ah* compliance of its products. In other words, academic debate is driven more by pragmatism of market logic rather than by the Ideals of Islam (Fang 2014; Rethel 2011). This would not have been the case perhaps if classical scholars of 16th century or before were present today. Ismail and Tohirin (2010) notes:

> three important aspects contributing to the systemic weaknesses of conventional economic system ... [are] the interest rate system, the fractional reserve system and the fiat money system ... Unfortunately, among these three only one, i.e., interest system can be avoided by Islamic banks ... Meanwhile the other two are unavoidably adopted by Islamic banks. (p. 190)

In this context, this chapter is an invitation to cover the gap by introducing aspects of theoretical analysis needed to create a foundation of an Islamic economic and monetary system in the contemporary world. The chapter uses the work of Grief, Hollingsworth and Schumpeter to develop a criterion to comprehend institutions in context of their historical and cultural peculiarity. The criterion is then used to understand the mainstream monetary framework of modern western economic thought as explained by ASE, which will then be compared with the Islamic monetary perspective. The chapter will also discuss the possible application of Islamic monetary perspective on community and village level in comparison to the macro monetary system of western origin.

5.2 Historical and Cultural Particularity of an Institution

The efforts to Islamize modern western design of institutions are seemingly done within a weak theoretical and philosophical premise (Javaid and Hassan 2013). It is apparently devoid of any understanding on how an institution is created, evolved and transformed over the period of time. Same can be claimed for the monetary institutions evolved in the capitalist order which were imposed on much of the world during the period of colonization (Javaid 2015a). Generally, institutions evolve through a historical process under the influence of the cultural norms and religion (or ideological roots) of host society (Greif 1994). The purpose of institutions is to facilitate various socioeconomic and political ends sought by the inhabitants of a society. Through the process of hit and trial spread across many generations, an institutional design reaches the level of maturity.

Likewise, changes in culture and meta-norms and subsequent changes in priorities of a society lead to an analogous change in the institutional structure as well (Hollingsworth 2000). This suggests that two culturally and ideologically distinct societies would have a distinct set of socioeconomic and political institutions, both designed to achieve distinct ends as well. Grief (1994) argues that it is unwise to expect institution emerge in individualistic (modern) to deliver results in a collectivist (traditional) one. An institution of western origin would either have to be significantly adapted to fulfil the requirement of the collectivist order or the collectivist order has to be transformed to become compatible with the requirement of the modern institutions. Hollingsworth (2000) and De Soto (2009) also agree.

The post-colonial world, in this context, presents an interesting example. The modern institutions like the free market, the constitutional democracy, judicial system, central banking system along with private banks, etc. all originated in Europe and were brought in by the colonial forces, despite the colonies having their own set of economic and political institutions embedded in their unique cultural and ideological disposition. There was perhaps an antagonism in the host societies and imported institutions. The traditional order of the host societies either had to be significantly transformed to become compatible or had to except the exclusion from the operational realm of the imported institutions (Gellner 2000; Polanyi 1944).

The traditional monetary system in the Muslim world was expected to maintain trust in the market, rather than maximizing returns on investment (Allouche 1994). The traditional mechanism to obtain an investment or a loan, to put money for safe keeping and to transfer from one place to another was all organized around traditional concept of money being a medium of exchange, a measure and a medium to store value (Niazi 2013). Money can be viewed also a 'social institution' (Simmel 2004) to keep the community bonded as it was used to facilitate the ones in need directly through charity or indirectly by giving relaxation to the debtor who needed more time to return the credit. The act of giving credit, investing money in a partnership, safekeeping someone's money and then honouring the terms agreed or returning the money as promised, for example, established trust. Money, therefore, can be assumed as a medium to establish and reinforce trust between people who lived together within extended families and communities (Javaid 2015b). Soundness of money (stability in its purchasing power over long periods), therefore, may be referred as a facilitator in this context.

The same may be true for the market system of European origin; however, there the concept of money changed from a facilitator - to a product to be sold in the market and maximize returns (Javaid and Suri 2015). The banks specialized in the sale and purchase of money. This new ontological position of money took precedence in the modern economy over its traditional role due to overarching influence of free-market institutions (including banks) over non-market spheres of the society. Using money to make more money was now the goal. This was the period in history when money perhaps became capital, financial capital to be specific. Machines, man, materials and land were also transformed into factors-of-production or into means to generate more capital.

The money was commoditized along with land and labour, and the same was imposed on the colonies during the period of colonization. The political machinery also reportedly backed such a transition (Polanyi 1944). Once forcefully imposed, the transformation had immense implications for the traditional societies and communities in the colonial world. The traditional society was turned upside down (Gellner 2000). The man became the facilitator of money, instead of money being a facilitator of man (Javaid and Suri 2015).

5.3 Origin of Modern Monetary System

The rise of modernism and replacement of traditional society in Europe is a common knowledge. The capitalist economy and liberal democracy took place of the hegemony of church and monarchy in Europe. The new market society advocated the values of individualism, competition, pursuit of material self-interest, progress and rationalism. The new system was 'characterized by the pursuit of material self-interest under freedom and ... cultural influence of reason' (Reisman 1998, p. 19).

Accumulation of capital is an embodiment of freedom and progress in capitalist society (Heilbroner 1994). Therefore, capitalist society, including its political and economic institutions, is organized to facilitate the process of capital accumulation and hence provides a free hand to the market where individual agents can compete with each other for profit maximization. Man, machine, material, land and any other item which can be used for producing goods or services are privately owned and traded for profit (Polanyi 1944).

Before modernization of Europe, traditional society was organized to preserve their collectivist order. The production was a household phenomenon managed by the tribe which operated more like a giant extended family, instead of an impersonal-rational-bureaucratic corporation which emerged later in Europe (Javaid and Suri 2016). Polanyi (1944) has noted how the tribal resources were transformed into factors of production. Money was another factor of production which was required in excess quantity to facilitate the transactions in a developing capitalist society.

The bimetallic currency was in short supply; despite influx of gold and silver from foreign lands, the short fall could not be covered. Many scientists experimented with alchemy to convert abundantly available metals into gold. The traders during that time begin to use credit in lieu of a mortgage as a medium of exchange. Receipts mentioning the owed amount by reputed traders begin to circulate in the market. Looking at the trend, Bank of England was formed, in view of Wennerlind (2011), to facilitate the process.

The banks, therefore, eliminated a great hurdle in the expansion of the capitalist economy and continue to do so till today (Schumpeter 2006). The role of the commercial banks to expand the money supply through credit creation through the FRB system has been acknowledged recently by Bank of England (McLeay et al. 2014). Since bank's profitability is dependent on advancing credit, which contributed in the expansion of money supply, therefore, it is illogical to assume that the banks would restrict themselves from doing so in a normative context where profit maximization is seen as the ultimate goal.

The only limit use to be the growth in the real economy, as the banks could only advance loans to the industry which intended to expand in real terms or consumers who wanted to purchase the products which they could not otherwise afford. Since the advent to financial markets (hedge funds, derivatives, etc.), the possibility of expansion is now perhaps endless. Nevertheless, advocating the growth of a consumer society – where every individual strives to maximize consumption – is in direct interest of the banking system. When the general public exhaust their income, they resort to the banks for loans to expand more (Javaid 2015a). Privatization of services like health care and education also goes very much in favour of the banking system, as it opens new venues to advance loans to the consumer.

The commercial banks, in a nut shell, create an economy where every individual owes money to the banks, whose value keeps increasing with constant inflation caused by continuous expansion of the money supply by the FRB system. Banks virtually own the real assets financed by bank loans through hypothecation, and gradual transfer of ownership of real assets to the banks when the debtors are not able to payback and opt for foreclosure. The commercial banks also create an atmosphere where the rich are treated better than the poor because of their assumed ability to generate better returns for the banks. The poor are excluded, therefore, from the circuit of capital and the pretext of credit unworthiness (which has been debunked by Mr. Yunus, founder of Grameen Bank). As a result, the banks perhaps become a harbinger of shifting the wealth to the upper strata of the society, becoming a source of increasing inequality. Banks does this mercilessly without any remorse; in other words, it appears that banking system may be considered as an embodiment of the dictatorial spirit of the capital (Javaid and Suri 2015). The raison d'être of doing so is established by the broader socioeconomic and political system having secular, liberal and capitalist orientation, of which the commercial banking is a part of. Table 5.1 outlines various levels of this system.

Table 5.1 The socioeconomic and political context of commercial banking system

Level 1: Informal institutions	Liberal, secular worldview; ontological and cosmological views based on materialism, Scottish enlightenment, virtuous man; wealthy and powerful ones (see Adam Smith's 'Theory of Moral Sentiments')
Level 2: Institutional arrangements	Liberal and secular state formation, social hierarchy based on aristocratic values, rich on the top, poor on the bottom, competition in markets between rich and poor, social Darwinism
Level 3: Institutional sectors	Interest-based lending, monetary system based on bank notes representing credit or debt, corporate culture; profit-maximizing institutions (corporates) seeking loan to finance operations and expansion
Level 4: Concrete organization	Private banks, central banks, insurance firms, corporations, cartels
Level 5: Output and performance	Consumerist culture, mass supply of debt, wealth and freedom and pleasure maximization for rich, increasing income disparity, industrialization of social functions (see Adam Curtis's documentary "'The Century of Self' made for BBC)

Note: Based on Hollingsworth (2000) framework of institutional analysis (For detailed analysis of the above, see my earlier paper (Javaid 2015a, b))

5.4 Austrian School of Economics on Modern Monetary System

ASE is a pro-secular and staunch advocate of free-market capitalism, just like other modern schools of economics. Their criticism of the commercial banking system's ability to expand to money supply through credit creation is the only concern for this paper. ASE believes that the FRB system of monetary expansion is responsible for inflation, or decrease in purchasing power, economic cycles and bank runs. Alfred Marshall,[1] quoted by De Soto (2009), argues:

> … if each bank could lend two thirds of its deposits, the total amount of loaning power got by the banks would amount to three times what it otherwise would be. If it could lend four-fifths, it will then be five times, and so on. The question how large a part of its deposits a bank can lend depends in a great measure on the extent on which the different banks directly or indirectly pool their reserves. (p. 215)

When money is deposited to the banks, it is lent to the borrowers while keeping a fraction as deposits; however, the depositors also can use their deposited money through cheques, bank drafts, pay orders, etc. Therefore, the money can be used by multiple individuals at the same time. The amount issued as credit is deposited in the same banks or some other bank. A fraction of the new deposits is kept and loaned again to someone else. When this happens, the amount of credit and amount of deposits increases simultaneously, while the physical stock of currency remains a fraction of the total credit and deposits. Money is, therefore, created out of nothing, argues De Soto (2009). Macleod (1906) noted the same a century ago,

[1] Alfred Marshall, "Memoranda and Evidence before the Gold and Silver Commission," December 19, 1887, in Official Papers by Alfred Marshall [London: Royal Economic Society, Macmillan, 1926], p. 37

Schumpeter (2006) also concurs. Recently, Bank of England published an article explaining how money is created through commercial banking system. This paper is a further confirmation to the phenomenon discussed above. The article explains:

> The reality of how money is created today differs from the description found in some economics textbooks. Rather than banks receiving deposits when households save and then lending them out, bank lending creates deposits. In normal times, the central bank does not fix the amount of money in circulation, nor is central bank money 'multiplied up' into more loans and deposits. (McLeay et al. 2014, p. 14)

The statistics of money multiplication is also officially published by central banks of respective economies. For example, a document on State Bank of Pakistan's website defines that a Money Multiplier 'is the ratio of stock of broad money (M2)[2] to the stock of reserve money (M0). The money multiplier is a measure of the extent to which the creation of money in the banking system causes the growth in the money supply to exceed growth in monetary base' (SBP 2012).

Banks have their own interest attached with the phenomenon as more credit creation means more profitability, presumably because combining the deposit and lending functions bank can perhaps earn multiple times over the same amount of currency. Such flexibility may not be available to any other forms of business, such that one unit of currency is expanded to as much as ten times (depending upon the reserve requirements established by the central banks), and each expansion would reap profit for the bank. Therefore, ASE is at the forefront to advocate the idea that business cycles are a result of credit expansion by the banks (de Soto 2009; Hayek 1953; Polleit 2011; Reisman 1998; Schumpeter 2006).

Nonetheless, this theory is not without criticism. Many believes that this theory incompletely explains the phenomenon of business cycle, as there are also other factors which inflate and deflate an economy (Caplan 2008; Friedman 1994; Krugman 1998; Tullock 1988). However, as far as inflationary period is concerned, there is also sufficient evidence to significantly correlate the credit expansion by the banks with 'monetary inflation' (Benati 2005; Hasan 1999; King 2001; Polleit 2005; Roffia and Zaghini 2007). The endogenous theory of inflation also asserts that banks are directly involved in this expansion leading to inflation (Bernanke and Blinder 1988; Niggle 1991). In view of Gordon (1975), many economists agree that the long-run inflation is caused by monetary expansion. Milton Friedman, who does not agree with ASE often, also once famously said 'Inflation is always and everywhere a monetary phenomenon' (Friedman 1994).

It is believed that when banks overlook the risks involved in the investments, they perhaps expand the credit to the point of a financial crisis. It is the job of regulatory institutions to keep an eye on the banks (McLeay et al. 2014). However, the way top executives in the banking system bypass such regulatory regimes to play havoc with the economy for their own self-interest is not a secret as well (Curtis 2011).

---

[2] M2 is the sum of all private, public sector deposits and M0.

5.5 Money Creation Through FRB System and Islamic Banks (IBs)

IBs are also required by the central banks to follow the FRB system (Ismail and Tohirin 2010). Therefore, it needs to be asked: would the criticism of FRB system of ASE apply on IBs as well? Would IBs contribute in long-term inflation through creation of credit? Can IBs theoretically contribute in economic cycles? How the ownership structure of the economy would be affected under the IBs operating on FRB? Can bank run happens on IBs in case of economic recession, or would IBs be able to fulfil their depositors request to release all the cash in case they demand to do so? Possible answers to these questions are discussed below.

5.5.1 *If Financing Is Asset Backed Will It Cause Inflation?*

Henry Thornton (1760 – 1815) who was a monetary theorist, and long-time Member of British Parliament argues that there are three flaws of the 'Real Bills Doctrine'[3] which assumes that 'inflationary over issue [of credit] is impossible provided money is issued on loans made to finance real transactions' (Humphrey 1982, p. 4). This doctrine though looks fine at theoretical level; however, looking more closely reveals its various flaws, which have been explained by Humphrey while referring to Henry Thornton (1760–1815). The three flaws are as follows:

1. *Single asset, multiple exchanges.* Any asset may exchange many hands, and during each transaction a financial intermediary may create credit money if required by the buyer of the asset. This would mean that a piece of land or a vehicle, for example, can be sold many times over, for all or some of these purchases of the same asset the buyer may seek the services of a financial intermediary. Each of such transaction can involve an intermediary, thus creating a debt each time for the same asset or a set of commodities
2. *Cost of debt leading to more debt.* The manufacturer after acquiring debt from a bank would add the debt servicing expense into the cost of goods, thus adding to the selling price; this increase would subsequently become an excuse for a further creation of debt when the whole seller would purchase the manufactured item from the manufacturer in case he used a financial intermediary for this purchase. This would make inflation a 'vicious circle'.
3. *Continuous inflationary spiral.* For example, when public take credit to meet their expanses, the money supply increase contribute to inflation, which tempts the manufacturers to increase prices and the worker to demand for more wages. Increased wages of the workers and debt servicing expense would further force the manufacturer to increase the price of his products, which would force work-

[3] 'Real Bills Doctrine' assumes that "inflationary over issue [of credit] is impossible provided money is issued on loans made to finance real transactions" (Humphrey 1982, p. 4).

ers to demand more wages and so on. Increasing prices would also increase the amount of credit required by the manufacturers to make purchases further causing the spiral to continue at a greater pace.

This suggests that even by claiming to be asset-backed IBs (along with their orientation to maximization of profit, market share, shareholder's value, while competing with conventional banks on the same lines) would expand the money supply and generate a money multiplier effect and would subsequently contribute in debasing the currency. In other words, inflationary effects of FRB may not be curtained by simply bringing assets backed-debt-based transactions in IBs (Meera and Larbani 2004; Zubair and Abbas 1987). Even if the money supply does not surpass the real goods in the economy, the cost of debt servicing at every stage of the supply chain would add to the cost of doing business, subsequently causing a rise in prices.

Continuous inflation due to expansion of money supply in a bank is perhaps tantamount to debasement of currency, defrauding of poor, and even equivalent to theft of purchasing power from the money supply (Meera and Larbani 2009). Unfortunately, this phenomenon is also reported in Islamic history; however, inflation in Islamic history in nominal terms has been primarily[4] due to the debasement of coinage by the monarchs to finance wars during the history of Ottoman Empire (Pamuk 2000). It can be deduced that IBs, with a FRB system and its inclination towards debt-based instruments, would allow IBs to contribute to the problem of inflation. This contribution may be lesser than the conventional banking system; however, empirical evidence is required to establish its magnitude.

5.5.2 Status of Private Ownership

Capitalism advocates private ownership of property, and it is believed to be its most distinguishing feature. Alan Greenspan has repeatedly emphasized about this in his autobiography and has declared it as a reason for success of American economy (Greenspan 2008).[5] However, it may be argued that private ownership in a capitalistic economy is gradually reduced by the dominance of financial markets (Ansari 2004).

Bank often requires a collateral against the credit it issues. The collateral remains under the hypothetical possession of the bank until the debt is paid off. This is known as hypothecation. It is not impossible, at least theoretically, that banking system might have an amount of collateral in its hypothetical possession equivalent to the amount of domestic debt existing in an economy (government is an exception). Furthermore, since the total money supply is a result of bank credit, therefore, the bank can also virtually own capital equivalent to the amount created through

[4] Other causes could include influx of gold and silver coins from outside like in war booty or shortage caused due to export to other areas where a higher price of product was offered, etc.

[5] See index entry 'Property Rights' in the cited book.

giving credit. As the credit grows, the money supply also grows, so does the amount of collateral. Same would be even truer for IBs, as they claim to own the asset before selling or renting it in various ways. IBs, however, do not give credit; they rather finance or invest, while apparently creating effects similar to their conventional counter parts.

The penetration of financial system, whether Islamic or conventional, in an economy may reduce private ownership of real asset to the degree of penetration and may replace it with the ownership of debt instead. At the time of recession (caused by excessive credit creation by the private banks in view of ASE), the amount of foreclosures and bankruptcies increases, which perhaps formally transfers the ownership of the real assets from the defaulters to the bank.

Monetary data available at central banks suggests that one of the biggest borrowers of the private banks is the government itself. When government uses the borrowed money for the first time, its purchasing power is intact; however, once the money flows in the economy, the money supply goes up causing the purchasing power to go down. If a poor fellow has $1000 in saving, which he legally earned through hard work, its purchasing power would be taken away without his consent, because government or the elite class borrowed more money into existence (Meera and Larbani 2009). It is referred as a form of hidden tax charged by the government through borrowing from the banks (Mises 1953).

Furthermore, with the penetration of such a financial system, more individuals are subsequently inclined to get indebted to finance their needs and wants. This is already happening in capitalist societies with a culture dominated with consumerist mentality (Wright and Rogers 2010). It has been noted that when public finance their assets like car, house, education of children, inventory or assets for their business, or grocery items from their credit cards (which are also now being offered by some IBs), a percentage of their income goes in the debt servicing. The more the debt, the more they have to pay back out of their disposable income. Henceforth, when the public is obsessed with buying products and commodities, personal savings rates may reduce accordingly (Sartell and Vierra 2012; Treeck 2007).

Therefore, it may be asked, what would happen to the institution of *Zakat*[6] and inheritance, once the concept of private property evaporates due to heavy dominance of debt and personal saving go away in debt servicing in a society where a debt-based Islamic financial system dominates the entire market? Banks may not be required to pay *Zakat* except which is applicable on their paid-up capital; they though become an agent to deduct *Zakat* amount from the deposits and submit it to *Bait-ul-mal*; therefore, it is the depositors who pay *Zakat* if the funds in their accounts are more than the qualifying limit (*nisab*). The same depositor could also be a client of the same bank or some other bank, who might have also availed financial ser-

[6] *Zakat* is equivalent to 2.5% of total savings which is above the prescribed limit and is in the form of cash, gold, silver or any other tradable commodity which a Muslim male or female has in his or her ownership; it is mandatory for him or her to pay to a poor who qualifies to receive *Zakat*. *Zakat* cannot be paid via an IOU.

vices, and pays an amount in debt servicing. This depositor will then eventually pay *Zakat* at the end of the year from his net savings after paying for debt servicing. In this context, it is not so surprising to note the severity of condemnation in various hadith[7] against the taking debt especially for luxuries of life.

Therefore, in an FRB system, the amount of net savings of the public may reduce. In pursuit of gaining market share, IBs are perhaps doing the same. If they continue to promote the idea of indebting oneself for the sake of increasing one's living standards, the resulting reduction in disposable income would perhaps make it increasingly difficult to pay *Zakat* due to the amount owed to IBs. Similar can be the case with inheritance, as increased level of personal debt may force the heirs to first payback the debt and then distribute the remaining assets among each other as per the ratios prescribed by *Shari'ah*.

5.5.3 Mitigating the Bank Run

Since the deposits in the banking system are only backed by a fraction of physical cash and securities, therefore, it is impossible for all depositors to take physical possession of the money stock equivalent to their deposits. In fact, banks can only release cash equivalent to the amount kept as reserve which is only a small fraction of the money they owe to their depositors. It can be argued that since conventional banks do not trade in commodities or assets, they only lend money on interest; therefore, in case of a bank run (all depositors demanding their money to be returned as they have lost trust in the bank), conventional banks will not have anything to return other than the fraction of the cash reserve they have. They might have a hold on the collateral (against the loans they have advanced); however, they can only acquire this collateral unless the borrowers have defaulted.

The case of IBs is different; as they don't loan money on interest, their transactions are perhaps equivalent to sale and purchase with differed payment; hence, they are required to acquire ownership of an asset before selling it, for example, in case of *Murabahah* or *Bai-Muajjal* contract. The customer might take possession of the asset and agree to pay on instalments, now till the time the banks receive all the instalments the ownership will remain at the bank equivalent to value of the asset minus the amount returned by the client as instalments.

---

[7] Prophet Muhammad (peace be upon him) has sought refuge from debt (Sunan Nisai, p. 264, vol. 8, Maktaba Al-Matboot Al-Islamia: Halb), termed the indebted person as a prisoner (Sunan Abi Dawood p. 119, vol. 2, Al-Maktaba Al-Asriya, Syeda: Beirut), has refused to lead namaz-e-janazah (funeral prayer) of the indebted person (Sunan Nisai p. 315, vol. 7, Maktaba Al-Matboot Al-Islamia: Halb), has informed that the soul of indebted person is suspended in his grave and his soul would not enter paradise unless his debt is paid off even if he is a martyr in a holy war (Sunan Nisai p. 314, vol. 7, Maktaba Al-Matboot Al-Islamia: Halb; Sahih Muslim 1501-2/3, Darul-Ahya Al-Taras Al-Arabi: Beirut). Prophet (pbuh) has even informed that a person who takes a debt unnecessarily or to fulfill any desire beyond his very basic need deserves the wrath of Allah (Mashkah Al-Masabiyh p. 579, vol. 1, Maktaba Al-Islami: Beirut).

Henceforth, an IB (Islamic bank) would either have cash or it would own an asset on the behalf of the depositor who in case of a profit- and loss-sharing account is the *Rabb ul-Mal* (investor) and bank is *Mudarib* (working partner). Therefore, in case of all depositors coming to IBs to take back their cash, the IB would either give cash, but if that is not available then IB would issue ownership receipts perhaps for the assets it might have in its possession. Since the depositor is *Rabb ul-Mal* and IB being the *Mudarib*, therefore, bank also reserve the right to hold payment of cash until the asset which were purchased from it are liquidated in the market. In *Mudarabah* contract, the depositor is also entitled to share the profit and loss of the bank, such that in case of an unprecedented loss, not caused by negligence of the bank, the depositor will bear all the loss. If IBs are not able to liquidate the assets in hard cash, as the cash in an economy is also only a fraction as compare to the total deposits, then central bank would act as a lender of last resort to protect the bank from defaulting.

However, in case of current account, the amount deposited in the IB is *Qard Hasan*; bank is allowed to use it for commercial purposes but is also bound to return the principal amount to the depositor as and when demanded. IBs, therefore, must keep cash in easy access equivalent to the amount deposited in the current accounts by the depositors, to fulfil their promise of return on demand all the deposits when required by all the borrowers. The risk of a bank run is although insignificant, though its ramifications are of historic proportions. Therefore, due to high risk, IBs may keep themselves prepared to mitigate the crisis by honouring all the claims when required. This however may significantly affect IBs profits.

5.5.4 Transfer of Wealth to the Elite

The promise of return of deposited amount with a surplus encourages the rich class towards hoarding, wealth accumulation and earning without participating in real economic activity. The elite deposits their money in profit-sharing accounts which the bank invest wherever it assumes it is safe to invest, like public limited companies. The money, therefore, keeps circulating among the elite. Furthermore, how the FRB system transfers the purchasing power to the elite without the consent of the public, poor in particular, has already been discussed (Meera and Larbani 2009). The IBs also favour the rich due to lesser risk involved, perhaps creating the same effects as their conventional counter parts. This may be evident from their lack of focus in the microfinance domain (Abduhu 2013) relative to the total market size of global Islamic finance industry.

5.6 Incoherence Between Western and Islamic Monetary Principles

The ultimate objective of an Islamic society may not be to enable every individual to unprecedentedly maximize his or her material affluence (Javaid and Suri 2015). In fact, this objective is nowhere in the *Maqasid al-Shari'ah* framework, which rather prioritizes protection of *deen*, followed by self, family, intellect and then lastly the wealth owned by the self and the society as a whole (Javaid and Hassan 2013). Wealth in *Maqasid al-Shari'ah* framework is referred in the context of protection of private property, instead of amassment or accumulation. The worldview within which Islam sets these priorities also defines the meaning of life, death and life in hereafter distinctly from a secular or a materialist worldview (Javaid and Hassan 2013). A society built on Islamic values, beliefs, principles, ideals (meta-norms) and worldview is unfortunately non-existent in contemporary post-colonial world. If it had been in existence, its monetary system may have been designed to accomplish the requirements outlined by Islamic meta-norms and evaluated accordingly. The monetary system may have focus on maintaining a medium of exchange which would perhaps keep its purchasing power to avoid any unpleasant situation to the debtor or creditor, as discussed earlier, or preserve the value of one's savings. The purpose would be to maintain the trust and cohesion, *Assabiah*, as suggested by Ibn-e-Khaldun (Mohammad 1998), between Muslims trading in the market. This is not possible when medium of exchange continuously loses its value, particularly when the elites of the society clandestinely take away the purchasing power through borrowing (Meera and Larbani 2009).

The monetary institutions developed in capitalism seemingly assume the ontological superiority of capital over that of a human being who rather has committed himself or herself to the continuous accumulation of capital, who is perhaps superior to the one who has not made such a commitment(Javaid and Hassan 2013). The form of capital in this context perhaps has been in continuous evolution since the advent of industrialization, continuously making it easier to facilitate the process of accumulation. The creation of Bank of England, the institutionalization of credit as a form of money perhaps facilitated such a transformation, which made the credit created in every transaction to be used as a medium of exchange. First, the gold backing was removed as its limited quantity restricted the expansion of monetary supply as and when needed by the political authorities or the industries (Wennerlind 2011). The paper receipts representing credit were then replaced with digital media in more recent times making it even easier to store, transfer and multiply the stock of money to the extent required. The digital representation of money apparently allows capitalists to surreptitiousness pursue capital accumulation anywhere on the planet. Imagine the hassle a billionaire would face while making payments worth millions of dollars in precious metals while travelling the world in comparison to the digital transfer of money. How difficult it would be to carry and how noticeable it would be to any concerned stakeholder? Due to the global mobility of digital currency in contemporary times, the capital now can move to any part of the world at a speed of light wherever there is a better opportunity for its multiplication (Javaid and Suri 2015).

The capital now moves in and out of nations on a short notice often affecting the stability of local economy (Helleiner 1998; Stiglitz 2004). The more an economy is dependent on the banking system, the more it may be affected by the international economic shocks (Kroszner et al. 2007). It appears that during such moments, the primary commitment of a capitalist is demonstrated when he or she often move capital to another place where its chances of accumulation or maintenance are better, irrespective of the consequences for the local economies. The economic crisis faced by Asian Tigers during 1990s is a case in point, where the interest of international investors was apparently prioritized over the interest of the population of East Asian countries (Sharma 2012). Recently, devaluation of Malaysian Ringgit due to flight of capital from Malaysian economy is perhaps another example (Pilling 2015).

One can argue that such crisis caused by the inflows and outflows also has been documented in history when the gold and silver coins were used (Pamuk 2000). The owner of the coinage (during old times) and international investors (during present times) has the right to take away their money, in whatever form, to anywhere they want to the only difference is that nowadays it is possible to transfer of money in or out of a region at a speed unprecedented in human history. This transfer of colossal amount of capital is done in a normative context which justifies the prioritization of maximization of one's self-interest over the larger socioeconomic consequences of doing so; previously, neither such a justification nor the mechanisms were present. Therefore, the impact of a quick and massive outflow of capital from an economy can be far adverse as compare to gradual devaluation of coinage during pre-industrial era.

What role IBs would play in such a scenario? The primary commitment of a bank is perhaps to its customers not with the well-being of the general public, so is perhaps true for IBs. Would classical Islamic scholars of the sixteenth century have allowed IBs to become part of an institutional framework which is committed to ensure the global sovereignty of capital at the cost of well-being of the general public? The debate perhaps warrants probing into some deeper questions, which are:

1. Do IBs intend to shape the market and monetary system in a way that it facilitates in the reinforcement or establishment of an Islamic society? Or IBs are the agents of global capital and reinforce the modern capitalist order in the post-colonial Muslim world while only superficially saving the religious segment of Muslim elite from *riba*, *qimar* and *gharar*, while excluding the remaining population?
2. Does accepting the western design of the monetary system is also an acceptance of the superiority of capital over man?
    (a) If the answer is yes, then what justification from Islamic point of view is available to back this claim?

(b) If the answer to above is no, then one must ask: what changes in the capitalist monetary system have been done to bring the ontological position of money where it should be as per Islamic worldview?
(c) If it is not possible to bring such a change, what alternatives are available for the segment of Muslim population who do not wish to be a part of the modern monetary system, or do so unwillingly?

5.7 Alternatives

From an Islamic perspective, a stable society would be where the atmosphere of trust and social cohesion is maintained, what Khaldun referred as *Assabiah* (Mohammad 1998). Money has its role in maintaining a stable society perhaps only when its value is established and stable (Simmel 2004). Therefore, all factors which contribute in fluctuation of its value, either through debasement, hoarding or transfer to another region, may be eliminated to the extent possible. This is unlikely in a global FRB-based-banking system where the elite and governments can manipulate the money supply for their advantage also at the expense of the masses, as discussed above. Many communities around the world have already opted for a local currency or exchange systems due to the problems with the mainstream system as discussed above.

5.7.1 Local Currencies

Local currencies are issued by a non-profit body and accepted by various registered businesses within a community. The value of the locally issued currency or community currency (sic) is either 'based on the value of the services or goods provided [or they can also be based on] the labour time required to produce such services or goods' (Collom 2005, p. 1566). Their value can also simply be equivalent to the national currency. The buyers are encouraged to use local currencies through discounts on purchases, while the businesses are encouraged to accept through increased number of recurring customers who owns the currency. The same businesses also pay salaries to their employees using the same who eventually spend it on the registered businesses. In some examples, the currency is deliberately made to lose a small fraction of its value after a predefined time, to discourage hoarding. Furthermore, there is no money market where the local currency can be invested to earn some profit; therefore, its only use is to buy local stuff or services (Collom 2005). As a result, the local business is boasted, new employment is created, and currency is kept constantly in circulation within a community (Ryan-Collins 2011).

Anyone who is interested to use the local currency can exchange the national currency with the local one at exchange kiosks, where they are often given some additional amount for free to encourage the conversion. The money comes into circulation only in a quantity which is to be used for exchange real products or services; therefore, there is no apparent possibility of inflation due to increase in quantity of circulation. Local currency can be printed or digitized through pay card system, each having unique ways to prevent counterfeiting. Any local currency initiative survives only when a significant number of businesses accept them in a community; unfortunately, the failure rate of such currencies is as high as 80% (Collom 2005). Some famous examples are as follows: Ithaca hours, BerkShares, Equal Dollars, Bay Bucks, Cascadia Hour Exchange, Life Dollars (digital), Downtown Dollars, Potomacs, Local Trade Partners, Brooklyn Torches, Crescents, etc. (Ellis 2012).

5.7.2 LETS (Local Exchange and Trading System)

A part from local currencies, LETS (Local Exchange and Trading System) is also being used by more than 2000 communities around the world (Collom 2005) where all the transactions are recorded in the form of debit or credit in the account of buyers or sellers managed by a centralized system. If a person or a business, registered into the system, wants to purchase something, then he or she informs the record keeper about the payment amount to be debited from his or her account, which is simultaneously credit into the account of the seller. Now, the buyer will have to sell something, either a product or service, to balance out the amount he owes to the system. The amount a person can borrow is limited to discourage free riding. No interest is charged on the loan created in the process of exchange, and members can indulge in any transactions as and when they please. This is a form of virtual currency whose value is mutually agreed by the community members in most cases, while sometimes it uses the value of national currency. The exchange, however, can only happen among registered members.

LETS, as opposed to local currency, requires a centralized system to maintain the records of each member, which are made public on periodical bases. The centralized system is often run by volunteers or by some local business. LETS is 'systematic barter' … 'LETS is not managed by a bank but by its members; therefore, this money is theoretically unlimited and economic activity need no longer be restricted by a lack of money' (Caldwell 2000, p. 4). A community which is cash starved can adopt it to economically empower its members through LETS system. Also in case of reduction in value of national currency due to extraneous reasons, a community using LETS or a local form of currency is least affected. Both LETS and local currencies are accepted and used within a particuarly community, so there is no possibility of flight of capital to other regions (Caldwell 2000; Collom 2005). The use of cell phone, mobile payment systems and payment cards has made it convenient to run and maintain both types of systems these days.

In a nutshell, these alternatives employed by thousands of communities around the world can help boost the local economy while protecting against the community member's hard-earned wealth from fluctuation in the national or international economy. The communities, therefore, can empower and develop themselves in a self-reliant manner. The social atmosphere in the community is improved with enhanced trust and social cohesion. When most of the products and services are locally produced, the transportation cost and reduced carbon foot prints are noted to be some of the positive externalities of such systems (Collom 2005).

Ryan-Collins (2011) and Jones (2011) have noted that the local currency or exchange system isn't without its own limitations such as:

- Local currencies which are issued only through the exchange of national currency can lead to financial exclusion of those who do not possess enough of national currency. LETS however can help in financial inclusion of people as it allows an able-bodied cash-less person to sell his skills in exchange of credit or make purchases in advance. Local currencies can be donated to economically marginalized people, however, that may risk devaluation due to increased circulation.
- The local currency or exchange system is run by non-profit organizations; their own sustainability can be a challenge. Printing of local currency is a major expense, while managing the record-keeping system in case of LETS system also requires human resource.
- The system in discussion is designed to facilitate the trade and not savings. The users therefore have to find alternative venues to save, particularly when the currency is meant to lose its value after defined time.
- Large projects such as infrastructure development or setting up of some industrial unit may not be financed with the local currency due to insufficient quantity.
- The system has its geographical limitations as going beyond can lead to governance issues.
- Since issuance is privately managed, therefore, one cannot rule out the possibility of over issuance, which can lead to more of local currency chasing the available good, causing a rise in prices.

5.7.3 Sound Money

ASE also advocates the idea of sound money which should be produced in the market not by an institution which is run or regulated by the government, rather by a private entity, subjected to commercial and criminal laws, under the supervision of the market itself. ASE also advocated pegging of the currency with a commodity such as gold or silver, whose value will be the benchmark to measure the value of other products or services. A region which is deprived of gold or silver will use any other commodity for that matter. This is one of the key differences between ASE idea of sound money and the local currency and LETS system. Other distinctions being the 'anti-globalization … counter-cultural greens and anti-capitalists' (Collom 2005, pp. 1566–67) stance of the communities which opt for their own currency or

LETS systems, whereas ASE is a staunch advocate of free-market capitalism. ASE perspective leaves some questions unanswered. For example:

- How the flight of capital from rural communities (where the possibility of its multiplication is lesser) to urban centres (where capital accumulation can happen at a much faster pace) of the country can be prevented? Or how regions with lesser economic activity would attract sound money which they do not possess in the first place?
- How the effects of international commodity markets on the price of gold or silver (or any other commodity in use as a medium of exchange) would be prevented?
- In case if the private issuer of sound money issue more gold-backed medium than it has gold, who would compensate the users if they face a loss in the purchasing power of their investments (the governments can provide subsidies to compensate, e.g. when they regulate the money supply)? Would there be some privately run insurance system for that matter? The same question is also valid for the community currency.
- The free-market context is now global and capital flows all over the planet to places wherever its possibility of multiplication is higher: how this would be done efficiently in the free-market context advocated by ASE, if the sound money is to be generated by the market itself? If capital is moved to other parts of the world by private investors, who would protect the larger population from the adverse effects of capital outflows?

The challenges with the mainstream monetary system and its alternatives, along with the questions posted above, deserve further investigation to create alternatives which are compatible with the meta-norms of an Islamic society. The plausibility of the future investigation of the subject is dependent on our agreement that the meta-norms and the design of socioeconomic and political institutions in Islam in comparison to the modern western alternative are not just different rather goes in opposite direction. In this context, the community currency and LETS concept discussed above deserve a thorough investigation as they are also practised by people who do not agree with capitalist ways of running the economy and politics. Perhaps their experience can help Islamic economist to develop an alternative closer to the one advocated by classical Islamic scholarship. Furthermore, any similar alternative should be made conducive of *zakat* system and should acknowledge the *Shari'ah* rulings related to the exchange of debt and other monetary matters.

5.8 Conclusion

The deductive analysis on the role of IBs in money creation phenomenon, in context ASE perspective on FRB system, suggests that IBs can possibly cause inflation, can contribute in economic cycles, can affect the ownership structure of the society where they operate and can also lead to bank runs. These claims can be taken as proposition to be empirically tested by future researchers. Furthermore, the article also stressed upon the broader level analysis of the institutional structures in context of their history, cultural particularity and meta-normative foundations. Without such an analysis, it is difficult to appreciate, let alone identify, alternatives which are compatible with the aspiration of Islam. It is because of lack of such analysis that contemporary scholarship of IBF is more driven by pragmatism and logic of capitalism (Javaid et al. 2017). Therefore, it is argued that Islamic scholarship should broaden the depth and breadth of their investigation to incorporate all dimensions of institutional analysis (see Table 5.1) to create better alternatives which are compatible with Islam's vision of a society

References

Abduhu, S. (2013). Islamic banking confined to the rich; Microfinance share less than 1pc. Retrieved 20 Aug 2017, from http://nation.com.pk/business/12-Sep-2013/islamic-banking-confined-to-the-rich-microfinance-share-less-than-1pc

Allouche, A. (1994). *Mamluk economics a study and translation of Al-Maqrizi's Ighathah*. Salt Lake City: University of Utah Press.

Ansari, J. A. (2004). Rejecting freedom and progress. *Jareedah, 29*, 47–224.

Benati, L. (2005). Long-run evidence on money growth and inflation. *Bank of England Quarterly Bulletin, 45*(3), 349–355.

Bernanke, B. S., & Blinder, A. S. (1988). Credit, money, and aggregate demand. *The American Economic Review, 78*(2), 435–439.

Caldwell, C. (2000). Why do people join local exchange trading systems. *International Journal of Community Currency Research, 4*(2015), 1–15.

Caplan, B. (2008). What's wrong with Austrian business cycle theory. Retrieved 20 Aug 2017, from http://econlog.econlib.org/archives/2008/01/whats_wrong_wit_6.html

Collom, E. (2005). Community currency in the United States: The social environments in which it emerges and survives. *Environment and Planning A, 37*(9), 1565–1587.

Curtis, A. (2011). *All watched over by machines of loving grace (documentary)*. United Kingdom: BBC.

de Soto, J. H. (2009). *Economic cycles. Money, bank credit and economic cycles*. Alabama: Ludwig von Mises Institute.

Ellis, B. (2012). Funny money? 11 local currencies. Retrieved 20 Aug 2017, from http://money.cnn.com/galleries/2012/pf/1201/gallery.community-currencies/index.html

Fang, E. (2014). Islamic finance in global markets: Materialism, ideas and the construction of financial knowledge. *Review of International Political Economy, 21*(6), 1170–1202.

Friedman, M. (1994). *Money mischief*. Orlando: Harcourt Brace & Company.

Gellner, E. (2000). Trust, cohesion, and the social order. In D. Gambetta (Ed.), *Trust: Making and breaking cooperative relations* (pp. 142–157). Oxford: University of Oxford.

Gordon, R. J. (1975). The demand for and supply for inflation. *Journal of Law and Economics, 18*(3), 807–836.

Greenspan, A. (2008). *The age of turbulence* (1st ed.). London: Penguin Books.

Greif, A. (1994). Cultural beliefs and the organization of society: A historical and theoretical reflection on collectivist and individualist societies. *Journal of Political Economy, 102*(5), 912–950.

Hasan, M. S. (1999). Monetary growth and inflation in China. *Journal of Comparative Economics, 27*(4), 669–685.

Hayek, F. A. (1953). *Monetary theory and the trade cycle*. New York: Sentry Press.

Heilbroner, R. L. (1994). *Twenty first century capitalism*. New York: W.W Norton & Company.

Helleiner, E. (1998). Electronic money: A challenge to the sovereign state? *Journal of International Affairs, 51*(2), 387–409.
Hollingsworth, J. R. (2000). Doing institutional analysis: Implications for the study of innovations. *Review of International Political Economy, 7*(4), 595–644.
Humphrey, T. (1982). The real bills doctrine. *Economic Review (Federal Reserve Bank of Richmond)*, 3–13.
Islahi, A. A. (2008). Monetary thought of the sixteenth century muslim scholars. *American Journal of Islamic Social Sciences, 4*(25), 46–60.
Ismail, A. G., & Tohirin, A. (2010). Islamic law and finance. *Humanomics, 26*(3), 178–199.
Javaid, O. (2015a). Methodology of institutional analysis and its implication for contemporary framework of Islamic banks. *Humanomics, 31*(2), 183–200.
Javaid, O. (2015b). The original socio-cultural and economic context for practicing shirkat-ul-aqd. *International Journal of Pluralism and Economics Education, 6*(4), 371.
Javaid, O., & Hassan, M. (2013). A comparison of Islamic and capitalist conception of economic justice. *International Journal of Economics, Management and Accounting, 21*, 1), 1–1),31.
Javaid, O., & Suri, A. W. (2015). Global financial capital vs. Islamic concept of wealth: The question of ideological dominance. *Journal of Islamic Business and Management, 5*(2), 117–134.
Javaid, O., & Suri, A. W. (2016). Bureaucratic system of management in Islamic financial institutions: Implications and alternatives for social inclusion. *Journal of Islamic Business and Management, 6*(2), 89–114.
Javaid, O., Mahmood, N., & Shamsi, A. (2017). The loss in meaning: Influence of strategy language and modern financial discourse on the working concepts in Islamic banking and finance. *Pakistan Business Review, forthcoming*.
Jones, S. D. (2011). Money and participatory governance: A review of the literature. *International Journal of Community Currency Research, 15*(A), 56–68.
King, M. (2001). No money, no inflation - the role of money in the economy. *Economie Internationale, 88*, 111–132.
Kroszner, R. S., Laeven, L., & Klingebiel, D. (2007). Banking crises, financial dependence, and growth. *Journal of Financial Economics, 84*(1), 187–228.
Krugman, P. (1998). The hangover theory: Are recessions the inevitable payback for good times? Retrieved 20 Aug 2017, from http://www.slate.com/id/9593
Macleod, H. D. (1906). *The theory and practice of banking* (6th ed.). London: Longmans, Green and Co..
McLeay, M., Radia, A., & Thomas, R. (2014). Money creation in the modern economy. *Bank of England Quarterly Bulletin, Q1*, 14–27.
Meera, A. K., & Larbani, M. (2004). The gold dinar: The next component in Islamic economics, banking and finance. *Review of Islamic Economics, 8*(1), 5–34.
Meera, A. K., & Larbani, M. (2009). Ownership effects of fractional reserve banking: An Islamic perspective. *Humanomics, 2*(25), 2.
Mises, L. V. (1953). The theory of money and credit. In *New Horizon*. Yale: Yale University Press.
Mohammad, F. (1998). Ibn Khaldun's theory of social change: A comparison with Hegel, Marx and Durkheim. *American Journal of Islamic Social Sciences, 15*(2), 25–46.
Niazi, A. K. (2013). *Money and its usage: An analysis in the light of Shariah*. Karachi: Darul-Ishaat.
Niggle, C. J. (1991). The endogenous money supply theory: An institutional appraisal. *Journal of Economic Issues, 25*(1), 137–151.
Pamuk, S. (2000). *A monetary history of the ottoman empire*. New York: Cambridge University Press.
Pilling, D. (2015). Malaysia's economic frailty is all too familiar. Retrieved 20 Aug 2017, from https://www.ft.com/content/96d3f610-50bb-11e5-8642-453585f2cfcd
Polanyi, K. (1944). *The great transformation: The political and economic origins of our time*. Boston: Beacon Press.
Polleit, T. (2005). Why money supply matters. Retrieved from http://mises.org/daily/2810

Polleit, T. (2011). Manipulating the interest rate: A recipe for disaster. Retrieved 20 Aug 2017, from http://mises.org/daily/2810.
Reisman, G. (1998). *Capitalism*. Illinois: Jameson Books.
Rethel, L. (2011). Whose legitimacy? Islamic finance and the global financial order. *Review of International Political Economy, 18*(1), 75–98.
Roffia, B., & Zaghini, A. (2007). Excess money growth and inflation dynamics. *International Finance, 10*(3), 241–280.
Ryan-Collins, J. (2011). Building local resilience: The emergence of the UK transition currencies. *International Journal of Community Currency Research, 15*(D), 61–67.
Sartell, E. A., & Vierra, A. J. (2012). Overview of the United States economy 1950-2011: Four lessons for Brazil. *World Review of Business Research, 2*(3), 1–11.
SBP. (2012). *Glossary: Statistical bulletin Feb 2012*. Karachi: State Bank of Pakistan.
Schumpeter, J. A. (2006). *History of economic analysis (reprint)*. London: Routledge.
Sharma, R. (2012). *Breakout nations: In search of the next economic miracle*. Noida: Gopson Papers, Ltd.
Simmel, G. (2004). *The philosophy of money*. London: Routledge.
Stiglitz, J. E. (2004). Capital market liberalization, globalization, and the IMF. *Oxford Review of Economic Policy, 20*(1), 57–71.
Treeck, T. V. (2007). A synthetic, stock-flow consistent macroeconomic model of financialisation. Retrieved from http://www.boeckler.de/pdf/p_imk_wp_06_2007.pdf
Tullock, G. (1988). Why the Austrians are wrong about depressions. *Review of Austrian Economics, 2*(1), 73–78.
Wennerlind, C. (2011). *Casualties of credit: The English financial revolution 1620 – 1720*. Cambridge: Harvard University Press.
Wright, E. O., & Rogers, J. (2010). *American society: How it actually works?* New York: W.W Norton & Company.
Zubair, I., & Abbas, M. (1987). *Islamic banking. IMF Occasional Paper No. 49*. Washington, D C: International Monetary Fund.

Part II
Monetary Policy, Policy Instruments and Financial Stability in Islamic Economy

Chapter 6
Islamic Finance and Participatory Financing Constraints in Pakistan

Azam Ali, Tanveer Kishwar, and Muhamed Zulkhibri

6.1 Introduction

In all the constitutions of Pakistan, elimination of *riba'* has consistently occupied an important position among the principles of policy of the state. However, the real efforts for economy wide elimination of *riba'* started during 1970s and most of the significant and practical steps were taken in early 1980s. Numerous measures were taken at that time to introduce interest-free banking in Pakistan. Banking and other relevant laws such as State Bank of Pakistan (SBP) Act 1956, Banking Companies Ordinance (BCO) 1962, Companies Ordinance, recovery laws, negotiable instruments act, etc. were amended to facilitate interest-free banking system. However, these efforts could not produce desired results due to the absence of *Shari'ah* compliance mechanism in place of proper homework at the level of central bank as well as that of the financial institutions to enable such a sudden shift.

Considering the lessons learnt from the earlier efforts, Islamic banking in Pakistan was re-launched in 2001 when the Government decided to promote Islamic banking in a gradual manner and as a parallel and compatible system in line with the best international practices. Since then, SBP has been playing a leading role in pro-

---

The views expressed in the paper are those of the authors and should not necessarily be considered as reflecting the views or carrying the endorsement of their organizations. Authors are solely responsible for any error and omission.

A. Ali
State Bank of Pakistan, Karachi, Pakistan
e-mail: azam.ali@sbp.org.pk

T. Kishwar
Jinnah University for Women, Karachi, Pakistan

M. Zulkhibri (✉)
Islamic Research and Training Institute, Islamic Development Bank, Jeddah, Saudi Arabia

M. Zulkhibri et al. (eds.), *Islamic Monetary Economics and Institutions*,
https://doi.org/10.1007/978-3-030-24005-9_6

moting and developing Islamic banking in Pakistan by putting in place an elaborate regulatory, supervisory and *Shari'ah*-compliant framework. Islamic Banking Department was established at SBP on 15 September 2003 with the mandate of developing and strengthening regulatory and *Shari'ah* compliance framework for Islamic banking industry and taking initiatives for the promotion of Islamic banking as a parallel and compatible banking system in line with the best international practices.

Islamic banking industry has grown tremendously since its re-launch in 2001 by SBP as a parallel and viable alternate solution to conventional banking. The industry has now attained a market share of 11.4% of the total banking industry assets by the end of 2015 and is expected to reach at 15% of the total banking industry by the end of 2018. However, one of the foremost challenges is to maintain its distinction over the conventional banking. Mostly, industry is replicating the products of conventional banking. Due to perception-related issues, the overwhelming reliance on fixed/predictable return-based modes may not be sustainable for the industry in the long run. Hence, efforts should be made to diversify their portfolio, especially on asset side and evolve participatory modes of financing.

The use of participatory modes like *Mudarabah* and *Musharakah* has been absent, particularly on the asset side of the bank's balance sheet. When some Islamic banks (IBs) execute *Musharakah* financings, it lacks true risk sharing as the return on *Musharakah* financing is based on conventional pricing benchmark. These practices have attracted criticism on the current model of Islamic banking. Hence, efforts should be made to evolve participatory financing modes, as also recommended by the Steering Committee established by the Government of Pakistan for the promotion of Islamic banking. Moreover, all the early reports of high-level commissions and committees have recommended that participatory financing (PF) like *Musharakah* and *Mudarabah* are the spirit of Islamic finance and therefore may be promoted.

In literature, it is widely accepted that Islamic banking and finance is truly reflected by participatory modes of financing such as '*Musharakah* and *Mudarabah*'. Islamic banks, contrary to conventional banks, are supposed to achieve greater socioeconomic objectives such as social justice, economic growth, efficiency and stability, and these objectives can be better served through the use of these participatory modes of financing (ISRA 2013). It is also viewed that these modes have the potential to better serve the stakeholders through equitable and broad-based distribution of risks and rewards among the entrepreneur, banker and depositors and promote stability of the financial and economic system.

The objectives of the study are threefold: (i) to examine the earlier efforts to revive and promote risk-sharing modes of financing (*Musharakah* and *Mudarabah*) with respect to the current international and local practices of Islamic banking industry; (ii) to identify the challenges and constraints currently faced by IBs applying the *Musharakah* and *Mudarabah* concepts; and (iii) to propose measures that would encourage a wider adoption of the *Musharakah* and *Mudarabah* financing contracts by IBs.

The remainder of the chapter is structured as follows. In Sect. 6.2, the previous studies on participatory finance are discussed. Section 6.3 provides an analytical review of current practices and experiences in participatory finance. Section 6.4 provides systematic identification of impediments of growth participatory finance. Section 6.5 presents our conclusion and recommendations.

6.2 Literature Review

Some of the other problems faced by adopting the risk-sharing finance are the risk of fraud, taxation system and highly complex nature of equity financing. For example, Sudan Islamic Bank in the application of *Musharakah* indicates that Islamic banks find it difficult to identify sound financing opportunities and expensive to employ specialists for financing. One of the dominant factor in the low level of application of *Musharakah* is the moral hazard (Khan 1995; Aggarwal and Yousuf 2000; Ahmed 2005). Dar and Presley (2000) argue that an imbalance between management and control rights is attributed as a major cause of lack of PLS in the practice of Islamic finance. Given this dichotomy, the agency problem gets accentuated, which may put the PLS at a disadvantage vis-à-vis other mode of financing. However, there is no theoretical reason to believe that PLS is inherently inefficient.

Iqbal and Llewellyn (2002) viewed that the most influential factor in the marginal application of *Musharakah* model is asymmetric information, which is the result of adverse selection and moral hazard problems. They also point out that the reduction of information asymmetry is a prerequisite for the implementation of an equity-based system. Ahmed (2005) describes three major areas where the Islamic banks find it difficult to finance under the PLS system, they are (i) participating in long-term and low-yield projects, (ii) financing the small businesses and (iii) granting non-participating loans to running businesses. Financing under the equity participation method is most risky for banks in developing countries due to major reasons such as lack of proper accounting, honesty, integrity and character of investors, insufficient number of skilled entrepreneurs and the presence of contrary laws and regulations.

Highlighting the importance of PLS-based financing, Chapra (2007) emphasizes that the socioeconomic benefits of the prohibition of interest may not be realized fully until the share of PLS modes rises substantially in total financing. It would hence be desirable for the use of PLS modes to gain momentum. However, Islamic bank faces operational difficulties, business ethics, bad projects with high-risk and overoptimistic prospective profit figures, lack of special regulatory framework, inefficient procedures and low level of expertise, high monitoring cost, inefficient tax system and high rate of illiteracy are some of formidable obstacles in the practical scope of PLS instruments. Chong and Liu (2009) mention several possible reasons for the poor adoption of the PLS paradigm in practice, like PLS financing encounters severe principal–agent problems, moral hazard problems associated with ex-post information asymmetry. The adoption of the PLS paradigm is constrained by competition as well as by best practices from conventional banking. Accordingly, PLS financing requires more costly monitoring.

Shinsuke (2010) indicates that from the viewpoint of microeconomics, the use of partnership-based instruments in Islamic finance get involved in the incentive problem, which implies that the use of partnership-based instruments cannot result in the most efficient solution owing to the asymmetry of information which further leads to adverse selection in the period before a contract is entered into and moral hazards in the period after a contract is entered into. Chattha and Bacha (2010) consider credit risk which arises from the extensive moral hazards inherent in the PLS contracts as one of the major hindrance factors in the implementation of *Musharakah* financing. Another aspect of low level of application of PLS mode is pointed out by Nihar (2011) that the low content of PLS contracts in the financial statements of the Islamic banks indicates competition has made the banks to modify their contracts for survival, and therefore, Islamic banking practices do not deviate substantially from a conventional bank.

6.3 Current Practices and Experiences

The Islamic finance and banking industry has grown tremendously during the past few years, evidenced by its assets' double-digit compound annual growth rate (CAGR) of 17% between 2009 and 2013. However, the industry has witnessed modest growth during 2014 and 2015 due to exchange rate depreciations in key Islamic finance markets, the withdrawal of a major issuer (Malaysia) in the global *Sukuk* market and the asset value contractions in the Islamic capital markets due to overall downward pressures in the global equity markets. The industry's assets are estimated to be worth US$2 trillion by the end of 2015, having grown from US$1.87 trillion as at the end of 2014.[1] This growth has come from across the world as evident in Table 6.1.

Table 6.1 Islamic finance segments by regions (US$ billion, 2015)

Region	Banking assets	*Sukuk* outstanding	Islamic funds' assets	*Takaful* contributions
Asia	209.3	174.7	23.2	5.2
Gulf Cooperation Council (GCC)	598.8	103.7	31.2	10.4
Middle East and North Africa (MENA) (exc. GCC)	607.5	9.4	0.3	7.1
Sub-Saharan Africa	24	0.7	1.4	0.5
Others	56.9	2.1	15.2	–
Total	**1496.5**	**290.6**	**71.3**	**23.2**

Source: IFSB Stability Report (2016)

[1] IFSB Industry Stability report 2015 and Islamic Finance for Asia report (2015) by IFSB and ADB.

6.3.1 Experiences of Malaysia

The enactment of the Islamic Financial Services Act 2013 (IFSA) in consort with the Financial Services Act 2013 (FSA) marks an important milestone in modernizing Malaysia's financial sector laws. Both the FSA and IFSA combine several separate laws to govern the financial sector under a single legislative framework for the conventional and Islamic financial sectors, respectively, namely, the Banking and Financial Institutions Act 1989 (BAFIA), Islamic Banking Act 1983, Insurance Act 1996 (IA), Takaful Act 1984, Payment Systems Act 2003 and Exchange Control Act 1953.

The introduction of FSA offers a new dimension to the regulatory framework for Islamic finance as it accords greater prominence to the *Shari'ah* contracts in Islamic finance transactions. The statutory foundation for a contract-based regulatory framework in FSA has enabled the issuance of *Shari'ah* standards that define the underlying *Shari'ah* principles adopted by Islamic financial institutions and support the effective application of *Shari'ah* contracts in the offering of Islamic financial products and services. This represents a significant step forward in aligning legal and regulatory principles with *Shari'ah* precepts and can serve as a useful benchmark for evolving more comprehensive regulatory frameworks globally that promote greater legal and operational certainty in Islamic finance.

As far as actual results are concerned, the total financing provided by Islamic banks in Malaysia reached RM 396 billion in 1H 2016. Deferred payment contract *Bai Bithaman Ajil* and the fixed margin *Murabahah* make up half of all financing. This is not peculiar to Malaysia's Islamic banking sector; in general, a sizeable proportion of Islamic banking and financing transactions globally are based on debt and deferred payment products. However, the share of *Musharakah* and *Mudarabah* financing constituted a very small portion of Islamic financial institutions (IFIs) assets. It can be evident from the fact that in April 2016 the share of *Musharakah* financing was only 8% of the total financing, while the proportion of *Mudarabah* was only 0.02%.

A research study (ISRA 2013) finds out the reasons of why *Mudarabah*- and *Musharakah*-based products constitute a very small portion of IFI assets. As per the study, there are a number of reasons why IFIs seem to be reluctant to operate or implement *Mudarabah* and *Musharakah*. These include high risk levels, the familiar role of the bank as a fund provider rather than a partner or investor, inadequate demand from customers, complexity in implementing the products, stringent regulations and lack of expertise and skilled staff. The Capital Adequacy Framework for Islamic Banks adopted in 2012 by BNM is also found to have a negative impact on the IFIs if they were to adopt *Mudarabah*- and *Musharakah*-based products.

6.3.2 *Experiences of Pakistan*

During 2015, the *Musharakah* financing in the total financing by IBs has been remarkably increased and reached to 14% in December 2015 as compared to 11% in December 2014. Apart from *Musharakah* financing, *Mudarabah* financing has yet to take a prominent space in the asset side of Islamic banking in Pakistan. The IBs have developed running *Musharakah* financing based on sharing the profit/loss on the ongoing operations of an entity/firm rather than permanent investment as an equity partner. IBs have introduced this product to meet the running finance needs of their customers. Moreover, IBs extended considerable financing under *Diminishing Musharakah* (DM) mode. However, DM may not be taken as pure profit and loss sharing *Musharakah* financing as it has been offered based on *Sharikat-al-Milk* rather than *Sharikat-al-Aqd*.

Figure 6.1 depicts the financing mix for 2014 and 2015 of the entire Islamic banking industry in Pakistan. As depicted, there are seven main modes of financing, which are being offered by IBs, namely, *Murabahah*, *Ijarah*, *Musharakah*, *Mudarabah*, *Diminishing Musharakah*, *Salam* and *Istisna*. Moreover, there are few other modes like *Musawamah*, *Wakalah*, *Qard*, etc. which are being offered by IBs but at limited scale and thereby have been classified in others category. In 2014, the total financing of IBs amounted to Rs. 422 billion. Of this, *Murabahah* constituted 30.1% (Rs. 127.2 billion), *Diminishing Musharakah* 32.6% (Rs. 137.7 billion), *Ijarah* 7.7% (Rs. 32.3 billion), *Salam* 4.5% (Rs. 19.2 billion), *Istisna*' 8.3% (Rs. 35.2 billion) and others 5.6% (Rs. 23.8 billion), whereas 11% of total financing in 2014 consisted of *Musharakah*-based products (Rs.46.5 billion), while *Mudarabah* financing has represented only 0.1% of the total financing (Rs. 0.2 billion).

In 2015, the amount of financing increased to Rs. 658 billion from Rs. 422 billion in 2014, posing 56% growth, almost double during the year. It shows that the IBs have efficiently diversified their portfolio mix during the year. Consequently, the share of *Diminishing Musharakah* reached to 31.7% (Rs. 208.7 billion), and it became the largest among all financing categories. Similarly, the shares of *Istisna'*,

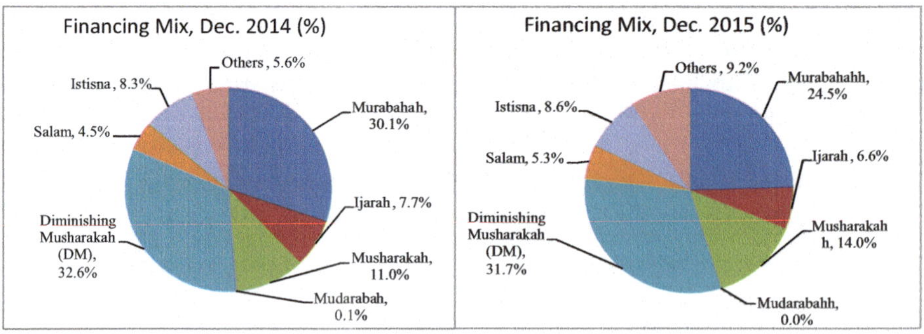

Fig. 6.1 Financing mix for Pakistan Islamic Banking Industry 2014–2015. (Source: State Bank of Pakistan)

Salam and others financing have also increased to 8.6% (Rs. 56.8 billion), 5.3% (Rs. 35.1 billion) and 9.2% (Rs. 60.4 billion). The share of *Musharakah* financing has increased to 14% and IBs have financed Rs. 92.1 billion under this participatory mode. However, the share of *Murabahah* financing has reduced to 24.5% (Rs. 161.6 billion). Moreover, already small share (0.1%) of *Mudarabah* financing has further shrunk to 0.03% (Rs. 0.1 billion) during 2015.

This recent increase in *Musharakah* financing (based on *Sharikat-al-Aqd*) can be attributable to some Islamic banking institutions (IBs) which started offering participatory mode of finance *Musharakah* or running *Musharakah* as an alternative to the running finance facility, being offered by the conventional banks. The product enables the customer to draw and deposit funds against running *Musharakah* limit offered by the bank. Although the underlying contract is *Musharakah*, the product is designed in such a way that the economic outcome of the financing becomes, by and large, akin to that of conventional running finance. This is due to the following facts:

(i) Profit/loss is determined according to gross rather than net profit of *Musharakah*.
(ii) The expected/desired/targeted profit is linked to Karachi Interbank Offered Rate (KIBOR).
(iii) Any return that is over and above of the KIBOR is passed on to the customer as a 'bonus'.

If we look at the amount of financing by IBs as of December 2015 (Figs. 6.2 and 6.3), Bank T, Bank S, Bank R and Bank Q represented more than 74% of the total financing. The total amount of financing offered by Bank T was Rs. 216.136 billion or 32.9% of the total financing, Bank S Rs. 106.627 billion (16.2%), Bank R Rs. 69.037 billion (10.5%), Bank Q Rs. 50.546 billion (7.7%) and Bank P Rs. 43.062 billion (6.6%). Three of these big four banks – namely Bank T, Bank S and Bank Q – have offered *Musharakah* financing products. Moreover, Bank P, Bank O and

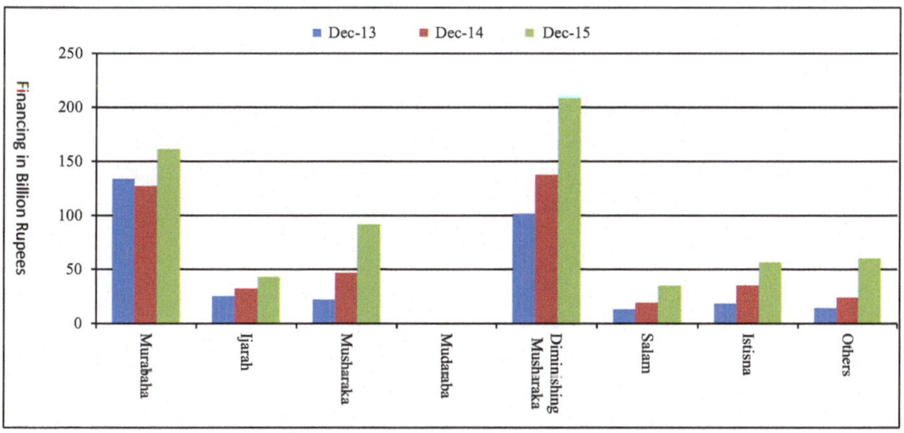

Fig. 6.2 Different modes of financing 2013–2015. (Source: State Bank of Pakistan)

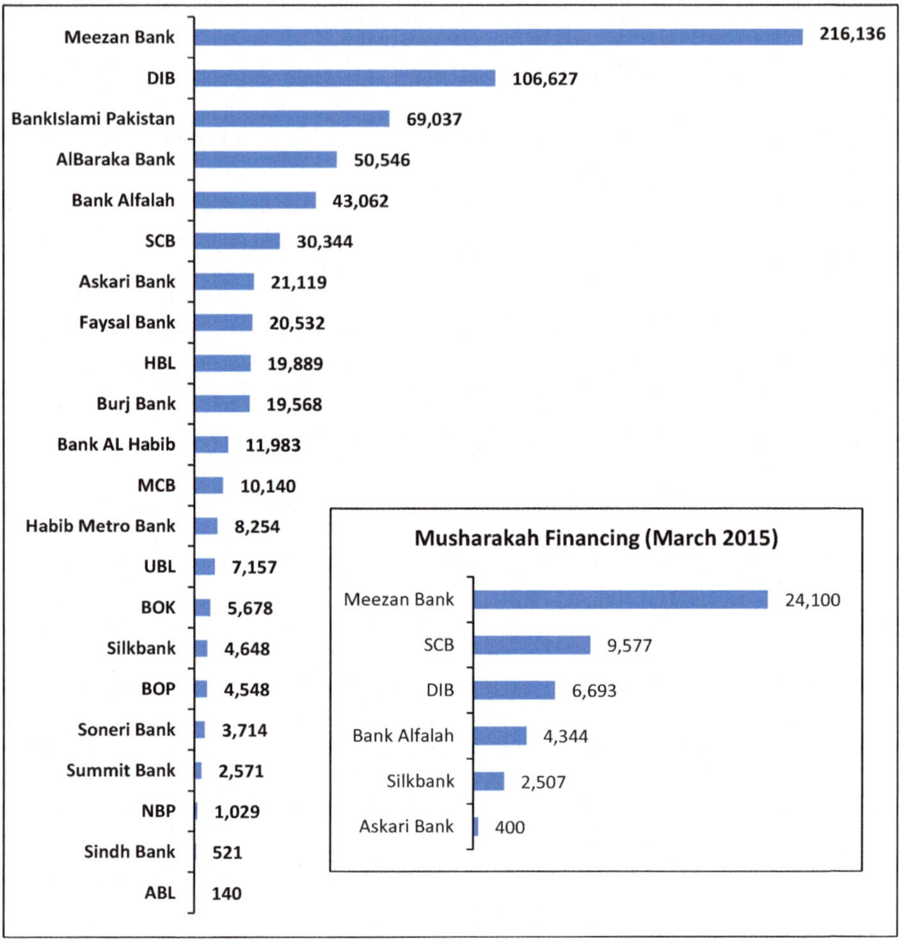

Fig. 6.3 Total financing of Islamic banking institutions (December 2015, million Rupees). (Source: State Bank of Pakistan)

Bank N have also extended running *Musharakah* facility (a replica of running finance facility) based on *Musharakah* principles.

Table 6.2 describes some general characteristics of the *Musharakah* products, which are currently being offered by few IBs.

6.4 Participatory Financing Constraints

Participatory financings (PF) are very flexible tools as these can be used to finance every economic activity from working capital finance to financing of huge infrastructure projects. However, there are certain challenges both on supply and demand

Table 6.2 *Musharakah* financing offering by the Islamic banking institutions

Bank	Bank P	Bank R	Bank Q	Bank S	Bank T	Bank O
Product name	Running *Musharakah*	Running *Musharakah*	Running *Musharakah*	Running *Musharakah* facility	Syndicated *Musharakah*	*Musharakah*
Type of product	Corporate and SME	Corporate	Corporate	Corporate and SME	Corporate	Corporate
Salient features	The product is based on *Sharikat-al-Aqd* whereby the IB and the customer enter into partnership. This financing facility is offered to the customers where the IB participates in the operating activities of the customer and shares profit and loss as per the actual performance of the business. Profit sharing ratios are decided at the start. The profit ratio of sleeping partner cannot be more than its share in *Musharakah*. Loss is shared on pro rata basis. In a syndicated facility, X bank (lead manager) and Y bank provided *Musharakah*-based financing of PKR 3 billion to a petroleum corporation. The corporation's share in *Musharakah* was PKR 200 million. The financing was used for the procurement of oil and LPG. Actual profit is distributed among partners according to agreed profit sharing ratio.					
Pricing	Expected/desired/targeted profit rate is linked to the KIBOR and is used for provisional distribution of profit. However, provisional profit is subject to the settlement on the basis of actual *Musharakah* profit.					
Volume	PKR 12.5 billion*	PKR 42.3 billion[a]	PKR 28.9 billion*	PKR 150 million*	PKR 350 million*	PKR 7.9 billion*

Source: Quarterly reports; *Annual Audited Accounts, ROCA data
[a]Annual audited accounts of the banks

sides in the implementation of *Musharakah* and *Mudarabah* financing products in true spirit. On supply side, major challenges include high level of risk, lack of human resource capacity and technical expertise of IBs, complicated documentation process, accounting and taxation issues, rights and obligations of IBs, legal and regulatory concerns, foreclosure issues, adverse selection and moral hazard problems, regulatory requirement of benchmarking with conventional benchmark 'KIBOR' and gaps in human resources, while on demand side, major concerns are dual banking system and customers' perception.

6.4.1 Supply Side Challenges

6.4.1.1 High Level of Risk

PF-associated risk is one of the main challenges in adopting these modes of financing. IBs have the following high-level inherent risks while engaged in PF:

(i) *Lack of technical expertise of IBs due to the absence of proper monitoring mechanism*: In the absence of any proper mechanism for evaluation of projects and companies, the banks are unable to measure the performance as well as the value of projects at the different stages of their business life cycle. Furthermore, mechanisms to be adopted in case of premature exit from the venture should be clear. According to Dar and Presley (2000), there is no serious problem with this (PLS) arrangement if the bank is able, and is allowed, to monitor business operations of the firm. However, proper monitoring mechanisms are yet to be devised for PLS.

(ii) *High level of risk weightages assigned:* Capital adequacy standards are not very accommodative to *Musharakah*- and *Mudarabah*-based products. High level of risk weightages has been assigned for such products, i.e. 400% as stated in IFSB Standard No. 15, whereas it is 1000% in BASEL III.[2]

(iii) *Shari'ah non-compliance risk*: *Shari'ah* non-compliance risk could also be a major concern in *Musharakah*- and *Mudarabah*-based products. Since the project would normally be a long-term project and has complex/hybrid structure, the bank might not be able to continuously monitor the project in order to ensure that it complied with the rules of *Shari'ah.*

6.4.1.2 Accounting and Taxation Issues

There are different accounting practices for banks and firms. Even within the banking sector there is no standardized accounting requirement for both *Musharakah* and *Mudarabah* financing products. Detailed and standardized accounting procedures are very much necessary to record, manage and evaluate performance of the projects financed through *Musharakah*- and *Mudarabah*-based products.

There is no explicit tax neutrality treatment provided under existing tax laws to customers availing Islamic banking services. This has resulted in high profile cases between the Income Tax Department and large tax payers such as Sui Sothern Gas Co. (SSGC, a big corporate customer and a large tax payer). SSGC received a notice from Federal Board of Revenue (FBR) wherein benefit of depreciation on their plant and machinery, which was financed on *Diminishing Musharakah* basis by an IB, was declined due to creation of joint ownership of IB and SSGC. If same facility would have been obtained from a conventional bank against mortgage of fixed assets and hypothecation charge against current assets, there would not be any tax liability on SSGC. Such unfavourable tax treatment on account of availing Islamic banking facilities can potentially have far-reaching negative consequences; thus appropriate amendments are very much essential to be incorporated in taxation laws.

6.4.1.3 Legal and Regulatory Concerns

Since re-launch of Islamic banking in early 2000s, State Bank of Pakistan has taken several policy initiatives to promote Islamic banking in the country through enabling legal, regulatory and supervisory frameworks. However, the current legal and

[2] Instruction for BASEL III implementation in Pakistan (Page # 5) issued under BPRD circular # 06 dated 15 August 2013(http://www.sbp.org.pk/bprd/2013/Basel_III_instructions.pdf).

regulatory frameworks still need to further strengthen in order to promote Islamic banking in general and participatory modes in particular. Following are few areas which need immediate attention:

(i) *BCO 1962 and SBP Act 1956:* Overall, the existing versions of both the laws fully support Islamic banking. However, the legal framework (Section 9 of BCO 1962) currently prohibits banks to engage in trade. Therefore, in order to provide legal cover to Islamic banks to do trading, an amendment is proposed in the BCO. Once the legal provision enabling IBs to engage in trade is in place, necessary regulatory instructions may be issued so that IBs do not misuse the legal cover. In order to expand PLS-based financing, IBs need to bridge their risk and rewards with that of the investment account holders (i.e. the depositors). For this purpose, the IBs have to mobilize deposits for specific areas/sectors/ventures and remunerate such deposits based on the performance of the sectors/ventures, etc. funded by such deposits. This aspiration demands an amendment in Section 26A of BCO 1962 to allow IBs to mobilize restricted deposits.

(ii) *Limits regarding equity financing/investments by banks:* As per section 23(2) of BCO 1962, a banking company cannot 'hold shares in any company whether as pledgee, mortgagee or absolute owner, of an amount exceeding thirty per cent of the paid-up share capital of that company or thirty per cent of its own paid-up share capital and reserves, whichever is less'.

(iii) *Joint ownership issues:* Under prevailing laws, it would be too costly for IBs to create co-ownership of assets financed through participatory modes due to dual/double stamp duty, property taxes and other registration charges.

6.4.1.4 Lack of Consolidated Supervision Framework

Under BCO 1962, IBs are allowed to act as '*Mudarabah* Company' under the provision of the *Modarabah* Companies and *Modarabah* (Floatation and Control) Ordinance 1980. Accordingly, IBs can establish an asset management company, a venture capital management company or a *Mudarabah* management company. Furthermore, IBs are also allowed to directly float *Musharakah* certificate or *Mudarabah* certificates. However, there are certain challenges associated with these options.

Though there are legal and regulatory frameworks available for IBs, there is a need to develop consolidated framework for PLS-based partnership avenues to facilitate in establishment of smooth working of *Shari'ah*-compliant asset management companies (AMCs), *Mudarabah* funds, PE ventures, etc. As already suggested to SECP, the *Mudarabah* sector as a whole may be transferred to the regulatory ambit of SBP and this proposal may be further evaluated and discussed at the highest level among GoP/MoF, SECP and SBP.

6.4.1.5 Foreclosure Issues

Earlier in the Financial Institution Recovery Ordinance (FIRO) 2001, the financial institutions were given the right to foreclose a mortgaged property without recourse to the court of law in case the client defaults. However, after a long-standing stay order against its implementation, the Supreme Court of Pakistan passed an order on 10 December 2013 whereby the provisions of Section 15 of the FIRO were held to be ultra vires the Constitution of Pakistan 1973. However, to safeguard the interest of stakeholders, SBP after consultation with PBA has proposed amendments in the law including alternative provisions to plug the void created by Section 15. But it would take time to promulgate the same in FIRO 2001.

Apart from the above-mentioned judicial issue, the litigation process usually takes 4–5 or more years to be concluded and resulted in operational and legal cost to banks. Even if the court decides in favour of the bank, the foreclosed property receives little interest from new clients due to its legal history. The situation for Islamic banking has complicated due to non-supportive conventional judicial system. There is no law which unequivocally governs the Islamic banking transactions. Secondly, the existing laws though have some supporting provisions for Islamic banking, but these are not enough to clearly distinguish between Islamic and conventional banking. Furthermore, judges (even in banking courts) are not well versed with Islamic banking concepts and practices, which ultimately lead towards further complications in court cases of IBs.

6.4.1.6 Rights and Obligations of IBs

Since the concepts of *Musharakah* and *Mudarabah* require the banks to share all the risks associated with the projects, they should be provided with an avenue to voice their views on the way the project is managed in order to make sure it is successful. However, this raises the issue of the extent to which IBs can be involved in the decision making of the board of directors. There is also the issue of compliance with current regulations regarding IBs combining the roles of financier and member of board of directors.

6.4.1.7 Adverse Selection and Moral Hazard Problems on Asset Side

There are serious concerns regarding asymmetric information that might limit IBs capacity to monitor and control projects financed using the *Musharakah* and *Mudarabah* modes. It eventually creates adverse selection and moral hazard problems for the banks. It is highly perceived that customers might not disclose the actual facts of the proposed project when they apply for financing from the IB. Customers usually maintain double book keeping and disclose minimal profits to avoid taxes and sharing lower profit rates with IBs.

6.4.1.8 Complicated Documentation Process

Financing under *Musharakah* and *Mudarabah* have been considered to be too complicated, especially in terms of the procedures and legal documentation. Normally, implementation of participatory models necessitates combining of different contracts in one product. Therefore, the documentation of such products might become very complicated in order to fulfil all the requirements of the contracts involved.

6.4.1.9 Regulatory Requirement of Benchmarking with Conventional Benchmark 'KIBOR'

The industry has previously requested for exemption from linking KIBOR to determine pricing for all modes of Islamic banking, especially for the profit sharing modes such as *Musharakah* and *Mudarabah* and for *Wakalah*-based products to achieve the true essence of Islamic finance. Ideally, the need for delinking KIBOR to determine pricing in Islamic finance modes cannot be overlooked. This is desirable because Islamic banking as the dominant segment in Islamic finance industry should go beyond the function of a financial intermediary whereby it also serves as a *wakeel* (trustee), custodian, partner, entrepreneur, buyer, seller, guarantor, etc. It will make Islamic banking more comprehensive and independent from the conventional benchmark and address key perception issues. However, the following practical challenges are involved in delinking KIBOR to determine pricing for all modes of Islamic banking.

- It will necessitate the development of an alternative benchmark rate for Islamic banking.
- No viable Islamic benchmark, with sound history of practical implementation, is currently available globally.
- Regulatory requirements in terms of capital adequacy are likely to increase in light of Basel III and IFSB Standard 15 and become prohibitive for equity investments.

6.4.1.10 Lack of Human Resource Capacity and Technical Expertise of IBs

Lack of expertise is another major concern in the implementation of *Musharakah*- and *Mudarabah*-based products. IBs lack the necessary human resources and technical expertise; for instance, project managers, product specialist, engineers and other professional who may be required to manage projects that are financed using *Musharakah* and *Mudarabah* modes. There is a high-cost associated with finding and hiring such experts for implementation and monitoring of *Musharakah* and

Mudarabah projects. Therefore, banks may not want to employ technical staff with limited job scopes.

There is also a human resource gap in the market. Due to limited avenues available with the higher educational institutions to graduate in Islamic banking and finance, fresh graduates do not meet industry requirements. On the one hand, commercial banker does not have enough *Shari'ah*-related knowledge/aspects about their products/services, and on the other hand, *Shari'ah*-related person does not have expertise in commercial banking practices/operations.

6.5 Demand Side Challenges

6.5.1 Dual/Parallel Banking System

Customers are continuously comparing Islamic banks with their conventional counterparts, especially in terms of the products they offer. Therefore, despite all the advantages that a dual banking system should offer, it also provides customers with the option of moving easily from one system to another. If they find that the product offered by one banking system is not suitable to them due to reasons such as costs (too expensive) or convenience (too complicated), they can easily look for similar products offered by the other system.

This has serious implications for the practice of Islamic banks in Pakistan or anywhere else where dual system exists. It happens because, to remain competitive, the IBs products would have to be similar to or in line with those being offered by their conventional counterparts. This also explains why financing products based on the concepts of *Musharakah* and *Mudarabah* remain unattractive for the Islamic banks, as conventional banks offer no products equivalent to them. Islamic banks may need a longer time to propagate the true concepts of *Mudarabah* and *Musharakah* to the customers and change customers' perceptions towards the Islamic banking system.

6.5.2 Customers' Perception

The theoretical part of *Musharakah* and *Mudarabah* concepts is perceived to be difficult to be practiced in the current circumstances. It particularly links with the profit sharing principle of *Mudarabah* and *Musharakah*, i.e. the profits will have to be distributed between the IBs and the project owners. However, some customers, who are looking for a source of financing, may not perceive a bank as a business partner. Therefore, they may wish to get financing through *Mudarabah*- and *Musharakah*-based products as depicted in Knowledge, Attitude and Practices (KAP) survey, but they may not want to allow access to their books/information including managerial accounts to bank's internal and external auditors, *Shari'ah* advisor and regulator (SBP) to oversee the running of their projects.

Customers are always looking for the cheapest alternative, and if *Mudarabah*- and *Musharakah*-based financing products are offered, they may cost more to the customers. This also happens due to the public's lack of understanding, in general, regarding the principles and purpose of Islamic banks. For them, what matters most is to obtain the funds needed to finance their projects at the lowest cost possible. Also, banks as a solution provider would provide the solution that best suited the needs of their customers. However, if the customers were to understand the principles that underlie Islamic banking practices, they might be willing to bear the extra costs.

6.5.3 Other Issues

In literature, following are the major issues restricting participatory financing that have been highlighted by various scholars: moral hazard and adverse selection, lack of interest of the bank management, unavailability of guidelines/regulations from the central bank, risk of loss, accounting problems, lack of interest from the customers, lack of committed, honest and skilful entrepreneurs, lack of expertise, lack of government legal support, unavailability of checks and balance mechanisms of *Musharakah* business and taxation issues.

6.6 Conclusions

Most of the financial service needs are met through trade or rental-based modes, such as *Murabahah*, *Ijarah*, *Salam*, *Istisna'*, *Diminishing Musharakah*, etc., which essentially bear a close resemblance to conventional debt-based instruments/products. On the other hand, profit-and-loss sharing modes, i.e. true *Musharakah* and *Mudarabah*, are employed minimally by IBs due to involvement of high risk exposure. Nonetheless, few IBs have started offering running *Musharakah*, which has gained significant proportion, but it lacks true spirit of profit and loss sharing mechanism propagated by Islam.

As Islamic banking is moving from niche to mainstream and gaining wider acceptability, it calls for a paradigm shift in terms of a well-balanced financing mix. The time is ripe to move beyond creating resemblance with conventional products to remain competitive in the industry. On the product development side, innovation and creativity is necessitated more than ever to promote participatory modes of financing and to make it the preferred choice for meeting the increasingly sophisticated and diversified financial needs. It cannot be stressed enough that IBs need to keep in mind the crux of *Shari'ah*-complaint banking at all times. They should aim at creating products that not only result in fair and equitable distribution of risks and rewards among its stakeholders but also promote stability of the financial system and create real economic value to the society in line with *Maqasid al-Shari'ah.*

Reasonably, it will take time and focus for participatory modes to reach from a negligible size to a significant share in the overall Islamic financing by IBs. Concentrated efforts are required to remove obstacles and anomalies at different fronts as highlighted in Sect. 6.5. Needless to mention, creating an enabling environment for IB to venture into participatory mode-based financing demands perseverance and dedication from all stakeholders, i.e. regulator, IBs, *Shari'ah* scholars, ministries and relevant accounting and business associations. A few recommendations and action points to facilitate IBs in exploring the feasibility of *Musharakah/Mudarabah*-based products are as follows:

6.6.1 General Recommendations

1. IBs need to spell out conceptually how *Musharakah* and *Mudarabah* transactions could be undertaken within the existing financial landscape.
2. IBs need to come up with suggestions and identify areas requiring new rules to be formed and existing to be amended with proper rationalization.
3. SBP may consider setting up indicative targets, initially in agriculture and SME sectors for participatory mode financing in relation to the asset base of IBs.
4. SBP may provide relaxations of specific prudential regulations such as per party and individual limits to encourage participatory finance by IBs.
5. SBP may consider allowing incentives in the calculation of CAR with regard to PLS-based financing products and services.
6. IBs/stakeholders need to develop guidelines/policies on participatory modes of financing with respect to risk management, investment objectives, return mechanism and exit mechanism.
7. IBs/stakeholders need to develop robust risk management framework entailing an effective monitoring and controlling techniques/tools for continuous watching performance of the corporate /partners.
8. Strategies for sound practices of corporate governance including *Shari'ah*, risk management and compliance review may also be developed.
9. The newly developed three centres for excellence in Islamic finance at IBA, LUMS and IMS Peshawar should be efficiently and effectively utilized to fulfil the human resource needs of the IBs. Specialize training programmes/workshops should be organized on regular basis by these institutes on participatory modes of financing.

In order to take the Islamic banking industry towards *Musharakah* and *Mudarabah* financing (MMF), it is proposed that a broad-based research and development task force (RDTF) for the same purpose may be established at SBP. The key objectives of the RDTF would be to review in detail the previous efforts/work done by various task force/committees, on the same issue/matter. After detailed review, RDTF may take up MMF-related matters like constraints faced in MMF, work in removing the identified constraints and develop a comprehensive framework/roadmap for IBs to offer MMF on large scale in Pakistan. It may be mentioned that globally, the share of MMF is also minimal and if SBP succeeds in establishing a sound and large MMF portfolio in Pakistan, this can also serve as a model for other countries. Accordingly, it is proposed that a RDTF on MMF at SBP may be established, chaired by the Director – Islamic Banking Department. The other members on the task force are recommended to be selected from PBA Islamic Banking, SECP, *Shari'ah* community, Federal Chamber of Commerce, accountancy/ auditing firms and academia.

(i) There could be some strategic alliance between IBs and *Mudarabah* creating synergies through availability of opportunities for diversification of asset portfolio for IBs and addressing the issue of financial constraint of other IFIs.
(ii) Can there be some benefit to IBs in calculation of CAR in case of *Mudarabah/ Musharakah*-based portfolio especially if IBs are able to generate special pool of funds/deposits for such portfolio?
(iii) There could be tax incentives for IBs for their income from *Mudarabah/ Musharakah* business. This may encourage them to enter into such ventures plus this incentive could be regarded as risk premium for using these modes.
(iv) In consolidated supervision perspective, it may be suggested that the *Mudarabah* sector as a whole may be transferred to the regulatory ambit of SBP and this proposal may be evaluated and discussed at the highest level among GoP/MoF, SECP and SBP.

6.6.2 *Specific Recommendations*

6.6.2.1 Exemption of Benchmarking with KIBOR for Participatory Modes of Financing

SBP may consider delinking of KIBOR benchmark to achieve the true spirit of participatory modes. However, while financing/investing via participatory modes IBs entail significant capital impairment or equity investment risk. Therefore, while granting exemption from KIBOR for participatory modes, IBs may be advised to meet the following conditions:

- IBs should ensure that adequate measures are in place as per Risk Management Guidelines for Islamic banking institutions issued vide IBD Circular No. 1 of 2008 particularly to mitigate equity investment risk in participatory mode-based products.
- For *Mudarabah*- and *Musharakah*-based products, IBs should ensure compliance with minimum *Shari'ah* standards issued vide IBD Circular No. 2 of 2008 and AAOIFI *Shari'ah* Standards No. 12 and 13 as adopted vide IBD's Circular No. 1 of 2013 and Circular No. 1 of 2010 respectively.

- IBs should submit the details of *Mudarabah*- and *Musharakah*-based products (new/revised) for delinking with KIBOR benchmark to Islamic Banking Department in line with IBD Circular Letter No. 2 of 2013 in the prescribed manner. The submissions shall also include:
  - Detailed mechanism for pricing under these modes with proper policies for risk mitigation
  - Amendments in agreements and related documents
  - Approval of IB's product by their *Shari'ah* board
  - Criteria for selection of firms/companies with whom IBs can execute *Musharakah* or *Mudarabah* contract.

6.6.2.2 Proposal for Tax Neutrality Treatment for Participatory Modes of Financing

Stakeholders need to make efforts to remove tax anomalies as well as create tax benefits on both demand and supply side to promote the use of participatory modes. In this regard, SBP has already proposed certain tax proposals to Federal as well as Provincial Governments to provide tax neutrality treatment to IBs. Among these tax proposals, SBP has proposed following clarification or amendments in existing tax laws to Federal/Provincial Governments for the promotion of participatory modes of financing:

- FBR may clarify that the financing availed by the customers of Islamic Financial Institution(s) licenced by State Bank of Pakistan (SBP) or Securities and Exchange Commission of Pakistan (SECP), as the case may be, under any Islamic modes of financing shall be treated at par with the financing obtained from conventional financial institutions for the purpose of computation of income tax liability under this ordinance.
- Benefit of depreciation should be allowed to customers of IBs despite having joint ownership of property pursuant to an arrangement of *Musharakah* financing or *Diminishing Musharakah* financing for calculating tax liability of the customers of Islamic banking institutions.
- In order to ensure tax neutrality for IBs as well as fulfilling the registration requirements with regard to sale/purchase of immovable property under the Registration Act 1908, the provincial governments may be requested to exempt the registration of sale/purchase of immovable properties for the purpose of extending financing facilities under Islamic modes of financing by IBs. Section 9A of Stamp Act 1899 empowers the provincial governments to do the needful as proposed.
- The Federal/Provincial Government may also issue a suitable notification for exemption of capital value tax for Islamic banking institutions on sale/purchase of immoveable property.

6.6.2.3 Proposal for Legal Amendments

The set of guidelines presented in the Report of the Commission on Banks and Financial Institutions (1992) for formulation of a *Musharakah Law* may be used as baseline to develop a robust legal framework for participatory modes of financing and to regulate the conduct of contracting parties undertaking financing on the bases of such modes.

6.6.2.4 Proposed Approaches Under Existing Legal and Regulatory Framework

Within existing legal and regulatory framework, there are essentially three non-exhaustive approaches through which IBs may venture into participatory models:

Approach A: Dedicated Subsidiaries of IBs Banks can set up subsidiaries under Section 23 of BCO as long as their business is 'incidental to banking business' or compliant with those listed in Section 7. Nonetheless, there is a ceiling requirement of 30% and issues of taxation, governance and return mechanism also need to be dealt. Possible options are:

1. *Asset Management Company*. A mutual fund setup for off market investment transactions may be a long shot and challenges include lack of precedence, double taxation and need of separate structure.
2. *Venture Capital Management Company*. It may be set up for funds of various risk appetites, exposures and objectives with challenges including double taxation and need of separate structure.
3. *Mudarabah Management Company*: It is entrusted to float and manage specific purpose or general purpose *Mudarabah*. It faces challenges same as mentioned above.
4. *Mudarabah*: A bank according to BCO can act as a management company. *Mudarabah* can be set up for specific or general purpose with no separate governance mechanism. Tax is exempted on manufacturing and financing *Mudarabah*.

Approach B: Direct Exposure of IBs IBs may invest through PTC's under Section 120 of Companies Ordinance or by using a simple *Musharakah* Agreement (The Guidelines for *Musharakah/Mudarabah* finance by *Musharakah/Mudarabah* Task Force 2010 [SBP] at Annexure E may referred). However, it can mainly be used for investment in businesses which are already in operation giving IBs no control over corporate management and legal framework. In other words, it will be constituted as a 'financing relationship' and not a real 'partnership'. Returns generated from such investments are pooled and distributed onwards as per existing profit and loss distribution mechanism. Challenges or issues pertaining to such form of *Musharakah* business include tax on profit, parallel book-keeping, lack of business knowledge, lack of incentives, risk transfer and under-reporting of CAR.

Approach C: Third Party Management Funds raised by banks may be given to third parties, i.e. a specialized venture capital company to engage in partnerships with clients. It may yield positive results due to its specialized role, separate management and permissibility in the existing structure, while possible hitches could be reputational risk, low degree of ownership and poor track record. In view of above, it may be concluded that in case of dedicated subsidiaries, *Mudarabah* seem to offer the most efficient structure. Direct exposure/investment by IBs may never be able to generate significant volume in the absence of incentives at both demand and supply sides. As for third-party arrangement, long-term relationships may not be sustained between IBs and third-party product providers except for their own subsidiaries.

References

Ahmed, H. (2005). Withdrawal risk, market discipline and efficiency in Islamic banking. In T. Khan & D. Muljawan (Eds.), *Islamic banking stability: The role of risk management, regulation and supervision*. Jeddah: Islamic Research and Training Institute, Islamic Development Bank.

Aggarwal, R. K., & Yousef, T. (2000). Islamic banks and investment financing. *Journal of Money, Credit and Banking, 32*(1), 93–120.

Chapra, M. U. (2007). The case against interest: is it compelling? *Thunderbird International Business Review, 49*(2), 161–186.

Chattha, J. A., & Bacha, O. I. (2010). Duration gap and net worth risk for Islamic and conventional banks: a comparative cross-country analysis. *Review of Islamic Economics, 13*(2), 5–33.

Chong, B. S., & Liu, M. H. (2009). Islamic banking: interest-free or interest-based. *Pacific-Basin Finance Journal, 17*(1), 125–144.

Dar, H. A., & Presley, J. R. (2000). Lack of profit loss sharing in Islamic banking: management and control imbalances. *International Journal of Islamic Financial Services, 2*(2), 3–18.

Iqbal, M., & Llewellyn, D. T. (2002). *Islamic banking and finance: New perspectives on profit sharing and risk*. Northampton: Edward Elgar Publishing.

ISRA. (2013). Challenges in the application of Mudarabah and Musharakah concepts in the Islamic finance industry in Malaysia. In *ISRA Research Paper No. 56/2013*. Kuala Lumpur: International *Shari'ah* Research Academy.

Khan, T. (1995). Demand for and supply of mark-up and PLS funds in Islamic banking: some alternative explanations. *Islamic Economic Studies, 3*(1), 39–78.

Nihar, K. L. (2011). *Shari'ah* based banking ad profit or loss paradigm. *International Journal of Management, 2*(1), 30–40.

Shinsuke, N. (2010). Reconsidering Mudarabah contracts in Islamic finance: what is the economic wisdom (hikmah) of partnership-based instruments? *Review of Islamic Economics, 13*(2), 65–79.

Chapter 7
Pricing Deposit Insurance Premium in Islamic Banks

Ibrahim A. Onour

7.1 Introduction

Due to frequent global financial crisis in the past 15 years, deposit insurance system attracted increasing attention of policy makers in the global banking industry. Deposit insurance aims to assure depositors that if their banks fail for any reason, their funds will be protected up to the limits on coverage. Demirguc-Kunt et al. (2005) show that most countries provide deposit insurance. The design of this part of the financial safety net differs across countries, especially in account coverage. Despite criticism, the usefulness of option pricing models based on Merton (1977) model for evaluating deposit insurance is the basis for many studies and application for pricing deposit insurance.

Most of the empirical literature on deposit insurance has focused either on the issue of over- or underpricing of deposit insurance or on how different design features affect the effectiveness of deposit insurance. Deposit insurance is considered overpriced (underpriced) if the deposit insurer charges more (less) for its insurance service than the cost of these services. Moreover, a growing number of studies have considered various factors such as dividend payout, interest rate risk, bankruptcy cost, regulatory forbearance, or closure policies based on the original Merton (1977) model; among others are Marcus and Shaked (1984), Ronn and Verma (1986), Duan et al. (1995), So and Wei (2004), Hwang et al. (2009), and Duan and Yu (1994, 1999).

Islamic deposit insurance is an arrangement to protect insured depositors against the loss of their insured Islamic deposits placed with Islamic banking institutions. The research on Islamic deposit insurance is still very primary as published research in this area up till now is confined to conceptual framework and its permissibility from

I. A. Onour (✉)
School of Management Studies, University of Khartoum, Khartoum, Sudan
e-mail: onour@uofk.edu

M. Zulkhibri et al. (eds.), *Islamic Monetary Economics and Institutions*,
https://doi.org/10.1007/978-3-030-24005-9_7

Shari'ah perspective.[1] As to the best of my knowledge, the current paper is the first in its kind dealing with empirical aspect of deposit insurance system in Islamic banks.[2]

The aim of this paper is to extend the empirical literature of pricing deposit insurance to Islamic banking system, which differ from the conventional banking system, in vulnerability to credit risk. As a result, the paper aims to fill part of this void by assessing empirically the deposit insurance premium of Islamic banking system of different environments. This paper aims to determine the cost of deposit insurance premiums in a number of Islamic banks operating in GCC, Malaysia, and Bangladesh to assess the appropriate insurance policy in each country with regard to risk-based versus flat rate premium policy. As further extension of this research it is possible to utilize the findings of this research, the cost of deposit insurance premium, to assess moral hazard behavior in Islamic banks.

The remaining parts of this chapter are structured as follows. Section 7.2 highlights models of Islamic deposit insurance. Section 7.3 illustrates the methodology of the research as well as the empirical analysis. Section 7.4 provides the conclusion.

7.2 Models of Islamic Deposit Insurance

To show how Islamic deposit insurance system operates, we illustrate two different models of regulatory framework of Islamic deposit insurance systems, the model of Malaysia and that of Sudan.[3]

Malaysia adopted in 2005 a dual deposit insurance system that applies separate deposit insurance systems for conventional and Islamic deposits. Both systems are managed by the Malaysia Deposit Insurance Corporation (MDIC). The operations of Islamic deposit insurance are funded by premiums paid by Islamic banks, as well as Islamic banking windows of commercial banks. During the years 2005–2007, the Islamic banks' premium were flat rates, but in 2008, the MDIC introduced risk-based variable premium rates to safeguard against moral hazard behavior of banks. According to this approach, an Islamic bank with higher risk pays a higher premium. Islamic deposits that are eligible for deposit insurance are savings, demand, and investment deposits included in the Islamic modes of finance, which include

---

[1] In the absence of prohibiting statement from Sunna and a verse from the *Quran*, a fundamental criterion for judging on permissibility of a certain action from *Shari'ah* perspective is public interest preservation, with no harm to any group or individual in that society as a result of that action. Then, as long as deposit insurance preserves public interest, it can be regarded permissible from *Shari'ah* point of view. For further elaboration on this view see discussion paper by IADI in the list of references.

[2] Onour (2014) paper uses the cost of deposit insurance premium to assess moral hazard behavior in banks in Sudan. However, the current paper differs in pricing deposit insurance premium for Islamic banks operating in 8 countries in Middle East and Asia.

[3] These two cases are the most cited in the literature of Islamic deposit insurance. For details, see IADI (2010).

safe custody (*wadiah*), loan (*qard*), cost plus (*Murabahah*), and profit sharing (*Mudarabah*). To ensure *Shari'ah*-compliant insurance system, MDIC adopted a contract of guarantee with fee (*kafalah bil ujrah*), in which depositors make placement with Islamic banks in the form of insurance deposits, and then Islamic banks pay *kafalah* fees to MDIC in the form of premiums. When any Islamic bank fails, the MDIC assumes the Islamic bank's obligation by reimbursing insured depositors.

Sudan has introduced a deposit insurance system in 1996, immediately after the enactment of the Bank of Deposit Security Fund (BDSF), which represents the administrative body of the deposit insurance system in the country. To guarantee *Shari'ah* compliance, the BDSF adopted the *takaful* contract for its deposit insurance. The BDSF operations of deposit insurance are funded by an annual flat premium rate paid by all Islamic banks operating in the country. The Ministry of Finance and Bank of Sudan (the central bank) each contribute 10% of the total value of deposits of Islamic banks at the end of each year (31 December). The BDSF manages its deposit insurance fund according to the following:

(a) Contributions to the *takaful* fund for the insurance of current and saving deposits are paid by Islamic banks, the Ministry of Finance, and the Bank of Sudan.
(b) Contributions to the *takaful* fund for the insurance of investment deposits under *Mudarabah* (profit sharing) are paid by the owners of investment deposits.
(c) In the case of financial insolvency of Islamic bank, the BDSF takes the bank obligation by reimbursing insured deposits.

7.3 Methodology

7.3.1 Pricing of Deposit Insurance

Many of the methods in the literature that have been developed to price deposit insurance are based on Merton (1977) option pricing model that portrays deposit insurance as a put option on the bank's assets. As such, this study follows Merton (1977) and many others for the empirical analysis. The following specification is developed:

$$p(d,\sigma^2)=\varphi(h_2)-\frac{1}{d}\varphi(h_1)$$

where

$$h_1 \equiv \left\{\log(d)-\frac{\sigma^2}{2}\right\}/\sqrt{\sigma^2}$$

$$h_2 \equiv h_1+\sqrt{\sigma^2} \tag{7.1}$$

where p is the price of deposit insurance per dollar of insured deposits, φ is the cumulative normal distribution function, $d = D/v$ is the current deposit-to-asset value ratio, and σ^2 is the variance of the logarithmic change in the value of the assets during the term of the deposits. This implies that as long as the deposit-to-asset ratio and the volatility of the assets remain fixed, the cost of deposit insurance is constant.

7.3.2 *Empirical Analysis*

Data employed in this study are taken from the Bankscope database for 25 Islamic banks operating in a number of Muslim countries including GCC countries, Malaysia, Bangladesh, and Pakistan for the year 2016. To estimate deposit insurance price based on Eq. (7.1), we used total deposit and total asset – sum of loans and cash – variables. Table 7.1 includes our estimation results. The insurance

Table 7.1 Deposit insurance premium

Bank	Country	Premium	Bank	Country	Premium
Al Rajhi Bank Public Joint Stock Company	Saudi Arabia	0.021855	Bank Islam Malaysia Berhad	Malaysia	0.00193
Bahrain Islamic Bank B.S.C.	Bahrain	0.001198	Public Islamic Bank Berhad	Malaysia	0.01105
Albaraka Islamic Bank BSC	Bahrain	0.02662	RHB Islamic Bank Berhad	Malaysia	0.04819
ABC Islamic Bank (E.C.)	Bahrain	0.049606	AmIslamic Bank Berhad	Malaysia	0.04231
Citi Islamic Investment Bank EC	Bahrain	0.042158	Affin Islamic Bank Berhad	Malaysia	0.01310
Islami Bank Bangladesh Limited	Bangladesh	0.016852	Alliance Islamic Bank Berhad	Malaysia	0.0264
First Security Islami Bank Limited	Bangladesh	0.027133	Kuwait Finance House (Malaysia) Berhad	Malaysia	0.03882
Social Islami Bank Ltd	Bangladesh	0.027861	Al Rajhi Banking & Investment Corporation (Malaysia) Berhad	Malaysia	0.03981
ICB Islamic Bank Limited	Bangladesh	0.002334	Kuwait Finance House	Kuwait	0.03936
BankIslami Pakistan Limited	Pakistan	0.019232	Alizz Islamic Bank S.A.O.G	Oman	0.04581
Dubai Islamic Bank Pakistan Limited	Pakistan	0.011913	Qatar Islamic Bank SAQ	Qatar	0.02846
			Qatar International Islamic Bank	Qatar	0.02664

premium varies across banks, with the highest rate of 4.8% for RHB Islamic bank of Malaysia to the lowest rate of 0.11% for Bahrain Islamic bank. Country-based variability of premium rates included in Table 7.2 reveals evidence of premium variability in 18 banks out of the total 22 banks in the sample. The highest variability of premium is noticed in Bahrain, Malaysia, and Bangladesh banks. For those banks revealing variable premium rates, it is recommended to apply risk-based bank-specific policy of insurance rather than flat rate policy.

To investigate further the association between insurance premium and risk, we employed regression analysis between insurance premium, as dependent variable, and credit risk as independent variable using cross-sectional estimation methods including pooled cross-sectional method and least absolute error regression method. Results of the two estimation methods in Table 7.3 indicate that there is statistically significant (at 5% significance level) evidence of positive association between insurance premium and credit risk, which is indication supporting risk-based insurance policy as opposed to flat rate policy.

Table 7.2 Deposit insurance premium policy

Country	Price premium (%)	Insurance policy	Number of banks
Saudi Arabia Average (min/max)	2.1 –	Sample[a]	1
Bahrain Average (min/max)	2.9 (0.1 /4.9)	Bank-specific Risk-based Insurance	4
BANGLADESH Average (min/max)	1.8 (0.2/2.7)	Bank specific Risk-based Insurance	4
Pakistan Average (min/max)	1.5 (1.1/1.9)	Bank-specific Risk-based Insurance	2
Malaysia Average (min/max)	2.7 (0.19/4.8)	Bank-specific Risk-based Insurance	8
Kuwait Average (min/max)	3.9 –	Sample	1
Oman Average (min/max)	4.5 –	Sample	1
Qatar Average (min/max)	2.7 (2.6/2.8)	Flat rate Insurance	2

Note: [a]Insurance policy cannot be decided due to sample limitation

Table 7.3 Deposit insurance and credit risk

Dependent variable	Pooled cross-section – OLS Independent variable (credit risk)		Least absolute error regression Independent variable (credit risk)
Deposit insurance	$\propto_0$	0.78	−1.37
	(p-value)	(0.86)	(0.78)
	$\propto_1$	0.64[b]	0.80[b]
	(p-value)	(0.03)	(0.02)
	R^2	0.22	
	LM[a]	27.4	
	(p-value)	0.06	
	Breusch-Pagan (LM)	190	
	(p-value)	(0.48)	
	AIC	3.73	
	LLF	−39.4	

Note: [a]LM test for cross-section heteroscedasticity significant at 10% sig level; [b]significant at 5% significance level

7.4 Conclusion

To price deposit insurance for Islamic banks, we employed Merton (1977) option pricing model using financial data from Bankscope database for 23 Islamic banks operating in GCC countries and other Islamic Asian countries. To estimate deposit insurance price, we used total deposit and total asset variables. Basic analysis of insurance premium results indicates there is significant variation of insurance premiums within banks in each country. The highest variability of premiums is noticed in Bahrain, Malaysia, and Bangladesh banks. To investigate further the association between insurance premium and risk, we employed regression analysis between insurance premium, as dependent variable, and credit risk as independent variable using cross-sectional estimation methods including pooled cross-sectional method and least absolute error regression method. Results of the two estimation methods indicate there is statistically significant (at 5% significance level) evidence of positive association between insurance premium and credit risk, which is an evidence supporting risk-based insurance policy rather than flat rate policy. As further extension of this research, it is possible to utilize its finding to assess moral hazard behavior in Islamic banks.

Appendix: Deposit Insurance Systems in Selected Countries

	Sudan law	Bahrain law	Jordan law
Board of Directors	1. The Governor of the Central Bank 2. The General Manager of the deposit insurance fund 3. Deputy Minister of Finance and National Economy 4. Director of the department of bank regulation at the Central Bank 5. Two members elected by the association of commercial banks 6. Two experts in banking chosen by the Minister of Finance and National Economy	1. Two experts nominated by the Governor of the Monetary Agency 2. Four members representing commercial banks nominated by the Governor of the Monetary Agency 3. A representative from each of: Ministry of Finance, Ministry of Justice and Islamic Affairs, Ministry of National Economy and Trade 4. A representative from a bank under liquidation	1. Governor of the Central Bank (chair) 2. Deputy Governor of the Central Bank 3. The General Manager of the Deposit Insurance Fund 4. Two members from the Ministry of Finance and the Ministry of Trade 5. Two members appointed by the Council of Ministers
Membership	All licensed commercial banks operating in the country	All licensed commercial banks operating in the country except those insured elsewhere outside the country	All commercial banks operating in the country, with exception of branches of Jordanian banks operating outside the country
Annual fees	Insured member pays annual fee of the rate 0.003 of its total current and saving accounts. And also 0.003 of its total investment account	Annual fee of 25 million Dinars divided between insured banks, based on proportion of each bank's deposits	Annual fee of 0.0025 of the total insured deposits, and possibly a higher rate for banks with higher risks, or when under liquidation

Source: adapted from IADI (2010)

References

Demirguc-Kunt, A., Karacaovali, B., & Laeven, L. (2005). Deposit insurance around the world: A comprehensive database. In *World bank policy research working paper No. 3628*. Washington DC: World Bank.

Duan, J.-C., & Yu, M.-T. (1994). Forbearance and pricing deposit insurance in a multiperiod framework. *Journal of Risk and Insurance, 61*(4), 575–591.

Duan, J.-C., & Yu, M.-T. (1999). Capital standard, forbearance and deposit insurance pricing under GARCH. *Journal of Banking and Finance, 23*(11), 1691–1706.

Duan, J.-C., Moreau, A. F., & Sealey, C. (1995). Deposit insurance and bank interest rate risk: Pricing and regulatory implications. *Journal of Banking and Finance, 19*(6), 1091–1108.

Hwang, D.-Y., Shie, F.-S., Wang, K., & Lin, J.-C. (2009). The pricing of deposit insurance considering bankruptcy costs and closure policies. *Journal of Banking and Finance, 33*(10), 1909–1919.

IADI. (2010). *Deposit insurance from the Shari'ah perspective. Discussion paper prepared by Islamic deposit Insurance Group of the International Association of deposit insurers*. Basel.

Marcus, A. J., & Shaked, I. (1984). The valuation of FDIC deposit insurance using option-pricing estimates. *Journal of Money, Credit and Banking, 16*(4), 446–460.

Merton, R. (1977). An analytical derivation of the cost of deposit insurance and loan guarantees. *Journal of Banking and Finance, 1*(1), 3–11.

Ronn, E. I., & Verma, A. K. (1986). Pricing risk-adjusted deposit insurance: An option-based model. *The Journal of Finance, 41*(4), 871–896.

So, J., & Wei, J. Z. (2004). Deposit insurance and forbearance under moral hazard. *Journal of Risk and Insurance, 71*(4), 707–735.

Chapter 8
Rate of Profit as a Monetary Policy Tool for Financial Stability

Trisiladi Supriyanto

8.1 Introduction

The changes of Indonesia central bank, Bank Indonesia (BI) from the use of BI rate as a reference which is noncontractual to BI 7-day repo rate which is contractual between BI and the conventional banks, have urged Islamic banking to look for a new benchmark reference rate for its liability and asset product pricing. The main reason is because the BI 7-day repo rate is determined by the supply and demand of lending and borrowing transaction between BI and the conventional banks, which will make use of interest rate as a main reference for the calculation of short-term liability product as a cost of funds and the long-term prime lending rate, which in turn will determine the management Islamic bank asset and liability.

As a consequence of the prohibition of interest instruments, Islamic financial system requires a substitution to the application of interest rate at the operational level, which is in accordance with Islamic principles. Alternative concepts for the substitution of interest is mentioned in the *Qur'an* as profits that derived from the commercial transaction without any exploitation, while in the economic literature of Islam, among others referred to as the "expected rate of profit" or "required rate of profit" (Choudhury 1997). Some classical economists call it as the rate of profit (Sraffa 1960). The neoclassical economist such as Henry Thornton (1965) refers the concept as a marginal rate of profit, while Wicksell (1934) called the concept as a natural rate of profit. In the concept of thoughts itself, there are disagreement among both conventional and Islamic economist.

The determination of profit rate for Islamic financial products and Islamic bonds is the key to create economic justice and stability in investment income and welfare of the society. The justice is seen in the form of a just and low business costs especially for the lower segment of society such as micro-entrepreneurs when

T. Supriyanto (✉)
Ibnu Khaldun University Bogor, Bogor, Indonesia

M. Zulkhibri et al. (eds.), *Islamic Monetary Economics and Institutions*,
https://doi.org/10.1007/978-3-030-24005-9_8

compared to interest rate system. With regard to financial stability, profit rate which will be used by Islamic banks and capital markets (bonds) should be guided by the return from the real sector. Hence, the study aims to find a substitute of the BI policy rate as a reference rate for the Islamic financial market transactions in determining asset and liability pricing such as deposits and financing cost. The substitute of BI policy rate as a reference rate for Islamic banking is important given the BI policy rate (noncontractual) has been replaced by the BI 7-day repo rate, which is contractual rate. The reference rate is determined by the supply and demand of borrowing transaction using the instrument of SBI (Bank Indonesia Certificate) in conventional money markets that are not based on the rate of profit derived from financial transactions in the real sector, which is in accordance with the principles of Islamic economics. The use of *Shari'ah Reference Rate* as a substitute for BI policy rate as a monetary tool is very important in determining the rate of profit for Islamic financial transactions.

8.2 The Rate of Profit: An Overview

The concept of rate of profit as a substitution of interest concept is very important, given the management of Islamic financial system today in some countries, both at the macro- and micro-levels, which does not have a clear concept (Fig. 8.1). At the macro-level, the use of the rate of profit concept is seen in central bank policy in countries that have implemented Islamic economic system either the dual banking system or full Islamic economic system (single economic system). Among both systems, the use of the concept in the financial system varies according to central banks in designing their monetary instruments.

At the micro-level, the application of the rate of profit concept is often facing a problem because there is no yardstick (benchmark) in determining the profit margin on natural certainty contracts such as the sale-based contract (*Murabahah*) and leasing-based contract (*Ijarah*) in Islamic banking practices. Furthermore, there is a difference in the use of profit rate, in particular, the sale-based contract (*Murabahah*). Some Muslim countries apply the rate of profit in *Murabahah* (called as a margin or markup) and *Ijarah* (called as *ujrah* or coupon), which are quoted fixed for long-term financing transaction. In Pakistan, *Murabahah* with a fixed rate of profit is used in the short, medium, and long term. In Bangladesh, the contract of *Murabahah* is used for short-term transactions, while the contract of *Bay 'muajjal* with installments is used for the purchase of long-term assets. In the United Kingdom, the contract of *Murabahah* is used in home financing transaction with a long period of 20–25 years. As a result, the entire applications of *riba* in Islamic financial institutions such as the interest rate formula, i.e., simple interest, compounded interest, fixed interest, variable interest, which are all determined in advance (predetermined), are all used in Islamic banking products in particular trade- and leasing-based financing such as *Murabahah* and *Ijarah* (Saeed 1996).

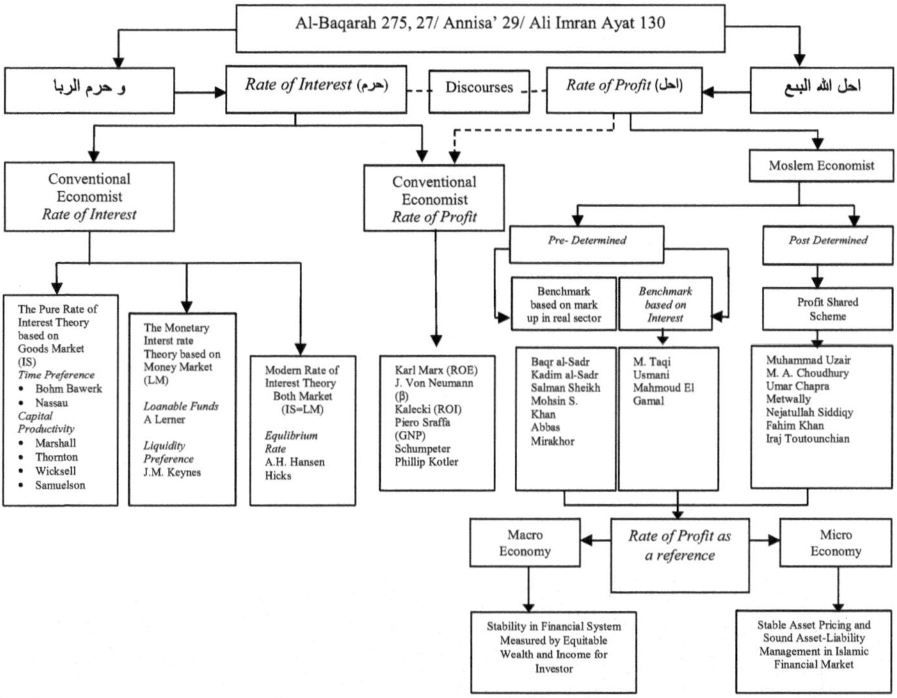

Fig. 8.1 The framework of rate of profit as *Shari'ah* reference rate. (Source: Author's own illustration)

Among the critical issues in the debate over the concept of rate of profit as a substitute for rate of interest concept is whether Islamic financial institutions have incorporated elements of *'iwadh* (countervalue for a benefit of the goods or service), or they just do the *ziyadah* (profit creation in the absence of activity in the real sector) in the determination of its rate of profit. According to the theory of Islamic rate of profit, to take a legal profit, a product must contain three elements (Rosly 2005): (1) the value added or value addition in a product as a result of the element of work (*kasb*), (2) risk taking (*ghurm*) due to the risk of price changes on goods that is traded, and (3) underwriting liability in case there is a defect in goods sold (*dhaman*).

In the practice, there is a difference of opinion in the use of contracts in the instrument of monetary operations, i.e., the rate of profit that is postdetermined (ex post), while the rate of profit is predetermined (ex ante). Countries that implement monetary instruments with the ex post rate of profit are Sudan, Iran, and Pakistan using the contract of *Musharakah* and *Mudarabah*, while countries that implement monetary instruments ex ante rate of profit are Malaysia and Indonesia using the contract of *Bay' al-Inah, Murabahah,* and *Ju'ala* (Rosly 2005; Omar et al. 2013). The differences are due to the differing views on the effectiveness of monetary policy to control the money supply. Instruments with ex ante rate of profit are considered more effective in controlling money in circulation.

Nowadays, Islamic banks in the financial center around the world are still using the LIBOR (London Inter-Bank Offered Rates), which is the average lending rate of the largest banks in London as a benchmark in quoting rate of profit to their products. The use of LIBOR as a benchmark is practiced in determining profit margin (rate of profit) of *Murabahah* or *Ijarah* for home financing, leasing, and other commercial financing such as financing of cars, motorcycles, and other consumer goods as well as pricing *Sukuk Al-Ijarah* (Islamic bond). The use of LIBOR or JIBOR is essentially the interest rate charged by five largest banks in the world financial centers such as London and Jakarta, which is basically the loan transactions between banks in the money market (not profit from real market), and this rate is determined by the forces of supply and demand for money (money supply and demand) as the cost of funds and is not based on the price of rent or rate of profit in the market for goods and services. In Indonesia, Islamic bank is still using SBI (Indonesia Central Bank Certificate) or JIBOR (Jakarta Interbank Offered Rate), i.e., interest rate average of the largest banks in Indonesia, in determining the Islamic financing price such as mortgages, multipurpose loan, and other financing as well as in determining the *ujrah* (leasing cost) on *Sukuk Al-Ijarah* in the capital market.

The use of LIBOR as a benchmark has raised pros and cons among Muslim economists. El-Gamal (2006) supports the conventional use of LIBOR as a benchmark or markup on Islamic sale-based product like *Murabahah*. The use of "Islamic Benchmark" is unnecessary, impractical, and dangerous because the implicit rate (rate charged) in Islamic financial product differs with the rate of interest in nature, depending on the quality of the underlying asset. However, Islamic benchmark is not deep and liquid enough to form a uniform rate implicit (uniform) as a benchmark transaction. The differences among Islamic economist in the opinion are regarding the use of LIBOR as a benchmark in Islamic financial market in general, which coexist with the conventional financial market globally. This is in contrast with other Islamic economist's opinions that prefer to use the economic value of time concept, which refers to the profit in real sector.

Malaysia and some other countries are using the LIBOR (London Interbank Offered Rate) as a reference in leasing-based product such as *Ijarah* or leasing, while Indonesia uses SBI plus in Indonesia Rupiah *Ijarah* transaction and SIBOR (Singapore Interbank Offered Rate) plus in US Dollar *Ijarah* Transactions. Therefore, it is now very urgent to have a standard on Islamic benchmark separated from conventional banks considering Islamic economics has different characteristics from conventional economy, especially in terms of determining the rate of profit as compared to rate of interest. Basically, the concept of rate of profit is the concept of ex post, while the interest is basically the concept of ex ante.

8.3 Research Methodology

The study conducts inferential research to find solutions for a new monetary instrument in accordance with Islamic principles and for the objectives of the *Maqasid al-Shari'ah* that can be substitute for interest rate as a reference rate which can realize economic justice (equitable distribution of income) and the prosperity of society (equitable distribution of wealth) through sustainable economic growth. This study uses the jurisprudence (*fiqh*) and Islamic economics approach to analyze the concept of rate of profit and its application. The approach utilized research documents by analyzing data or facts which are composed from both primary and secondary data. The study also uses analytical survey to draw conclusions.

8.4 Results and Discussion

8.4.1 Money Market and Shari'ah Monetary Operation by Bank Indonesia

The biggest challenge in the Islamic financial market today is creating a *Shari'ah* interbank money market instrument and the monetary policy tool in accordance with Islamic principles and to meet the objectives of *Shari'ah* (*Maqasid al-Shari'ah*). As shown in Fig. 8.2, the *Maqasid al-Shari'ah* in Islamic financial system is to create economic justice, which is to achieve equitable distribution of income and wealth as well as the stability of the financial system. The transaction *Shari'ah* interbank money market between BI and the Islamic bank is in the form of an auction or a classical repo SBI-S, whereby it is divided into two transactions, i.e., loan contract (*al-Qard*) and guarantees (*ar-Rahn*). According to Islamic principles, compensation should come from profits on real transactions either on the purpose of monetary contraction or monetary expansion (productive expansion). Profit can only be obtained by working or through trading backed by the asset/project assets in the real sector.

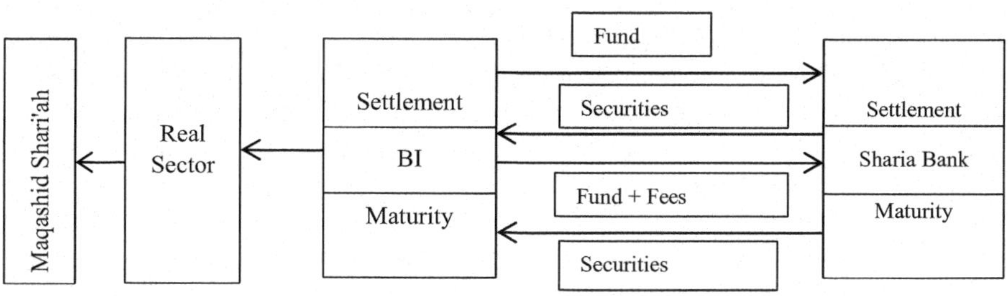

Fig. 8.2 Ideal *Shari'ah* compliance repo transaction mechanism for *Maqasid al-Shari'ah*. (Source: Author's own illustration)

In general, the transaction between Islamic and conventional interbank money market is the same, whereby the market is trading instrument for liquidity/short-term investments with a maximum term of 1 year and payment is made by credit notes via clearing or funds transfer. Money market has an important role for the bank to manage its liquidity position and trading to create profits for the banks, for the government, and for the BI to do an open market operation (OMO), although the OMO in this case cannot be effectively used in countries that financial markets are less developed such as Islamic financial market. The OMO is important because it is setting the reference rate (BI rate) that will be used by the banks as the benchmark to price any asset and liability product of the bank. Money market is used by the government as a place to sell short-term debt instrument (Treasury Bill or Treasury Notes) or in Indonesia is called T-Bills/*Shari'ah* T-Bills (SPN/SPN-S).

Money market is used by BI to conduct OMO in the form of (i) monetary operations; (ii) standing facilities through application FPJPS (hort-Term Facility Loans) to help the bank overcome difficulties in short-term liquidity due to mismatch, as part of the lender of the last resort; and (iii) deposit facility in the form of placement of funds by the Islamic bank in the form of Bank Indonesia Deposit Facility (FASBIS). In addition to these three monetary tools, beyond the money market operation, BI uses reserve requirement tools. For Islamic banks, the reserve requirement ratio is connected with the ratio of FDR (Financing to Deposit Ratio) that should be at least 80%. This suggests that the portfolio of Islamic banks entirely goes into the real sector with the consideration that the other portfolios such as *Sukuk* and *Mudarabah* Interbank Investment (IMA) are basically an investment in the real sector.

In the latter discussion, rate of profit term is referred to as the profit rate that the Islamic bank distributes to third-party fund investors and other banks at the end of the month. *Shari'ah* monetary operation is conducted to achieve the operational target of monetary control in Islamic banks in order to achieve the ultimate target of monetary policy of the central bank (Bank Indonesia 2008).[1] The operational target is the adequate liquidity in the form of base money (M1), which is currency and demand deposit in Islamic banks and M2 in the form of savings, deposits, and repos with the central bank. The operational target of monetary policy is conducted by influencing Islamic banking liquidity through monetary contraction or monetary expansion.

Shari'ah monetary contraction is a reduction in the liquidity of banks through *Shari'ah* monetary operations, while *Shari'ah* monetary expansion is an addition of bank liquidity through monetary operations must fulfill Islamic principles expressed in the form of a *fatwa* (*Shari'ah* opinion) from fatwa authority. *Fatwa* of DSN (National *Shari'ah* Board) for the *Shari'ah* money market has been issued in 2002 No. 37/DSN-MUI/X/2002, which says: "The underlying reasons why this fatwa was issued is the reality that Islamic banks may experience liquidity shortages or excess liquidity as a result of differences in the placing and taking of funds, as well

[1] Bank Indonesia, Bank Indonesia Regulation No.10/36/PBI/2008 on *Shari'ah* Monetary Operation, Indonesia.

as to improve the efficiency of fund management." The general provisions of the *fatwa*: (i) interbank money market based on interest is not justified according to *Shari'ah*, (ii) interbank money market based on *Shari'ah* is the short-term financial transactions among the participants based on the principles of *Shari'ah*, and (iii) the participants were Islamic bank as the owner or the receiver of funds and the conventional banks as the owner of the funds only. Special provisions on the *fatwa* are as follows: (i) contracts that can be used in the interbank money market based on the *Shari'ah* principles are *Mudarabah (Muqaradah)/Qirad, Musharakah, Qard, Wadiah,* and *Sarf,* and (ii) transfer of ownership of the money market instruments that used this transaction can only be sold to third party once. Islamic monetary operations with repo transaction by BI are currently done with two instruments along with the price:

8.4.1.1 Repo and SBI (Bank Indonesia Certificate) Shari'ah-Based Auction

(a) Bank Indonesia *Shari'ah* Certificate (SBIS) auction is conducted to absorb the excess liquidity (monetary contraction) through OMO with Islamic banks which are nonproductive because funds absorbed is not used for the real sector and at the maturity date of SBIS, the principal payments will generate monetary rewards for *Ju'ala* so that it will create additional liquidity which is nonproductive as well because of the occurrence of printing money that is not based on real transactions. SBIS time period is 1 week, 2 weeks, and a maximum of 1 month with a minimal amount of Rp 500 million (Table 8.1). Cut Off Time (COT) at 14:00 pm. The SBIS cannot be traded in the secondary market; thus, such a

Table 8.1 The government repo transaction volume and frequency

Year	Transaction volume (Rp trillion)		Total	Daily average	Frequency
	Outright	Repo	(Rp trillion)	(Rp trillion)	
2002	105.7	25.3	131.0	0.5	16
2003	327.7	10.0	337.7	1.4	51
2004	502.1	11.5	513.5	2.1	112
2005	512.2	107.4	619.5	2.5	102
2006	795.3	24.8	820.1	3.3	138
2007	1364.0	93.0	1457.0	5.9	232
2008	866.9	170.6	1037.5	4.2	156
2009	717.0	117.7	834.7	3.4	156
2010	1091.2	139.5	1230.7	5.0	194
2011	1466.0	428.8	1894.8	7.7	295
2012	1334.8	929.6	2264.4	9.2	407

Source: Bank Indonesia

mechanism does not have a role in the development and deepening of the Islamic financial market.

(b) Repo SBIS or *Shari'ah* Interbank *Mudarabah* Money Market Securities (SIMA) is not based on the principles of debt/borrowing funds to gain interest but based on classic repo transaction, namely, lending the money with the contract of *Qard* by the BI to Islamic banks (BUS) and the Islamic bank giving the collateral with contract of *al-Rahn* through nonauction mechanism with the repo cost: BI Rate + 300 basis points. This repo cost is determined by the BI as an obligation to pay as a penalty because BUS/UUS not fulfill the agreed period of SBIS purchasing agreement. This practice will lead to nonproductive effect of monetary expansion (nonproductive liquidity management). SBIS term of repo transaction is 1 day. Repo transaction is arranged between the window times, i.e. 2:00 p.m. to 5:00 p.m. after interbank clearing results were announced. Repo fees will be charged on the following day (2nd leg) on maturity.

8.4.1.2 Shari'ah Repo Based on Government Sukuk (SBSN)

(a) Reverse Repo Transaction is a conditional sale transaction of securities by banks to the central bank with the obligation to repurchase in accordance with the price and the agreed period. Islamic banks (BUS) can repo securities with Government *Sukuk* (SBSN) instrument. SBSN is government securities (SBN) issued based on Islamic principles, as evidence for the inclusion of the assets of SBSN either in rupiah or in foreign currency. SBSN could in the form of Wholesale *Sukuk* (code IFR – Indonesia Fixed Rate) and Retail *Sukuk* (code SR), PBS (Project-Based *Sukuk*) and SPN-S (Treasury Bills *Shari'ah*). The assets of SBSN is an object of financing and/or state property with economic value, such as land, buildings, or other than land or buildings, that in order to issue SBSN be used as basis for the issuance SBSN so intent SBSN issuance is to finance the state budget or the project development and the publisher is direct government or company issuing SBSN (UU 19 in 2008). BI can participate in the inaugural auction (primary market) SPN-S and selling SBSN/PBS in the secondary market. For that, BI needs to stock building by purchasing SBSN in the secondary market, given the implications of Article 56 of Law No.23 of 1999 as amended by Law No. 3 of 2004 which prohibits the central bank purchases government securities in the primary market because it is a form of giving direct credit.

(b) In relation to the *Shari'ah* OMO, which is part of the monetary operations, BI may conduct reverse repo SBSN with the promise of redemption by the bank at maturity in accordance with the price and time agreed. This transaction will be done after BI has purchased SBSN through auctions on the primary market for SPN-S (Islamic Treasury Bills) issued by the Ministry of Finance or Purchase Government PBS (Project-Based *Sukuk*) in the secondary market. SBSN reverse repo transactions are conducted by using contract of al bay (buying and selling), accompanied by *Wa'ad* (promise) by the bank to the BI in a separate document to resell back the SBSN within a certain price agreed. Although the contract used is in accordance with the Islamic principles, SBSN Reverse Repo is currently not intended to develop and deepening the Islamic financial market and only a part or a supporter of the main Islamic monetary instrument with SBIS (Sitorus 2015).

In Indonesia, the government securities repo market is relatively underdeveloped, the percentage of repo transactions on average less than 10% of all government securities transactions in the secondary market even though the number tended to increase from year to year. BI is also active in repo transactions with banks in the management of money market liquidity. BI's balance sheet in 2012 is recorded transactions amounting up to Rupiah 100 trillion, or up from Rupiah 69 trillion by the end of 2012. Compared to the United States and Japan, which are by volume, repo transactions represent 40% of all transactions, the debt repo transactions in Indonesia are still small.

8.4.1.3 Repo in the Intraday Liquidity Facility (FLI)

To support the creation of good financial systems and transactions that are quickly and accurately, since 2000 BI has developed a payment system known as Bank Indonesia Real Time Gross Settlement System (BI-RTGS). To reduce the risk of failure of the transaction due to the gridlock in the BI-RTGS system, BI provides intraday liquidity facility (FLI) with auto-repo transaction. FLI can only be used if a bank has securities as collateral and has transferred its securities to the collateral account for the FLI. The amount of funding ceilings depends on the market price of the type of securities as collateral and haircut of the securities. FLI includes FLIS (*Shari'ah* Intraday Liquidity Facility) for Islamic banks. FLI and FLIS are provided during the operational hours of BI-RTGS system and shall be paid on the day of use FLI /FLIS.

8.4.1.4 Repo Transaction in Islamic Short-Term Funding Facility (FPJPS)

Short-Term Funding Facility, herein after referred as FPJP, is a standing facility of the BI to the Bank to address the liquidity problems experienced by banks, both conventional banks and Islamic banks (FPJPS). Short-term liquidity problem is a condition experienced by the banks in general because of a mismatch in the rupiah cash flow so that the bank cannot fulfill the obligations of the Statutory Reserves determined by the BI (Reserve Requirement). FPJPS given is calculated based on the estimated number of bank liquidity needs up to meet the reserve requirement. FPJPS duration is firstly given for 14 days and then can be extended up to 90 days. Collateral of FPJPS can be SBSN and SBI-S or financing assets; in this case, SBPU-M as mentioned earlier also can be used as collateral of FPJPS in case the

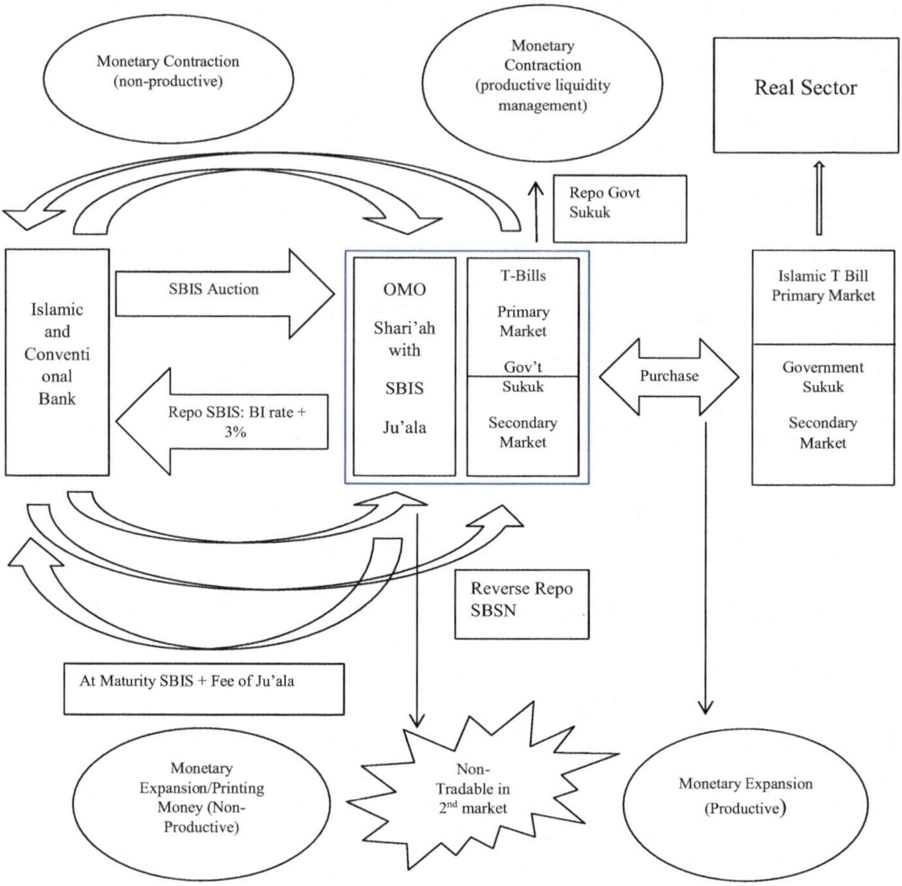

Fig. 8.3 *Shari'ah* open market operation through SBIS auction and government *Sukuk* repo. (Source: Author's own illustration)

bank does not have SBSN and SBI-S. BI will charge for the FPJPS facility: BI rate plus a margin of 300 basis point (Fig. 8.3).

8.4.1.5 Non-repo Bank Indonesia Shari'ah Deposit Facility (FASBIS)

FASBIS is deposit facility provided by Bank Indonesia to a commercial bank conducting business based on the *Shari'ah* principles to place their excess funds in Bank Indonesia. Owners of the FASBIS are recorded in Bank Indonesia Securities Settlement System (BI-SSSS) by not issuing securities (scriptless), such as SBIS, so that the FASBIS is not transferable. Auction method and other requirements are the same as SBIS auction.

8.4.2 The Impact of the Shari'ah Monetary Policy Transmission with Repo Transaction

If we analyzed the BI monetary policy today, the monetary policy is taken to affect the national aggregate demand made through the monetary policy transmission mechanism by using the interest rate channel and did not take another channel, that is, the exchange rate channel, the asset price channel, and the credit channel. The BI since July 2005 formally began to use the interest rate as the operational target, by setting the BI rate as the reference rate target. In the early stages, the BI rate is the reference (benchmark) for the 1-month SBI discount rate with the banks which is done every week with a certain volume so that the 1-month SBI discount rate can be maintain at the level of the BI rate by a certain range. BI rate change means indicate a change in attitude or *stance* of monetary policy is reflected in the discount rate movement around the BI rate.

Problems in Islamic bank today, the return for the SBI-S is not determined by the profit (rate of profit) derived from the real sector, which can be categorized as *ziyadah* (profit without countervalue in the real sector). Therefore, either monetary contraction or monetary expansion in Islamic banking is nonproductive because it does not have underlying in real sector such as SBSN. SBI-S moves around the BI rate and reverse repo SBIS uses penalty as a pricing base: SBIS +3%. BI rate change, in with the banking intermediation process, is expected to affect both deposit bank interest rate and rate of financing Islamic banks to the public. The big question is whether the interest rate channel is also be able to form the BI rate as a reference rate for the BI monetary operations in Islamic banking. In theory, Islamic monetary policy transmission channel should be based on the rate of profit, which is the profit coming from the distribution rate that is the right of investor (Islamic Bank Deposit Profit Rate or Profit Rate of Islamic Interbank Bank Money Market-IMA) as shown in Fig. 8.4.

Shari'ah monetary operations aimed at achieving the operational target of monetary control *Shari'ah* in order to support the achievement of the ultimate target of monetary policy of Islamic banks (PBI No.10/36/PBI/2008 regarding *Shari'ah* Monetary Operations). The operational target is adequate liquidity in the form of Islamic banking as M1 and M2 (including repo). Then, the achievement of monetary policy operations carried out by influencing *Shari'ah* bank liquidity through monetary contraction or expansion.

In a further development, in line with the development of the banking industry in the country that is more efficient, since October 2008, BI adjusted the BI rate policy previously as a references discount rate for 1-month SBI (not contractual), which is now converted into a contractual repo rate of Interbank Money Market term 1 day or overnight. BI rate determined by the Board of Governors (RDG) BI is done once a month. Monetary operations carried out to maintain the movement of interbank rates overnight remains in BI rate corridor with a certain margin, for example, BI rate plus minus 100 bps (1%). Interbank interest rate is the price that is formed through a mechanism in the interbank money market over the counter (OTC).

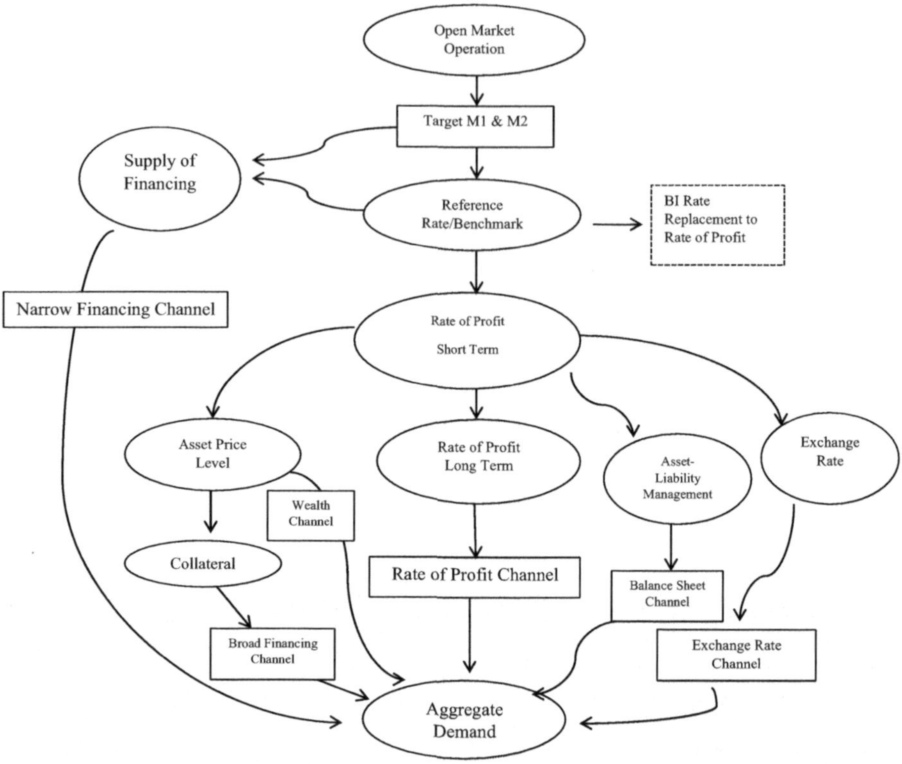

Fig. 8.4 The relation between the *Shari'ah* open market operation and the rate of profit. (Source: Ismail 2010)

Interbank period ranges from 1 day (overnight) up to 1 year, but interbank transactions dominated by transactions with a maturity overnight. Additionally, BI rate and JIBOR (Jakarta Interbank Offered Rate) an indicative interest rate deals in the interbank transactions in Indonesia, which is widely used as a benchmark rate on many financial transactions in Indonesia for transactions denominated in Rupiah. Recent development is that BI policy taken is to remove the use of BI rate period of 6 months as a reference and replace with an interest repo rate between BI and banking for a period of 7 days.

8.4.3 The Use of Rate of Profit as a Reference Rate in Islamic Bank

Problems of using BI rate or JIBOR in pricing the *Shari'ah* asset or investments for short-term liquidity management in the framework of monetary policy have long been debatable. Controversy occurred in the use of BI rate or JIBOR as a benchmark or as a reference rate. BI rate or JIBOR is formed by the demand and supply of money in the conventional money market lending and borrowing transaction with interest rate, and therefore is not based on profits in the real sector/productive sector. Nevertheless, Islamic banks in some financial centers are still using the LIBOR (London Inter-Bank Offered Rates) or the average lending rates of the largest banks in London as benchmark. While in Indonesia, Islamic banks are still using JIBOR (Jakarta Inter Bank Offered Rates) or the average interest rate the largest banks in Indonesia in determining the interest rate of Islamic financing such as mortgages, car financing, and other multipurpose financing.

The use of LIBOR as a reference is basically using the interest rate charged by the five largest banks both in financial centers such as London, the loan transactions between banks in the money market (money market) which is determined by forces of supply and demand for money (money supply and demand) as the cost of funds. This means LIBOR is not based on the market price of profits in goods and services transaction. For example, in the case of *Murabahah* car financing transaction or *Ijarah Muntahia bi-Tamlik* house financing transaction, the Islamic bank should use as the profit in the leasing market in real sector transaction and the bank should mark to market the profit to this benchmark.

El-Gamal (2006) supports the use of conventional benchmark such as LIBOR as a benchmark that is the markup on buying or selling. The use of "Islamic Benchmark" is unnecessary, impractical, and dangerous because although he admits that the implicit rate (rate subject to actual) in Islamic financial is different, depending on the quality of the underlying assets, the Islamic benchmark in the Islamic financial market is not deep and liquid enough to form a uniform rate implicit (uniform) as a benchmark transaction. The diversity of the contract that has been used in Islamic benchmark such as the sale-based product (*Murabahah*), lease-based transaction (Ijarah), profit-sharing transaction, and others compared to conventional bank that only use debt-based contract makes Islamic benchmark more difficult to be developed. In contrast, Khan and Mirakhor (1989) find that in the Islamic economic system, the rate of profit on financial assets is determined by the rate of return of bank financing which will be used as a benchmark. This means that the use of LIBOR as a benchmark in Islamic financial market is impermissible.

Khan (1995) finds that the Islamic discount rate can be benchmarked from the returns on the deposits in Islamic bank. The reason is as follows: to use the concept of time value of money, we need a portfolio, where the risk is almost nonexistent and can be ignored so that only pure risk exists in a reasonable time frame. So, only the rate of return of the portfolio that is not risk can represent the discount rate. Only the diversification of the portfolio that can reduce the risk or, in other words, the rate of return on the projects that have been distributed can be a proxy of the time value of money. Rate of return as it approaches will reflect the risk to be borne associated with uncertain time. Therefore, he proposed the rate of profit or equivalent rate of deposits of Islamic banks to be able to represent the Islamic discount rate, because it was obtained after the Islamic bank distributes deposit funds earlier to projects that diversified into various segments and get a return of the project. The return from the project then will be paid to deposit holder. This return is called the rate of profit of *Mudarabah* deposit.

On the use of a discount rate in the early days of Islam, Al Sadr (1961) describes that Islam already contained the concept of discount rate in sale-based transaction. The price is cheaper if we pay cash, but when the goods are purchased by installments within a specified period, the price is more expensive. Furthermore, in the monetary policy in the early days of Islam, in order to increase investment, the profit level of goods sold by installments will be lowered. The monetary policy operation by raising or lowering the selling price of *Shari'ah*-based instrument by installment purchase contract that is practiced in the days of the Prophet, thus, can be used as a theoretical basis for the central bank's monetary policy in interest-free system. It also shows that the cash price and the price of delay may be different. Price delay is greater due to the possibility of profit (rate of profit) on the turnover of goods during the delayed time.

Based on this study, it can be concluded that the reference rate of profit as a replacement for the BI rate, which is in accordance with the Islamic principles, is the equivalent rate of profit of the transaction between BI and Islamic bank in IMA (Indonesia Interbank *Mudarabah* Investment). The Islamic bank will offer a profit-sharing ratio and give the *Mudarabah* certificate to BI named SIMA (IMA Certificate). This *Shari'ah* open market operation (non-SBIS) is recommended with the consideration that BI is prohibited to provide loans directly to the government, either using SIMA or Government *Sukuk* securitization, which can be seen in Fig. 8.5.

The *Shari'ah* repo contract with BI that will produce Rate of Profit as a Reference Rate for Islamic Bank is explained as follows:

1. The repo transaction (repo or sell outright to maturity) with SIMA will be using *Mudarabah* contract with revenue sharing because the contract is an agreement of direct financing to customers of Islamic banks in which the funds obtained from BI as *rabb ul-mal* and the Islamic bank acts as *mudarib*. This will produce rate of profit coming from real sector directly.
2. The repo transaction with Government *Sukuk* such as SBSN will be using *Musharakah* contract between BI and the Islamic bank. This transaction is basically similar to the OMO conducted in Sudan by the Government *Musharakah* Certificate (GMC). The consequence of this contract is: if the Islamic or BI want to do the reverse repo agreements, the parties should seek permission from the other party. This transaction will also produce rate of profit that is coming from real sector through government investment (Fig. 8.6).

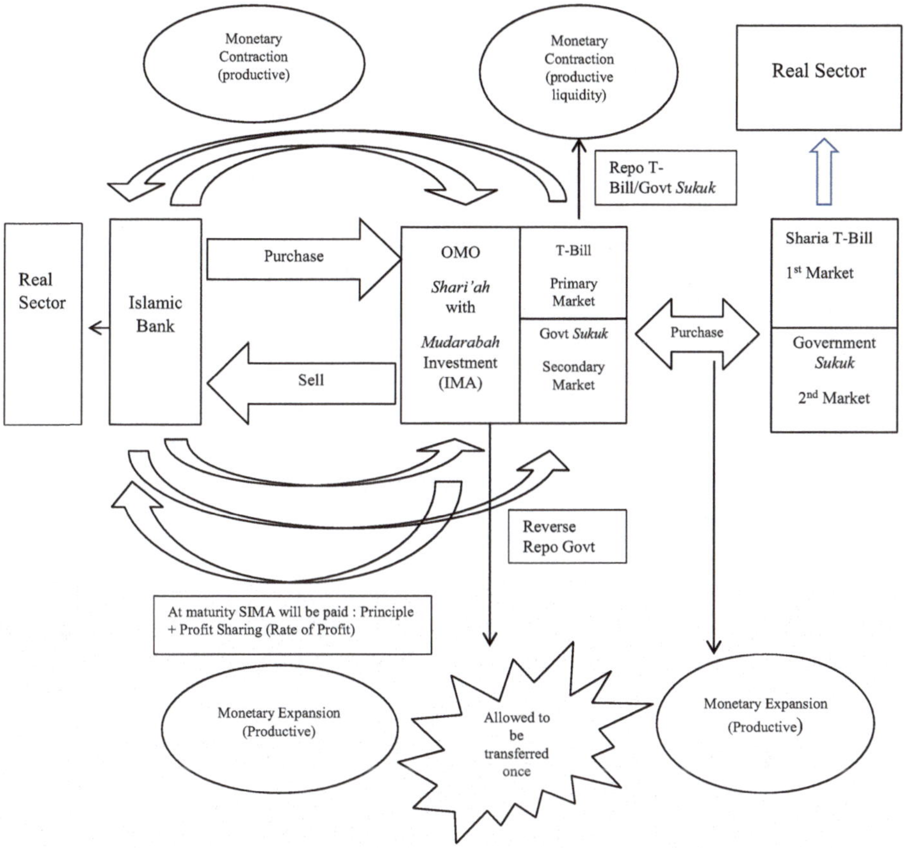

Fig. 8.5 Recommended *Shari'ah* open market operation using *Islamic* reference rate. (Source: Author's own illustration)

8.4.4 Risk in Repo Transactions with SIMA/SBSN

In practice, repo transactions with SIMA/SBSN have some risk:

(a) The risk of default if at maturity Islamic bank is unable to pay. Therefore, to mitigate this default risk, SIMA Repo transaction must have high-quality collateral such as SBSN (Government *Sukuk*). This transaction will push Islamic bank to have at least a portfolio of SBSN about 10% of the total portfolio if the BI requires high-quality collateral. This deal will create revenue-shared rate of profit as a reference rate for Islamic bank.

(b) Market risk can also occur if the market price of pledged collateral SBSN is lower than the specified SBSN price when the repo agreement is made. However, this scheme has lower market risk if Islamic bank use previous BI reference rate for SBIS reverse repo transaction that charged the Islamic bank by SBIS rate + 3%. This reverse repo charged can be higher than the rate of profit on the deposits of Islamic banks which depends on the macro-economic conditions. If Islamic bank is still using the BI rate as a reference/benchmark to determine the equivalent rate for the deposits in the Islamic bank, the repo cost by using the SBIS will be higher than the IMA funding with other Islamic bank. For example, when Islamic bank does the repo using the SBSN instrument like SR01 (S*ukuk* Retail 01) with *Ijarah* contract, the repo cost will be more expensive than the rate of profit on the deposits of Islamic banks.

(c) Liquidity risk can occur if BI purchases as part of the securitization of SBSN with Islamic bank to solve liquidity problems, the repo contracts should be followed with *Wa'ad* contract; otherwise, the BI will have to fine other party to sell the security with lower price.

8.4.5 The Benefits and the Advantages of Repo Transactions Shari'ah

Repo transactions can provide advantages in terms if at maturity the debtor is not able to buy back the guarantee or default, then the guarantee will become the property of the creditors. Creditors could benefit if such securities turned out to be

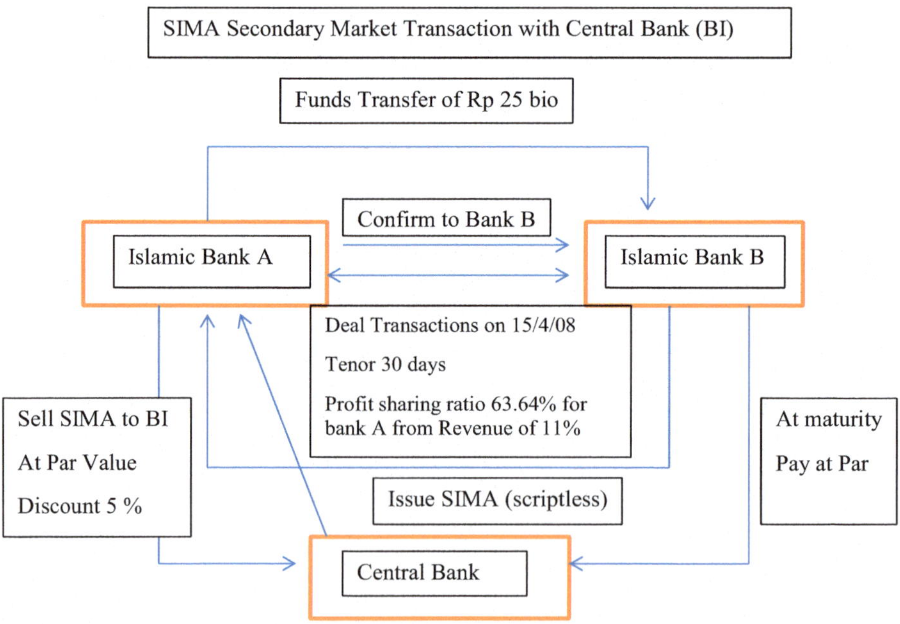

Fig. 8.6 Illustration of SIMA transaction in *Islamic* secondary interbank money market. (Source: Author's own illustration)

sold at a higher value than the price at the time of the repurchase agreements has been made at the inception. In the case of declining interest rates, the majority of SBSN will be traded at prices above 100% (par) and higher. This position will be reversed in the case that interest rate in an increasing trend. The price of the majority of the SBSN will go lower if *Ijarah* contract is using fixed coupon. This fixed and long-term quoted coupon price will create high duration and convexity or sensitivity of the SBSN price. Rising reference rate of SBI will make SBSN prices to fall. The price of SBSN is strongly influenced by the reference rate (BI rate) in accordance with this formula:

$$d(\text{VSBSN}) = -D \times dR + C/2 \times DR/(1+R) \quad (8.1)$$

where VSBSN is price of SBSN, *D* is duration, *C* is convexity, and *R* is reference rate (BI rate). For example, Government *Sukuk Ijarah* SR01 Series with 12% *Ijarah* coupon with maturity February 25, 2012, had ever reached the price of 107.72 or appreciated 7.72% above the cost of *Sukuk*. However, the Government *Sukuk* Series IF8 price with coupon of 8.8% maturing March 15, 2020, had reached 98.5 price or suffered a capital loss of 1.5% of their principal amount (Bloomberg Company 2010).

The price movement of financial assets of *Shari'ah* that can experience a capital loss (the wealth decline) as assessed by the BI reference rate will lead to the instability of the Islamic financial system, due to the instability of the assets and liabilities of Islamic banks, which in turn affects the wealth of the society who invest funds in Islamic banks. The instability in *sukuk* price could theoretically be overcome if the reference rate used is the rate of profit on the transaction deposits *Mudarabah*, which is determined and follows the rate of return of financing in the real sector. This ex ante rate of profit based on the revenue sharing will create the duration and convexity of the Islamic bank asset, which will always be close to zero. The prices of Islamic bank financial assets will be stable at the issuance price (at par).

Some benefits of using the repo transaction with SIMA and SBSN instrument include the following:

(i) The use of SIMA/SBSN will increase transaction on the secondary Islamic interbank market so that it can contribute to the development and the deepening of the Islamic financial markets.
(ii) Encourage the economic activity in the real sector and improve the welfare when: (a) SBSN purchased by the bank, it will help the liquidity of the government to finance the state budget and improve the general welfare, and (b) SIMA was bought by the central bank, it will increase the liquidity of the Islamic financial market and contribute to the Islamic bank market depth.
(iii) Improve coordination among government agencies, i.e., Ministry of Finance, the central bank, and the FSA, so as to improve the effectiveness of the monetary operations and budget funding through Islamic financial secondary market.

(iv) Increase participation of Islamic financial participants with the additional instruments. It will increase the investors' base other than Islamic financial institutions (nonbank financial industry), such as corporate, insurance, cooperative, and others.
(v) Increase market share of Islamic financial market as more and more investors are investing and the more public funds are absorbed well in the Islamic money market and capital market.

8.5 Impact of Islamic Monetary Policy with the Rate of Profit

The impact of monetary policy on the economy through the rate of profit in Islamic banking is achieved through the expansion of money supply (M1 and M2) by BI and can be done through the reduction of the rate of profit short-term transactions using the instrument of IMA (decrease the profit-sharing ratio for the deposits of Islamic banks). It will lower the cost of capital and will directly stimulate investment. On the other hand, consumers will save less and prefer to consume now rather than postpone the consumption, causing aggregate demand to increase. Furthermore, the transmission of monetary policy through rate of profit will improve banking intermediation through financing channel and the balance sheet channel. An expansive monetary policy would affect Islamic banks refinancing cost.

The fall in financing costs will increase investment and consumer spending that will contribute to the economic growth. Monetary policy will have a greater influence on small firms because they depend more on bank loans compared to medium and large firms that can raise funds directly from the capital markets through the issuance of shares and bonds. Monetary policy is also transmitted through the prices of financial assets, which in turn impacted the aggregate demand. Monetary expansion policy determined by the rate of profit that corresponds to a profit in the real sector will not cause the rise and fall of asset prices, which will eventually lead to wealth effects (i.e., increase wealth and prosperity), which is in accordance with the purpose of *Shari'ah.*

To support this qualitative research, a quantitative validation is carried out to assess the influence of interest rates as a reference on the net profit margin. The case study uses net profit margin growth data of Bank Syariah Mandiri (BSM) from May 2004 to May 2009. The year 2004–2009 is chosen because there was an interest rate hike from 7.25% to 12.25% due to the financial crisis in the United States. This condition is ideal to assess the effect of interest rate hike on net profit margin of Islamic bank. Bank's net profit margin is calculated from the portion of an Islamic bank profit from the customer as net margin (NM). The model used in this study is a multiple regression time series model as follows:

$$\text{NPM} = \propto + \frac{\beta_1 \text{RSA}}{\text{RSL}} + \beta_2 \text{SBI} + \beta_3 \text{FDR} + \beta_4 \text{CAR} + \beta_5 \text{NPF} + \varepsilon \tag{8.2}$$

where NPM is net margin to deposit, the ratio of RSA/RSL is rate sensitive assets/rate sensitive liabilities, FDR is financing to deposit ratio, SBI is interest rate (Bank Indonesia Certificate), CAR is capital adequacy ratio, and NPF is non-performing financing. The result from the statistical analysis is as follows:

$$\begin{gathered} \text{NPM} = 1.127 - 0.015 RSA - 0.028\text{SBI} - 0.0225\text{CAR} \\ (0.372)\ (0.004)\quad (0.002)\quad (0.027) \\ R^2 = 0.801 \end{gathered}$$

From the results, it can be interpreted that a 1% increase in the SBI rates will cause a decrease in the rate of profit amounted to 0.228%. This empirical data can be concluded that the nature of the instability of Islamic banks to interest rates hikes with the same risk of conventional banks. In other words, the rate of profit of Islamic banks is similar to the interest margin of conventional banks. Therefore, the rate of profit resulted from the central bank transaction with Islamic banks and Islamic bonds in the capital market should be reference to the profits in the real sector, which is inherently low in duration (volatility), as it will bring stability to the overall economy.

8.6 Conclusion

The current Repo SBI S transaction in Islamic banking practice does not create Islamic banking intermediation in the real sector because it is intended only for monetary operations, namely in the framework of monetary contraction and expansion in the absence of underlying transactions in the real sector. On the other hand, the Islamic Repo transaction can create Islamic banking intermediation which can be done through SIMA with *Mudarabah* profit-sharing scheme and the securitization of SBSN. However, with 5% market share of Islamic banking, the monetary policy will not be effective through the Repo transaction with Islamic bank.

The use of the rate of profit as a reference rate through *Mudarabah* profit-sharing system which is determined by the rate of return derived from the real sector will create a cash basis reference rate that produces stability on financial markets. Islamic repo transaction in Islamic interbank market should be supported by BI to contribute the development and the deepening of the Islamic financial market. The Islamic repo transactions with the instrument of SIMA and SBSN in large volume will create rate of profit as a reference rate as an alternative of BI 7-day repo rate for Islamic banks.

References

al-Sadr, M. B. (1961). *Iqtisaduna*. Beirut: Dar al-Fikr.

Bank Indonesia. (2008). *Bank Indonesia regulation no.10/36/PBI/2008 on sharia monetary operation*. Bank Indonesia: Jakarta.

Bloomberg Company. www.bloomberg.com. Accessed on 4 June 2010.

Choudhury, M. A. (1997). *Generalized theory of Islamic development financing*. London: The Edwin Mellen Press.

El-Gamal, M. A. (2006). *Islamic finance: Law, economics and practice*. New York: Cambridge University Press.

Ismail, A. G. (2010). *Money, Islamic banks and the real economy*. Singapore: Cengage Learning.

Khan, M. S., & Mirakhor, A. (1989). The financial system and monetary policy in an Islamic economy. *Journal of Research in Islamic Economics*,. King Abdul Aziz University, *1*(1), 39–57.

Khan, M. F. (1995). *Essays in Islamic economy: Time value of money and discounting in Islamic perspective*. Leicester, UK: The Islamic Foundation.

Omar, M. A., Abduh, M., & Sukmana, R. (2013). *Fundamentals of Islamic money and capital markets*. Wiley.

Rosly, S. A. (2005). *Critical issues on Islamic banking and financial markets: Islamic economics, banking and finance, investments, Takaful and financial planning*. Milton Keynes: AuthorHouse.

Saeed, A. (1996). *Islamic banking and interest: A study of the prohibition of Riba and its contemporary interpretation*. Leiden: E.J. Brill.

Sitorus, T. (2015). *Indonesia's bond market: Theory and practices*. Jakarta: Rajawali Press.

Sraffa, P. (1960). *Production of commodities by means of commodities: Preclude to a critique of economic theory*. Bombay: Vora &, Publishers PVT. LTD.

Thornton, H. (1965). In F. R. von Hayek (Ed.), *An inquiry into the nature and effects of the paper credit of Great Britain*. New York: Rinehart.

Wicksell. (1934). *Lectures in political economy, (trans.), E. Classen*. London: Routledge.

Chapter 9
Stress Testing and Reverse Stress Testing: An Approach for a Resilient Islamic Financial Industry

Samir Alamad

9.1 Introduction

Before the recent global financial crisis, liquidity risk was considered as a second-order risk in terms of impact, while now is considered a major risk class. It showed us how rapidly a risk, which sparks as a market or credit risk, transforms into a liquidity event and how quickly it develops into a systemic issue. Consequently, it led financial markets and financial authorities to consider the liquidity risk in stress testing frameworks (TATA 2013). Therefore, stress testing in the financial sector is an important aspect of the liquidity risk management framework for the stability and resilience of the financial market. The primary objective is for any financial market to hold or have access to sufficient and timely liquidity under both normal and stressed circumstances to enable it to continue as a solvent institution to meet its obligations as and when they fall due (BCBS 2009).

Stress testing has become an important risk management technique that is used by financial institutions as part of their internal risk management practices and, through the Basel II capital adequacy framework, is promoted by financial regulators. Stress testing alerts the management of Islamic financial institutions (IFIs) to adverse unexpected outcomes related to a variety of common risks and provides an indication of how much capital or funding might be needed to be held to absorb losses should large shocks occur (BCBS 2009).

The liquidity stress testing is typically divided into macro and micro stress testing. The main difference between micro and macro stress testing is that the former is conducted by individual IFIs in accordance with their risk profile. This is done as part of their risk management framework and its objective is limiting the likelihood of failure of the institution. While the latter, i.e. macro stress testing, is usually

S. Alamad (✉)
Aston University, Birmingham, Aston, UK

M. Zulkhibri et al. (eds.), *Islamic Monetary Economics and Institutions*,
https://doi.org/10.1007/978-3-030-24005-9_9

applied by central banks and supervisors to assess the resilience of the financial sector and the capital markets as a whole (Schmieder et al. 2011).

On the other hand, stress testing, whether macro or micro, includes scenario and sensitivity testing with different objectives for each one of them. Scenario testing uses a hypothetical future state of the world to define changes in risk factors affecting the Islamic financial market (IFM) or IFIs' operations, whereas sensitivity testing involves an incremental change in a risk factor (OSFI 2009) that would build up to form a risk of viability of the entity. We move in our analysis between IFIs and IFM according to the context and the flow of the discussion. This is because IFIs are an important component of the IFM and are the drivers and end users of its financial instruments. Therefore, there is a strong correlation between the two, and it is important to incorporate both aspects in the discussion of this paper to provide a fuller picture.

This study provides an insight into the real practices of stress testing as a risk management tool within an Islamic financial market that exists in the UK as a highly sophisticated and regulated financial centre. Although the regulatory approach for financial market infrastructure adopted by the ECB (European Central Bank) regulates the market in the member states including the UK, so far until the Brexit (the UK exit from the European Union) arrangements are agreed, this approach includes IFM without any special treatment or considerations of its specific requirements. Therefore, IFM actors must negotiate locally, e.g., in the UK which is the case study here, possible arrangements that do not contradict compliance with *Shari'ah*, or find other alternatives.

This study is conducted as a case study of the Islamic financial market in the UK and its institutions with the following objectives: (i) to identify the different types of stress testing that IFMs undertake in their liquidity modelling, (ii) to explore how liquidity risks relating to IFM and its institutions are managed and (iii) to suggest a best practice stress testing approach in line with existing approaches in the IFM. The chapter is divided into various sections; first it sets out the design and methodology of the study, then stress testing in IFIs and IFM is discussed in section three, section four analyses the dynamics of the liquidity position of the IFM and its institutions, section five sets out the discussion of the findings of the study, and then a conclusion is drawn in section six with suggestions of avenues for future research.

9.2 Study Design and Methodology

The analysis in this paper is drawn from a study conducted in the UK. In order to identify and understand the practice, Schatzki (2005, p. 476) argues that it "requires considerable 'participant observation': watching participants' activities, interacting with them (e.g., asking questions), and ideally attempting to learn their practices". Thus, a proximity to the field is required (Garfinkel 1967; Jönsson and Macintosh 1997).

An understanding of field study research was adopted, in which the researcher inquires into a field of practice and makes sense of their observations by adductive reasoning, i.e. by moving back and forth between data and theory (Ahrens and Chapman 2006).

The manifold practices involved in managing risks within the IFM and its financial institutions may not be fully illustrated by the case study. However, it does provide an understanding of the actions of the management team in IFM. This facilitates the possibility to carry out the research by providing feedback and recommendations (Czarniawska 1999).

The case study was conducted over a period of 8 months on a full-time basis. Formally, the research is based on a combination of three types of data: risk monitoring data and regulatory reporting, archives and participant observation (Dyer and Wilkins 1991). To obtain rich data, the daily treasury and capital market activities were observed as they went on outside the artificial interview situation. This also enabled an increased acquaintance with market actors.

The authorisation and reporting documents for the projects and products researched in relation to the issuance of *sukuk* and the use of other financial instruments generated the archival and reporting data. Each time a risk report is produced or annual update to stress testing scenarios is completed, it had to be authorised by the relevant management committee and the board of directors and this was another source of data. Stages, gates and authorisation criteria were described in the risk framework process manual and regulatory submissions, which were also studied carefully.

Data from the observation was retrieved from within the normal activities of the IFI. Risk reports, stress testing scenarios for IFIs and meetings were attended. Additional observations took place during the normal course of business, direct conversation and by overhearing and observing communications and actions of daily operations of the IFI and wholesale market management function.

9.2.1 Case Analysis

Empirical material about the risk management process was used to inform our analysis of stress testing approaches and practices in this study, as well as by data on regulatory stress testing and requirements. An assessment of the risks faced in ensuring self-sufficiency and liquidity adequacy in a possible volatile market, liquidity cash flows and results of stress testing, as set out in the regulatory requirements of BIPRU 12, is also included in this material. Also, for *Shari'ah* noncompliance risks, these risk control and reporting frameworks were monitored (Flyvbjerg 2001) as shown in the sections that follow.

9.3 Stress Testing

Stress testing originated not in finance but in engineering, where it was utilised as a technique to test the stability of an entity or system under adverse conditions. In finance, it was conceived initially to test individual portfolio performances or the stability of institutions. More recently, to consider the impact institutions may have on the economy, similar techniques have been employed to test the stability of groups of financial institutions (Borio et al. 2012). Hence, in 2014 the Bank of England announced the first concurrent stress test of the UK financial system, building on the EU-wide stress testing of the European Banking Authority (EBA) (Bank of England 2014).

Data analysis showed that within stress testing there is also scenario testing and sensitivity testing and can be divided into micro and macro stress testing. Scenario testing uses a hypothetical future event or financial climate to define changes in risk factors affecting an institution's operations. The time horizon appropriate for the business and risks being tested is used as the time of measurement (Peria et al. 2001).

The findings revealed that a key challenge with scenario analysis is that translating a scenario into balance sheet impact, changes in risk measures, potential losses or other measures of adverse financial impact is not a definite calculation. Instead, it could vary depending on the test design and type of scenario used (Board of Governors of the Federal Reserve System 2012). In contrast, sensitivity testing involves an incremental change in a risk factor and is typically conducted over a shorter time horizon. Fewer resources are required to conduct sensitivity testing; thus it can be used as a simpler technique for assessing the impact of change in risks when a quicker response or when more frequent testing is needed (OSFI 2009).

Whereas macro stress testing is designed to assess resilience of the whole financial system and usually run by the government or central bank, micro stress testing is designed and run by individual IFI to assess its resilience. (Fell 2006). Any stress testing, whether micro or macro, has four elements as presented by the findings of this paper. The first is the set of risk exposures subjected to stress. The second is the scenario that defines the shocks that stress those exposures. The third is the model that maps those shocks onto an outcome (or impact), tracing their propagation through the system of IFM. The fourth is a measure of the outcome on various relevant structures and products of the IFI or IFM. These factors are consistent with Borio et al.'s (2012) analysis.

The role of stress testing in risk management in the IFM (Peria et al. 2001) as the analysis shows is that:

- It provides information on the sources of risk in a portfolio that is relevant for decision makers at all levels of management in an IFM or an IFI.
- At the managerial level, it enables a comparison of risks across different asset classes and exposures and highlights the need for risk limits and controls.

- At executive level, it provides a way of comparing the risk profile of an IFI or capital market products with the risk appetite of the owners, helping to guide decisions on the optimal allocation of capital within that operational approach.
- For all levels of market participants, it provides help to determine if the return on a product or position is commensurate with the level of risks.

9.3.1 Liquidity Stress Testing

To achieve liquidity adequacy, an IFM or IFI should conduct stress testing. Through such stress testing an organisation can work to identify vulnerabilities related to liquidity adequacy considering both market-wide and IFI-specific stress events. Stress testing, if conducted effectively, assists a financial organisation to identify and quantify the depth, source and degree of potential liquidity and funding strain and to analyse possible impacts on its cash flows, liquidity position, profitability and other aspects of its financial condition over various time horizons (Board of Governors of the Federal Reserve System 2012).

The analysis of the data in this financial sector shows that a primary liquidity risk is funding run-offs in an IFI-specific event. The assumptions that IFIs utilise are based on a combination of IFI-specific historical data, industry data from prior stress events and/or best guess estimates. However, some IFIs add an extra cushion to the assumed outflows when using IFI-specific historical data, to factor in their perception that data largely based on stable historical periods may not adequately proxy depositor behaviour during a future stress event (BCBS 2006).

Several factors impact the severity of funding/deposit outflows in a stress scenario. These include the IFI's balance sheet, the length of crisis duration, the IFI's relationships with its client, the ability of the IFI to raise funds quickly within the capital markets and the share of deposits protected by deposit insurance (BCBS 2006).

In simulations of crisis scenarios, it is estimated that funds exiting the IFI would be in the single digits as a percentage figure and for a few IFIs assuming outflows could be in the low double digits. This reflects an assumption that retail clients would be reassured by deposit insurance which exists in some jurisdictions and so would not withdraw their deposits, but what would give the same comfort to corporate investors and depositors on the IFM level (Matten 2009; BCBS 2006).

The safety net of insurance is not applicable for corporate, IFI and government deposits. The impact of this is demonstrated in our findings which show that the typical worst-case scenarios reflect outflows within a one-month time period of between 20 percent and 50 percent for particular deposit types which depend on the IFI's credit rating. For a more accurate simulation, some IFI's make finer breakdowns according to the type of client and the relationship between the client and the IFI, for example, distinctions between domestic and foreign depositors or per geographical regions of an IFM (GARP 2011; BCBS 2006).

IFIs make several assumptions during these simulations: firstly, that they will roll over finances as they mature to protect their franchise; secondly, that any deposits with a time restriction will not be withdrawn until maturity, and at maturity, some percentage will be renewed; and finally, that developed countries retain convertible currencies, certain assets remain liquid and the repo and securitisation markets remain open (Van Den End 2010). However, it is argued that this is not always the case, and in wide stress scenario access to liquidity in the financial market becomes tight and more expensive.

Despite this positive forecast, most IFIs recognise that assets may entail haircuts (depending on the scenario). Some move this analysis further and assume that even secured funding would not be available, with the exception of funds from a central bank. However, this funding source is generally not available for IFIs in a *Shari'ah*-compliant way. The disruption of intra-group cash flows is also a possible concern to many IFIs as has been shown recently in 2015/16 low oil price environment (and most recently in the GGC diplomatic row started in June 2017 and its cross-border impact on financial institutions) and less cash flow from GCC (Gulf Cooperation Countries) IFIs to their subsidiaries elsewhere. This was evident by the analysis of collected data.

IFIs also conduct additional stress tests, unpredicted rapid requirements for liquidity that may occur due to a triggering event which causes products or services to require funding. An example of this could be a credit downgrade of an IFI. This may then induce an application for additional collateral for derivative transactions or wholesale funding from counterparties of the IFIs. Other common triggers include funding requirements for liquidity backup arrangements and credit enhancements for securitisations. According to the findings of this study, the most frequently used crisis time period stress tested is for one month or less; this is conducted by more than half of IFIs. Crises lasting two or three months are a time period used by one-quarter of IFIs, with the remainder testing crises lasting six months or longer. A range of different time durations are tested by a few IFIs (BIS 2010a; BCBS 2006).

9.3.2 Regulatory Requirements and Guidance

Current imposed regulatory requirements in the UK (BoE 2014) and generally in Europe, which aim to ensure some resilience of the financial system and capital market, are set out in accordance with BIPRU 12.4. These regulatory requirements state that a firm must conduct regular stress tests to:

- Identify sources of potential liquidity strain
- Ensure that current liquidity exposures continue to conform to the liquidity risk tolerance established by that firm's governing body
- Identify the effects on that firm's assumptions about pricing

BIPRU 12.4 sets out the requirements in relation to carrying out liquidity stress testing including:

- Stress tests should consider both short-term and protracted stress scenarios and both IFI-specific and market-wide difficulties.
- The assumptions used in stress testing scenarios should be regularly reviewed to ensure that their nature and severity remain appropriate.
- The results of the stress tests are reviewed by senior management and reported to the governing body.

Furthermore, an IFI must, where relevant as the findings of this study show, assess the impact of its identified stresses on the appropriateness of its assumptions relating to (BoE 2014):

- Correlation between funding raised from the financial markets
- The effectiveness of diversification across its sources of funding
- Additional margin calls and collateral requirements
- Contingent claims, including potential draws on committed lines extended to third parties or to other entities in the firm's group
- Liquidity absorbed by off-balance sheet vehicles and activities (including conduit financing)
- The transferability of liquidity resources
- Access to central bank market operations and liquidity facilities (this is currently not an option for IFIs in Europe as no *Shari'ah*-compliant option is available)
- Estimates of future balance sheet growth and possible impact
- The continued availability of market liquidity in many currently highly liquid markets
- Ability to access secured and unsecured funding (including retail deposits)
- Currency convertibility
- Access to payment or settlement systems on which IFIs rely
- Considering its operating regulatory and political environment, e.g., IFIs operating in Europe and the required stress and possible uncertainties resulted from the UK exit from Europe

According to our findings, an IFI should ensure that the results of its stress tests are:

- Reviewed by its senior management and board of directors
- Reported to that IFI's governing body, specifically highlighting any vulnerabilities identified and proposing appropriate remedial action
- Used to develop effective contingency funding plans
- Integrated into that IFI's business planning process and day-to-day risk management
- Considered when setting internal limits for the management of that IFI's liquidity risk exposure (Ali 2012)

9.3.3 Liquidity Risk Stress Testing Framework

The objective of a liquidity risk stress test for an IFI as shown in the collected data is to:

- Identify key risk factors including *Shari'ah* requirements and drivers affecting assets and liabilities
- Design scenarios which align with assets and liabilities
- Test the resilience of funding sources and *Shari'ah*-compliant alternatives under idiosyncratic and systemic disruptive events (BIS 2008, 2009, 2010a, b; TATA 2013)

Based on the analysis of the data collected and the regulatory requirements as interpreted and implemented by IFIs in the UK, Fig. 9.1 sets out a proposed liquidity stress testing framework that helps in planning ahead for market shocks and long-term survival of the IFIs and IFM performance. This framework comprises four stages:

(a) Assess

To design relevant stress scenarios for an IFI, it is critical to understand the composition of its balance sheet. As the arrangement of assets and liabilities and their behavioural characteristics is unique to each IFI along with the operating structure, jurisdiction and approach of the IFI, this is reflected in its balance sheet. Additionally, an awareness of the impact of the *Shari'ah*-compliant structure IFIs are based upon is one of the most crucial elements in designing relevant stress scenarios.

(b) Identify

Once the balance sheet has been assessed, the next most influential aspects are liquidity risk factors or other market drivers. The inception of liquidity risk

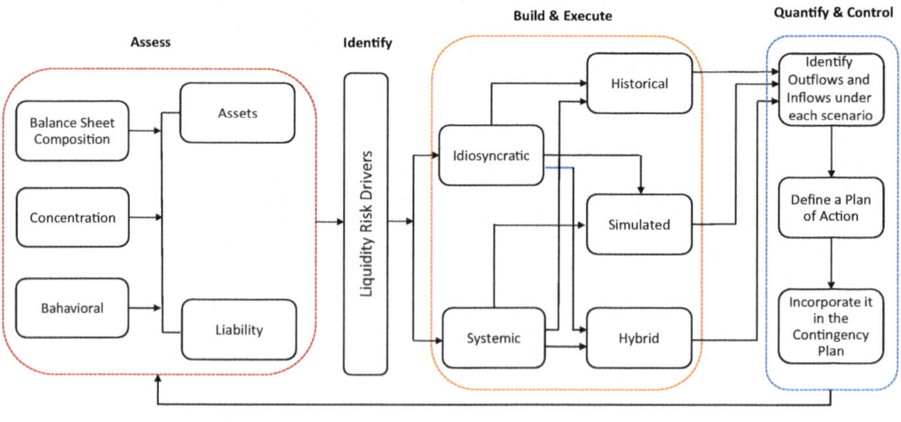

Fig. 9.1 Liquidity risk stress testing framework (Source: author's own illustration)

commonly lies within a credit risk, market risk and/or an operational risk event or a combination of these risk classes. The risk factors to be considered for designing scenarios are sizable because the canvas of liquidity risk is therefore larger than any other form of risk. Therefore, to aid in identifying the main risk factors from the larger population, the analysis of the concentration of assets and liabilities and their behavioural profile is necessary.

(c) Build and execute

In addition to building familiarity with the balance sheet, the previous two steps (Assess and Identify) ensure that the factors affecting it, such as the various requirements of Islamic finance principles that capital market's products, are also considered.

IFIs are required by regulators to create scenarios that are both in accordance with their *Shari'ah* governance operation and take into consideration both idiosyncratic stress and system-wide stress. This makes the Build and Execute phase of the framework more computationally challenging. However, the scenarios created are very dependent on the quality of the data used to design them. Therefore, if the correct data is not available, this can cause significant issues.

(d) Quantify and control

After development, each scenario is subsequently executed. Those scenarios which get negative net cash flows are examined and probabilities of occurrence considered. Each of the identified negative cash flow scenarios is categorised under headings of Bad, Severe and Catastrophic, based on the IFI's priorities and policies.

To counterbalance the impact of these cash flows, a plan of action should be clearly defined. Using the unencumbered asset pool is one of the key tools of counterbalancing. To assess the *Shari'ah*-compliant means available for countering liquidity stress under different scenarios, guidelines prescribed by the Basel Committee on Banking Supervision (BCBS) for the classification of High-Quality Liquid Assets (HQLA) should be considered.

9.3.4 Micro Stress Testing

Micro-prudential stress tests focus on the traditional role of IFIs establishing an emergency capital provision as a buffer against loss or other market shocks, shielding the deposit insurance schemes created by relevant regulatory authorities. The emphasis is on resolving insolvent IFIs to reduce any impact on IFMs on "prompt corrective action". The capital ratio set by Basel is key to address this matter (Barfield and Venkat 2008). Micro stress tests are designed to provide certain variables and assess their impact; these are listed below:

- Designed to assess resilience of individual IFIs considering the *Shari'ah* implications on equity-based products such as products based on Mudarabah or *Wakalah*
- Mainly run by individual IFI for institutional risk management
- Often ignores behaviour of competitors

(a) *Elements of Micro-Prudential Stress Testing*

There are also certain elements that should be embedded in any micro-prudential stress tests; these elements are set out below (Barfield and Venkat 2008).

- *Purpose:* The goal of any micro-prudential stress tests is to value assets owned by the IFIs correctly and determine that adequate measures for loss bearing capacity are in place to protect it in the event of a financial shock and to avoid possible taxpayers' bailout (FCA 2014).
- *Scope:* The scope of any micro-prudential stress tests is to analyse one IFI at a time to assess its resilience or using data from multiple IFIs to obtain reliable and correct information about the value of individual IFI's assets.
- *Liability Considerations*: Counting the amount of junior debt and equity and balances of insured deposits is one of the key aspects on the liability side of the balance sheet. The required loss absorbency is calculated as a ratio relative to asset risk, e.g., debt-based assets, such as *Murabahah* financing, would require less ratio in contrast to equity-based financing, such as *Musharakah* and *Mudarabah.*
- *Asset Considerations:* The process of assessing credit risk in relation to different assets determines the level of enterprise risk; this process would ensure that loss absorbency on the liabilities' side is tied to asset composition to balance the position on the balance sheet. A capital ratio adjustment therefore naturally emerges to inform the basis for regulatory supervision.
- *Output:* Developing a response plan about whether to wind down an IFI and determining the right time to sell its assets to maximize shareholders and creditors recovery.

9.3.5 Macro Stress Testing

Macro-prudential stress testing focuses on whether IFIs and the IFM system have the capacity to support the economy by assessing its combined balance sheet. According to the data analysis, a key objective of this stress is avoiding systemic runs on many IFIs by wholesale creditors. That systemic run would lead to a contraction of inter-banking credit and would have a damaging effect to the broader economy. To avert this aggregate deleveraging in events of systemic distress, recovery steps should focus on raising new capital measured in key global currencies, such as US Dollars, Sterling or Euro rather than on merely satisfying regulatory capital ratios (Fell 2006). Although IFIs are required to regularly carry on required stress testing, due to the small size of the IFM in Europe, any contraction in this market would not have a damaging impact on the broader economy.

Thus, macro stress test scenarios are designed to assess resilience of financial system rather than individual IFI only. Like micro-prudential stress tests, macro-prudential stress tests also have certain elements that should be observed when undertaking a stress test, as emerged from the data analysis. These elements are provided below (Schmieder et al. 2012).

(a) *Elements of Macro-Prudential Stress Tests*

- *Purpose:* Limiting the likelihood of costs of aggregate fire sales of assets, defaults and contraction of credit is the primary purpose of this stress.
- *Scope:* The test should be designed to assess the entire financial system. This design should examine any entity in the financial system that contributes to fire sales, whose default to meet its obligation is of a systemic nature that can exacerbate a credit crunch and has follow-on effects.
- *Liability Considerations:* The importance of assessing the impact of wholesale funding in the IFM, which can lead to a credit crunch or fire sale, is a key to prevent the impact of such event on that scale. Meeting capital adequacy requirements would be subject to the health of the overall financial system.
- *Asset Considerations:* Because illiquid assets in the financial system can lead to fire sales of such assets, asset liquidity is critical to any stress event. The risk of illiquid assets depends on both default risk, type of assets under Islamic finance principles and fire sale risk. For example, debt-based assets would be considered illiquid to some extent due to the *Shari'ah* restrictions on trading in debt obligations. This does not mean that such debt-based assets cannot be liquidated; the issue here is about time considerations to be able to do so.
- *Output:* The output of any stress testing indicates to its users whether the financial system is resilient enough or it has some weaknesses to deleveraging, which might exacerbate adverse shocks (ECB 2008). IFIs operating in developed financial and capital markets are required to incorporate the above stress tests in their modelling and operations. However, this would follow certain dynamics tailored to the way IFIs operate and the different structure of their wholesale products, which are so far limited.

9.4 Dynamics of IFIs' Liquidity Position

The dynamics of an IFM is dependent on the available sources of liquidity and funding, which are limited in contrast to the traditional capital and financial market. IFIs usually have several potential sources of liquidity as presented by the collected data, these sources of liquidity include

- Customers' *Mudarabah* and *Wakalah* deposits
- Cash flows from maturing transactions
- Reverse *Murabahah* and *Wakalah* transactions in the interbank market (including those with break clause agreements)
- A well-diversified Islamic marketable assets portfolio
- Liquidity asset buffer, usually sovereign *sukuk*
- Shareholders' support

9.4.1 Factors Which Might Impact Liquidity Position

There are various factors that would impact the position of an IFM and its medium-to long-term survival and resilience. IFIs should consider such factors in their stress testing based on their products and direction dictated by the underlying Islamic finance instrument. These factors are discussed below (ECB 2008).

(a) *Retail Assets*

The case analysis shows that IFIs' retail assets primarily comprise of secured financing for the purposes of commercial and residential property. This includes home finance, buy to let, leasing and commercial finance products. These products are structured usually as an *Ijarah* with diminishing *Musharakah* (leasing under a partnership arrangement), leasing ending with ownership, reverse *Murabahah* or *Murabahah* (credit sale), with term ranging between 7 and 30 years.

Inherently these asset products provide low levels of liquidity risk as the cash flows associated with them are known well in advance, via their payment schedules.

(b) *Wholesale Assets*

Usually IFIs' portfolio of wholesale assets is composed of commodity *Murabahah* and *Wakalah* deals, and *Sukuks* held as part of banks' liquidity asset buffer requirements and other investments.

(c) *Retail Liabilities*

Retail liabilities usually are provided via Internet, post, telephone and branch network. As a result, IFIs are susceptible to a sudden and material withdrawal of retail funding, particularly in situations where there is a retail-based crisis in confidence in banking in general or if compliance with *Shari'ah* may be called into question.

(d) *Wholesale Liabilities*

IFIs utilising unsecured wholesale markets for funding are exposed to refinancing risk, particularly those that rely on short-term financing to fund their businesses, as was demonstrated during the credit crisis which began in 2007.

9.5 Discussion

Stress scenarios have been developed with the objective of assessing risks to both sides of the IFI's balance sheet. This paper has considered such stress events and analysed them in accordance with the collected data from the IFI and the IFM as the case study of this paper. These key scenarios as emerged from the findings include:

- One off scenario causing significant doubt over the IFI's financial stability and withdrawal of retail funds
- Challenge to the IFI's status as a wholly *Shari'ah*-compliant bank leading to loss of confidence and retail withdrawal of deposit and business, also possible withdrawal of wholesale placement with the IFI
- Market-wide liquidity shortfalls resulting a default of a major counterparty(s)
- A *Shari'ah* non-compliance event and economic downturn
- A combination scenario covering the impact of idiosyncratic and market-wide stress on the IFM

Specifically, incorporating the analysis above as emerged from the data, the following scenarios have been considered as shown in Table 9.1.

As the findings have shown, IFIs currently maintain a small holding of eligible liquidity assets comprising Sukuks and other sovereign issuance, but do not currently maintain a significant portfolio of other marketable assets, so the concept of applying haircuts or discounts of varying severity becomes less important in this context. Therefore, given the absence of a portfolio of marketable assets, the methodology adopted by IFIs for stress testing primarily focuses upon the loss of retail deposits, particularly acceleration of treasury deposits, coupled with delinquency in both its wholesale and retail assets.

IFIs operating in Europe have drawn upon actual experiences gained during the recent economic crisis and accordingly the stress factors utilised within the revised scenarios are based upon management's expert judgement, actual experience and a high degree of conservatism.

Table 9.2 below details the approach taken to derive the stress factors for each event type and the relevant analysis associated with each driver as an impact on the IFI and its position in the IFM and ability to raise funds.

9.5.1 *Reverse Stress Testing*

To ensure the output of stress testing is accurate and close all possible gaps, a reverse assessment starting with output would provide a strong indication of any gaps. Reverse stress testing, therefore, would further identify and highlight events that may lead an IFI to become insolvent because its business model is no longer viable. A stress scenario or combination of scenarios that lead to question the viability of the business model of an IFI is an important risk management tool. This tool helps identify possible combinations of stress scenarios and concentration of risk within an IFI that might not be usually given due attention in regular course of stress testing (CEBS 2010).

Table 9.1 Stress testing scenarios

Event	Scenario	Impact
Event 1 Idiosyncratic event	Well-publicised rumour that an IFI is suffering a severe financial distress and may default imminently resulting in a severe retail and wholesale outflow for two weeks followed by a sustained leakage of funds thereafter	There may be an immediate "flight to quality" as larger deposit investors move assets into more traditional "safe havens" such as cash, gold or government *sukuk* and smaller deposits move balances away from the IFI The IFI would be unable to access funds in the unsecured wholesale markets until its financial situation had been clarified The IFI's top treasury/term depositors accelerate their maturities and demand immediate repayment of their funds (threatening high-profile public campaign to damage the IFI's name if not accepted and pledging support to redeposit at a later date if their requirements are met) General market liquidity would not be affected, enabling the IFI to request early repayment of commodity Murabahah contracts from its counterparty banks The IFI's position could deteriorate if confidentiality from "break-clause" banks is not maintained, and/or the IFI does not make a public statement of reassurance.
Event 2 Collapse of a major wholesale causing market-wide loss	Major event, e.g., collapse of a major market counterparty(s) causing severe disruption primarily to wholesale markets, with some impact to retail markets possible	The IFI suffers a wholesale counterparty(s) default. The loss is not deemed recoverable within the time horizon of a liquidity stress test and is, therefore, the expected inflow of maturing funds from the defaulting counterparty within the first 3 months of the stress event do not materialise Wholesale markets would effectively be closed until some market normality had been restored. This could impact the IFI's ability to access wholesale markets and make use of available funding lines for a period of 3 months Payment systems continue to work effectively
Event 3 Combination	A combination of the scenarios described above impact simultaneously	Combination of all impacts for each of the scenarios described above

(continued)

Table 9.1 (continued)

Event	Scenario	Impact
Event 4 *Shari'ah* non-compliance event	Challenge to IFI's status as wholly *Shari'ah*-compliant bank or claiming that some wholesale financial instruments or sukuk in the market are not compliant with *Shari'ah* leading to loss of credibility due to: Prominent *Shari'ah* scholar issuing a fatwa against the IFI's products or such products in the IFM, such as Mufti Usmani's fatwa about *sukuk Mudarabah* in 2009 Failure to adhere to or ineffectiveness of controls allowing launch of non-compliant asset/liability products	Commercial and home finance products may be switched to alternative providers Loss of deposits as a proportion of the religiously rigid/religiously inclined if deposit profit rates are not competitive, look to re-invest elsewhere and cancellation of finance deals
Event 5 Economic downturn	Economic downturn – An economic slowdown resulting in rising unemployment, an increase in consumers facing debt-repayment difficulties and increases in arrears on both secured and unsecured finance facilities leading to property repossessions, which would in turn depress property prices further	Reduced applications received for secured finance facilities; existing customers experience financial hardship, with payment arrears increasing and some repossession instructed. Collateral may be insufficient to cover the outstanding debt/finance on some facilities Expected withdrawal of retail and wholesale funds from depositors to supplement loss of income from increased unemployment

IFIs, like its conventional counterparts, are encouraged to consider stress events beyond normal day-to-day business operations that may lead to events with systemic implications on the financial system; this is achieved by conducting a reverse stress testing. For example, an IFI with a substantial exposure to complex sukuk issuance or structured credit products for consumers and commercial finance should consider what kind of event would have led to widespread losses that would affect its viability and are contagion and systemic (BCBS 2009).

As a result of this exposure the IFI would have then assessed its hedging strategy and the type of *Tahawut* instruments it has in place and ascertain whether this strategy would be robust enough in a stressed market event. Such a market stress would be linked to a lack of market liquidity options and increased counterparty credit risk. Hence, and subject to applying the appropriate judgments by the IFI, this form of stress test can unmask hidden vulnerabilities in hedging strategies or other behavioural reactions that would impact the IFI.

Table 9.2 Stress testing factors

Event type	Stress factors
Scenario 1 Severe retail withdrawal	Outflow of 20%/10% (Type A/Type B) of maturing retail term and treasury deposits (non-renewals of contractual deposits) with a severe retail outflow in the first two weeks followed by a sustained leakage of funds thereafter (Retail Funding Risk) Outflow of 20%/10% (Type A/Type B) of retail demand/instant access deposits in total with a severe retail outflow in the first two weeks followed by a sustained leakage of funds thereafter (Retail Funding Risk) Outflow of 20%/10% (Type A/Type B) of notice accounts that are not already on notice and can contractually be withdrawn within the stress period (Retail Funding Risk) The largest treasury/term deposit/notice products clients instruct the immediate withdrawal of their funds – threatening public relations campaign to damage the IFI's name if demands not adhered to (Franchise Viability Risk) The IFI will honour existing pipeline business (committed but undrawn) regarding finance facilities (Off- Balance Sheet Risk) Any wholesale funding is withdrawn (Wholesale Funding Risk) Inflows arising from planned management actions detailed in the IFI's Contingency Funding and Market Response Plan
Scenario 2 Collapse of a major wholesale counterparty, leading to a market-wide loss	A wholesale counterparty default for the largest wholesale counterparty where maturity of the funds occurs within the next 3 months is suffered and is not recoverable within the 3-month stress test horizon (non-marketable asset risk) No new treasury funding obtained during the entirety of the 3-month stress Inflows arising from planned management actions detailed in the IFI's Contingency Funding and Market Response Plan
Scenario 3 Combination	The top largest treasury/term deposit/60-day notice account clients instruct the immediate withdrawal of their funds – threatening public relations campaign to damage the IFI's name if demands not adhered to No new funding obtained during 0–8 days Outflow of retail term/treasury deposits (as above) Outflow of retail instant access deposits (as above) Outflow of notice accounts (as above) A wholesale counterparty default for a major wholesale counterparty (c100% of LECB) is suffered and is not recoverable within the 3-month stress test horizon The IFI would honour existing pipeline business (committed but undrawn) all finance facilities Any wholesale funding is withdrawn Inflows arising from planned management actions detailed in the IFI's Contingency Funding and Market Response Plan
Scenario 4 *Shari'ah* non-compliance	Outflow of 2% of retail demand deposits in total with a severe retail outflow in the first two weeks (Retail Funding Risk)
Scenario 5 An economic downturn	Downturn in economic climate resulting in: 25% of secured assets' finance monthly payments fail to be paid in the month 25% of SME monthly payments fail to be paid in the month (Non-Marketable Asset Risk)

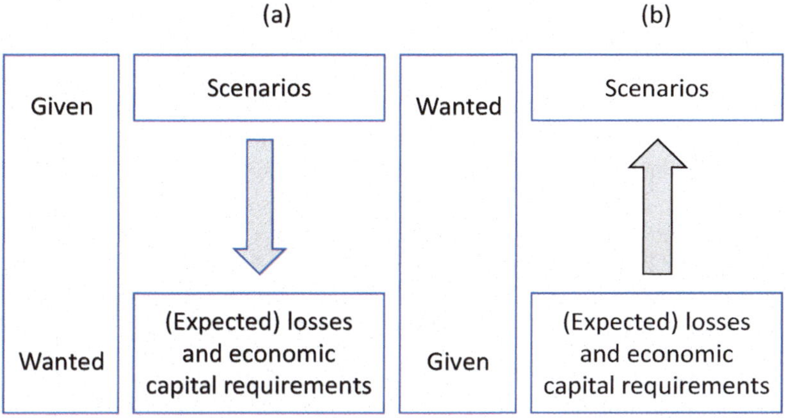

Fig. 9.2 (**a**) Regular and (**b**) reverse stress tests (Source: author's own illustration)

Prior to the financial market crisis of 2008, such an assessment was viewed to be of little value by most senior management of financial institutions since the scenario had low likelihood to happen. However, banks now consider the importance of examining tail events and evaluating the actions to deal with them. Some financial institutions reported benefits in using this type of stress test to identify hidden vulnerabilities and concentration of risk in their business model. A well-executed reverse stress test (Fig. 9.2) also includes enough diagnostic support to investigate the reasons for potential failure or run on an IFI (Grundke 2011).

Reverse stress tests, as depicted in Fig. 9.2, are not intended to be a substitute for regular stress tests as the findings from the collected data showed; rather, they are intended to be a supplement. According to the supervisory authorities, banks should be allowed to carry out quantitative as well as qualitative reverse stress tests, especially in the beginning when this concept is first applied.

9.5.2 *Stress Testing Limits (IFI Case Study)*

IFIs could perceive stress testing to be a straightforward process. In practice, however, as findings of this study revealed, this process is often neither easy nor transparent when it is implemented in practice. This is because stress testing is largely based on a number of assumptions made by senior management of IFIs as to what risk factors to consider for a stress, how to combine scenarios to be stressed, what values to consider and what is the applicable time frame to analyse.

Nonetheless, all assumptions are carefully considered, and an IFI is required to address challenging tasks of sifting through stress output and results to identify what implications the test outcome might have on an IFI and inform the decision of how IFIs should manage their risk-taking activities (BIS 2010a, b).

Carefully considered limitations of stress test are that there are no various probabilities attached to an IFI's stress results. Stress testing helps provide an answer to an important question that any IFI should carefully consider; this question is "How much could be lost?" The interviewed participants of IFIs fully agreed that the answer to this question is not straightforward or as informative as would the answer be to the question "How much is likely to be lost?" (BIS 2000). The absence of probability measuring tools exacerbates the challenge of ensuring transparency and the seeming arbitrariness of stress test design, an issue that is acknowledged by the interviewed risk experts.

The case IFI has not set any hard limits on its liquidity risk stress tests. However, in order to support its liquidity risk appetite, it has adopted the following limits:

- Maintaining a minimum of 100% ratios for NSFR and LCR
- Maintaining a prudent contractual maturity profile to allow the IFI to meet its entire contractual non-retail liabilities over a 2-week, 1-month and 3-month period
- Maintaining a maximum of 40% of retail fixed term deposits maturing in a rolling 3-month period
- Ensuring that wholesale funding with a residual maturity of <12 months never equates to more than 20% of the entire retail and wholesale funding portfolio

The relevance and applicability of "trigger points" for use in "stressed scenarios" are periodically reviewed by the IFI. The findings of this study suggest that this process should ensure that management of IFIs remains informed as to the suitability of existing liquidity management practices, the liquidity vulnerabilities facing the IFI and the appropriateness of mitigating actions currently employed. As part of this process, management should consider appropriate remedial actions to address the IFI's vulnerabilities and use these to develop and shape the IFI's response via the Contingency Funding and Market Response Plan.

9.6 Conclusion

Rule 12.1 of the Internal Capital Adequacy Assessment (ICAAP) of the Prudential Regulations Rulebook requires IFIs in Europe to carry out stress tests and scenario analyses as part of its obligations under the overall Pillar 2 rule. The regulator further expects IFIs to consider any impacts of the adverse circumstances on their capital resources over a three- to five-year time horizon[1].

This section summarises IFI's stress testing framework and the information on requirements under stressed conditions. IFIs perform stress tests at least annually when reviewing the ICAAP document.

The main purposes of stress testing and scenario analysis are:

[1] This requirement is included in rule 12.3 of the Internal Capital Adequacy Assessment part of the PRA Rulebook

- Quantifying how much capital might be absorbed or additional capital add-ons would be required if an adverse event(s) occurs
- Providing a check on the outputs and accuracy of the IFI's risk assumptions and assessments
- Exploring the sensitivities in longer-term business plans and how capital needs might change over time

Stress tests and scenario analysis typically refer to a wider range of parameters being varied at the same time to assess the impact of adverse events on the IFI's financial position. When defining the stress test scenarios IFIs should take into consideration:

- Economic outlooks, in particular the ones related to its region(s) of operations
- Internal information available through MI, financial statements and similar documents
- Prudential regulations supervisory statements, frameworks and guidelines

The board and senior management should, then, discuss, challenge and approve the stress scenarios to ensure that they are sufficient in scope and robustness. Once the stress scenarios have been completed, the stress tests performed and the related information included in the ICAAP, the senior management consider them and provide its recommendation to the board of director for approval. The board will review and agree the conclusions reached. At this stage, the board role, therefore, is to ensure that stress testing is performed in an appropriate rigorous and comprehensive manner and has a key role in deciding whether the IFI's risk strategy requires revisiting or adjustment following the result of the stress tests. It also assesses the possible remediation actions required by the management of an IFI in case the stress tests will crystallise.

It has been concluded by financial regulators and financial institutions that monitoring liquidity risk and undertaking stress testing as a risk management tool for liquidity is extremely important to understand the components of the balance sheet and its behaviour in the event of extreme stress scenarios, which are becoming more likely. When an IFI properly designs and executes stress tests, this process allows the management of an IFI to prepare a response strategy and put the required action plan in place. These plans enable the IFI to incorporate scenarios where matters could go wrong and the resulting adverse impact that follows.

We have established that stress tests provide valuable and important information in relation to possible future results. However, like any other risk management tools it has limitations and it does not guarantee absolute certainty about the implications of considered scenarios and potential impacts.

Moreover, actors in the IFM/IFIs should be mindful that activities and assumptions they consider for stress testing are not limited to reflect only their past experiences. Instead they should think of a much broad range of scenario possibilities. It is acknowledged here that there is no single stress test that would estimate accurately the impact of all stress events and scenarios. Thus, an IFI must fully appreciate and consider any stress testing limitations and uncertainties. As a result of such limitations, it needs to use stress tests alongside other risk management techniques to reach a sound risk management and business decisions that are justified by the results of those tests for its ongoing resilience. A future research is encouraged to explore further liquidity tools and risk management approaches for IFM. Also, the position and impact of the structure of various IFM's *Shari'ah*-compliant instruments in a market-wide stress scenario and how this is done in practice without compromising *Shari'ah* requirements of the relevant structure.

References

Ahrens, T., & Chapman, C. S. (2006). Doing qualitative field research in management accounting: Positioning data to contribute to theory. *Accounting, Organizations and Society., 31*(8), 819–841.

Ali, S. S. (2012). State of liquidity management in Islamic financial institutions. *Islamic Economic Studies, 21*(1), 63–98.

Bank of England. (2014). *Stress testing in the UK banking system: 2014 results*. London: Bank of England.

Barfield, R., & Venkat, S. (2008). Liquidity risk management. In *The Journal-Global Perspectives on Challenges and Opportunities*. London: PricewaterhouseCoopers.

BCBS (2006). *The management of liquidity risk in financial groups*. Basle: Basel Committee on Banking Supervision.

BCBS (2009). *Principles for sound stress testing practices and supervision*. Basle: Basel Committee on Banking Supervision.

BIS. (2000). Stress testing by large financing institutions: Current practice and aggregation issues. In *April 2000*. Basle: Bank for International Settlements.

BIS. (2008). *Basel committee on banking supervision- principles for sound liquidity risk management and supervision, September 2008*. Basle: Bank for International Settlements.

BIS. (2009). *Basel III: international framework for liquidity risk measurement, standards and monitoring, December 2009*. Basle: Bank for International Settlements.

BIS. (2010a). *Basel committee on banking supervision-iInternational framework for liquidity risk measurement, standards and monitoring, December 2010*. Basle: Bank for International Settlements.

BIS. (2010b). *Basel III: A global regulatory framework for more resilient banks and banking systems, December 2010*. Basle: Bank for International Settlements.

Board of Governors of the Federal Reserve System. (2012). *Guidance on stress testing for banking organisations with total consolidated assets of more than $10 billion*. Washington, D.C: Board of Governors of the Federal Reserve System.

Borio, C., Drehmann, M., & Tsatsaronis, K. (2012). Stress-testing macro stress testing: Does it live up to expectations? In *BIS working papers No. 369*. Basle: Bank for International.

CEBS. (2010). *CEBS guidelines on stress testing*. London: European banking authority.

Czarniawska, B. (1999). *Writing management: Organization theory as a literary genre*. Oxford: Oxford University Press.

Dyer, W. G., & Wilkins, A. L. (1991). Better stories, not better constructs to generate better theory: A rejoinder to Eisenhardt. *Academy of Management Review., 16*(3), 613–619.

ECB. (2008). *EU banks' liquidity stress testing and contingency funding plans*. Frankfurt: European Central Bank.

FCA. (2014). *Stress Testing and Contingency Funding*. London: Financial conduct authority.

Fell, J. (2006). *Overview of Stress Testing Methodologies: From Micro to Macro*. presentation to the Korea Financial Supervisory Commission/Financial Supervisory Service-International

Monetary Fund Seminar on Macroprudential Supervision Conference on Challenges for Financial Supervisors, Seoul, November 7, 2006.

Flyvbjerg, B. (2001). *Making social science matter*. Cambridge: Cambridge University Press.

Garfinkel, H. (1967). *Studies in ethnomethodology*. Cambridge: Polity Press.

GARP. (2011). A new regulation for liquidity risk. In *Global Association of Risk Professionals*. New Jersey.

Grundke, P. (2011). Reverse stress tests with bottom-up approaches. *The Journal of Risk Model Validation, 5*(1), 71–90.

Jönsson, S., & Macintosh, N. (1997). CATS, RATS, and EARS: Making the case for ethnographic accounting research. *Accounting Organizations and Society, 22*(3–4), 367–386.

Matten. (2009). *Stress testing liquidity and the contingency funding plan*. PRMIA Members' Meeting, February 24, 2009.

OSFI. (2009). *Stress testing: Sound business and financial practices*. Ottawa: Office of the Superintendent of financial institutions.

Peria, M. S. M., Majnoni, G., Jones, M. T., & Blaschke, W. (2001). Stress testing of financial systems: An overview of issues, methodologies and FSAB experiences. In *IMF working paper No. 01/88*. Washington DC: International Monetary Fund.

Schatzki, T. R. (2005). The sites of organizations. *Organization Studies, 26*(3), 465–484.

Schmieder, C., Claus, P., Maher, H. (2011). Next Generation Balance. Sheet Stress Testing, IMF working paper. April, WP/11/83.

Schmieder, C., Hesse, H., Neudorfer, B., Puhr, C., & Schmitz, S. W. (2012). Next generation system-wide liquidity stress testing. In *IMF working paper WP/12/3*. Washington DC: International Monetary Fund.

TATA. (2013). *A stress testing framework for liquidity risk*. Mumbai: TATA Consultancy Services Limited.

van den End, J. W. (2010). Liquidity stress-tester- do Basel III and unconventional monetary policy work? In *Working paper No. 269*. Amsterdam: De Nederlandsche Bank.

Chapter 10
Liquidity Risk Management in Islamic Banks: Evidences from Malaysia

Muhammed Habib Dolgun and Adam Ng

10.1 Introduction

After the global financial crisis, there are discussions in terms of liquidity risk management of banks, and in this context, many new tools, regulations, and mechanisms have been introduced by regulatory authorities. Islamic banks are also being governed by these tools and regulations. Liquidity risk is one of the important issues that needs attention in terms of resilience of Islamic banking sector. It can be defined as a shortcoming to cover financial liabilities and its management is related to managing the expected and unexpected cash outflows. A scrutiny of this important issue in an Islamic banking context is crucial to promoting efficiency, growth, and resilience of the Islamic financial industry. While there are several studies on the performance, growth, and efficiency of Islamic banks, empirical studies from the regulatory and supervisory perspectives are limited. In addition, the Islamic financial markets in Muslim-majority countries are still in their infancy stage. Accordingly, these markets may not be able to withstand challenges and risks stemming from adverse systemic and financial shocks.

In this context, it is well recognized that sustainable liquidity risk management is central to banks' continuous financing and protection against systemic risks (these risks include herding, unstable capital flows, vulnerable financial structures, and liquidity risks of counterparties, asset managers, market liquidity, business cycle, and other market anomalies). The Islamic banking industry is confronted with

M. H. Dolgun (✉)
INCEIF, Selangor, Malaysia, and Central Bank of the Republic of Turkey, Ankara, Turkey
e-mail: habib.dolgun@tcmb.gov.tr

A. Ng
Research Management Centre, INCEIF, Petaling Jaya, Selangor, Malaysia
e-mail: adam@inceif.org

M. Zulkhibri et al. (eds.), *Islamic Monetary Economics and Institutions*,
https://doi.org/10.1007/978-3-030-24005-9_10

several challenges regarding liquidity management. Since an Islamic Financial Institution (IFI) is not allowed to use interest-based financing resources from interbank money markets or other resources (such as using interest-based central bank's facilities via open market channels) and is not allowed to transfer its debt, Islamic banks have disadvantages concerning liquidity management compared to conventional banks. Also, it is a well-known fact that there is a dearth of *Shari'ah*-compliant securities or highly liquid *Sukuk* in many jurisdictions (IFSB 2015a).

Furthermore, even there are several *Shari'ah*-compliant *Sukuk* or securities in some jurisdictions, the secondary markets for these assets are thin or underdeveloped. The absence of *Shari'ah*-complaint lender of last resort (LoLR) facility in many countries places further constraint on Islamic banks' ability to mitigate liquidity risk (Mohammad 2015). Having the relevant lender of last resort facility may promote moral hazard behaviour of these banks and consequently attenuate the efficiency of liquidity management. However, without such facility, Islamic banks could not protect themselves against sudden liquidity changes or increasing stress in market liquidity. These factors and many others can impact the performance, growth, and portfolio management of Islamic banks as well as confidence of investors. Moreover, the distinctive behaviour of Islamic banks concerning asset-liability management, capital adequacy requirement, loan portfolio risk-taking, and interbank demand hinders their capacity to undertake a comparable liquidity transformation as their conventional counterparts.

In 2013, the Basel Committee issued a revised liquidity coverage ratio (LCR) to help local authorities to strengthen their liquidity regulations in order to promote a more resilient banking sector (BIS 2013). This was followed by the net stable funding ratio (NSFR) in October 2014.[1] These requirements need to be complied by respectively January 2015 and January 2018. In 2015, with some changes, the IFSB adopted the LCR and the NSFR for Islamic banks (IFSB 2015b). The implementation of liquidity coverage ratio (LCR) under the new standards may be challenging for Islamic banks. While the LCR and the NSFR are designed to improve banks' resilience to short-term liquidity shocks by holding high-quality liquid assets (HQLA) as reserve, these requirements compel Islamic banks to keep cash on their books due to lack of short-term highly liquid and *Shari'ah*-compliant financial assets.[2] Consequently, the efficiency, resiliency, and profitability of Islamic banks can be adversely affected.

At present, *Shari'ah*-conscious investors are at disadvantage when it comes to participation in the financial services provided by Islamic banks. At the financing end, they face financing rates higher than lending rates of conventional banks. Meanwhile, on the other side of the banks' balance sheet, they receive a lower profit

[1] See the document of the BIS, "Basel III: the net stable funding ratio" (http://www.bis.org/bcbs/publ/d295.htm).

[2] The IILM was established to facilitate cross-border liquidity management among Islamic financial institutions by making available a variety of instruments of acceptable features and characteristics. However, the IILM instruments have not reached a sustainable critical mass due to its infancy.

share compared to interest rate paid by conventional banks. Facing these, the *Shari'ah*-conscious investors may opt out from the Islamic financial system or from the financial system. The uneven treatment that these investors receive would likely jeopardize financial inclusion, which is purported to be one of the goals of Islamic finance. Accordingly, there is a need to improvise the current regulatory framework including the liquidity standards such that the interest of these investors is protected and financial inclusion is enhanced. The liquidity standards can be effective in protecting these investors and strengthen the financial inclusion of those who are unwilling to be bankable under the conventional banking due to religious reasons.

The chapter attempts to demonstrate that Muslim-majority countries may well be able to fortify their financial system against asset price sensitivities and global financial shocks by reforming their regulatory framework of liquidity management such as to facilitate further development of Islamic banks toward achieving the objectives of Islamic principles. The foregoing discussion highlights the importance of liquidity risk management. Accordingly, the paper has the following objectives: (i) to examine the short-run and long-run determinants of liquidity holdings of Islamic banks and (ii) to examine the effects of credit on liquidity risks of Islamic banks and assess the impact of net cash outflows on liquidity risk of these banks.

For these objectives, this chapter seeks to fill the gap by examining the liquidity risk management of Islamic banks in Malaysia. Section 10.2 highlights the main purposes and introduces the research background and explains the research problems. Section 10.3 provides related literature review. Section 10.4 provides an overview about Basel requirements, Islamic banks, liquidity management, their regulations, and supervision framework. Section 10.5 provides the theory and measurement of liquidity risk. Section 10.6 provides the comparative results of the short-term and long-term determinants of banks' liquidity holdings based on a liquidity model. Section 10.7 discusses the findings and policy issues.

10.2 Motivation and Research Questions

Liquidity risk management bears important implications for Islamic banks' activities. It is encouraging banks to reduce the risks on their balance sheets and facilitating the liquidation of assets in a crisis. In the conventional literature, various studies conducted on liquidity risk management and identification of liquidity risk determinants. An illustrative list of these studies includes Aldasoro and Faia (2016), Bonner (2014), Wagner (2007), Banerjee and Mio (2014), Leykun (2016), and Hong et al. (2014). These studies highlight the importance of effective liquidity risk management and hence the need to continuously identify factors that account for banks' liquidity risk. Among the factors considered to be significant are capital adequacy ratio, total loan to total asset ratio, total deposit to total asset ratio, and net cash flows (Leykun 2016; Hong et al. 2014). Despite their acknowledged importance to liquidity risk of conventional banks, whether they are central to Islamic banks remain largely unknown. The limited understanding of liquidity risk of Islamic banks serves as motivations and justifications for this paper. More precisely, this chapter evaluates the liquidity risk management of Islamic banks by taking the Malaysian Islamic banking system as a case study. It is hypothesized in this chapter that there are many factors that affect liquidity formation of Islamic banks. In line with the stated research objectives, the paper raises the following research questions to be addressed:

1. Can the liquidity requirement ratio of Islamic banks be explained by financial factors such as the stock of *Sukuk*, credit, deposits, and return on equity (ROE)?
2. Can the liquidity requirement ratio of Islamic banks be explained by macroeconomic factors such as inflation, interbank money market rate, or government bond rate?
3. Do these determinants affect liquidity risk of Islamic banks in the short-run or in the long-run or both?

10.3 Literature Review on Banks' Liquidity

Malaysia started to the Islamic banking in 1983; however, it changed its regulatory framework before many countries and has become one of the leaders in Islamic finance. Bank Negara Malaysia (BNM) has the biggest role in this success. It introduced the Interest-Free Banking Scheme in 1993 (Mohamad et al. 2013; Amin 2016) and the Liquidity Framework for Islamic banks in 1998 before many central banks. BNM is the first central bank that has started to have the dual banking system, which aims to increase awareness among Islamic banks for better liquidity management and adoption of efficient liquidity management by introducing this liquidity framework. BNM allowed Islamic windows in 1999 and now there are 16 licensed Islamic banks[3] and the Malaysia's Islamic banking sector represents 21.9% of domestic banking sector and 9.6% of global Islamic banking assets (IFSB 2015a). Malaysia established Islamic Money Market in 1994 for effective liquidity management of Islamic banks and there are many products available for Islamic banks' mitigation of liquidity risk (Obiyathulla 2008).

Malaysia is one of the important leaders in Islamic finance, which has double-digit growth rate in recent years (IFSB 2017), and liquidity risk management of Islamic banks in this country has significant repercussions for all Islamic banks in other countries. Liquidity risk is inherited in mismatch between assets and liabilities of banks. It is defined as a shortcoming of assets to cover liabilities (Banerjee and Mio 2014) as a result of unexpected cash outflows (Kumar 2008) and it is also defined as the risk inherited in the maturity transformation of short-term deposits into long-term loans (Vodova 2013; Bonner 2014). Liquidity risk is one of the results of tight liquidity position (AbdulGaniyy et al. 2017).

[3] http://www.bnm.gov.my/index.php?ch=fs_mfs&pg=fs_mfs_bank.

The Basel III liquidity framework is expected to lead to implementation challenges for Islamic banks in coming years due to the limited availability of high-quality liquid assets and difficulties in calibrating the structure to suit the practices of Islamic banks. Unfortunately, the effects of these liquidity standards on Islamic banks have not been analysed by many types of research. There are only a few studies on these regulatory issues. Islamic banks have some structural differences from conventional banks in the context of contracts and the liability side of their balance sheet (Verhoef et al. 2008). Deposits of Islamic banks are composed mainly of three classes of accounts: Current account deposits, saving deposits, and investment deposits. Investment accounts are divided into restricted investment accounts and unrestricted investment accounts. In practice, however, most Islamic banks hold high levels of excess cash.

There are different channels that show importance of robust liquidity risk management framework for Islamic banks. Yaacob et al. (2016) study Malaysian Islamic banks' liquidity risk management and find that an increase in capital adequacy ratio for Islamic banks in Malaysia is related with a decline in liquidity risk exposure. They also reveal that there is positive significant relationship between financing liquidity risk. Ariffin (2012) also studies liquidity risk management of Malaysian Islamic banks, and he reaches a conclusion that the global financial crisis has little impact on the extent of liquidity risk in the Islamic banks and, for the year 2006, the relationship between liquidity risk and return on assets (ROA) is positive, whereas for 2007, there is a negative relationship. He also suggests liquidity risk may lower ROA and ROE because of lack of stable and cheap fund during the crisis for Islamic banks with larger gap, which increases their cost of funding.

Mongid (2015) explores the liquidity risk management of small Indonesian Islamic banks and claims that liquidity risk of Islamic banks is determined by capital adequacy as well as asset management and leverage. But the shortcoming of his study is that the effects of macroeconomic factors or economic environment variables were not included in the model such as inflation rate, central bank fund rate, or interbank rate. One of the recent studies on empirical analysis of the bank-specific, financial, and macroeconomic determinants of the performance of Islamic and conventional banks in Pakistan has been done by Rashid and Jabeen (2016). By using an unbalanced annual panel data and the Generalized Least Square (GLS) regression, they showed that the performance of Islamic banks could be explained by operating efficiency, deposits, and market concentration and claimed that the lending interest rate negatively impacts the performance of Islamic banks.

Islamic banks in many countries show greater potential for growth that intensifies the specific challenges for these banks that need to be evaluated differently from conventional banks. For this reason, many international organizations, supervisory and regulatory authorities, and policy makers have examined various aspects of Islamic financial intermediation, each from their own perspective. Even though Islamic banks have to keep significant funds as cash to meet regulators' requirements, Ismal (2010) suggests that Indonesian Islamic banks have historically managed liquidity well, though the industry is too fragile. He shows a trade-off between self-insurance against liquidity risks and opportunity costs of holding liquid assets. A proper understanding of the macroeconomic situation and regulatory framework is, therefore, important for addressing this trade-off. In this context, Saeed and Izzeldin (2014) suggest that a decrease in default risk is associated with lower efficiency levels. However, Alam (2013) finds that regulations increase the technical efficiency for Islamic banks and suggest that Islamic banks appear to be technically efficient in stricter regulatory conditions. However, tighter regulatory conditions improve risk-transfer ability of banks, which results in avoiding risk-sharing contracts. Since Alam's (2013) study covers data for the year 2006–2010, new studies are needed to evaluate the effects of Basel reforms on Islamic banks' efficiency that are based on more granular data.

Macroeconomic control variables can also influence the behaviour of Islamic banks in managing liquidity according to Mohamad et al. (2013) based on the evidence of Malaysian banks. The same result was found by Krasicka and Nowak (2012) who suggest that Malaysian Islamic banks have responded to economic and financial shocks in the same way as Malaysian conventional banks. Using parametric and non-parametric classification models, Khediri et al. (2015) find that Islamic banks are, on average, more liquid and profitable than conventional banks. On the other hand, specific studies on determinants of liquidity management of Islamic banks have shown that the probability of occurrence of irregular liquidity withdrawals and a liquidity run is very moderate in these banks. This may be the direct result of the satisfactory performance of Islamic banks and the confidence of their depositors (Ismal 2010).

It is accepted that short-term instruments are more liquid than long-term assets. Short-term excess liquidity is managed through the money markets. Several countries have developed money markets for Islamic banks, where Islamic banks can convert their asset into liquid assets when needed. These mechanisms allow Islamic banks to manage liquidity while staying profitable. Islamic banks may have excess liquidity because of the regulatory framework that requires achievement of the requirement of the LCR standards. This excess liquidity can decrease Islamic banks' profits and limit their market share. Variously, for Islamic financial system, Akhtar (2007) suggests that regulators should adopt different approaches. Haan and End (2013) find that most banks hold more liquid assets against liquid liabilities than strictly required. However, specific needs of Islamic financial institutions should be taken into consideration when the regulatory framework is developed (Hesse et al. 2008). It is claimed that risk-sharing feature of Islamic banks may ease to absorb external shocks and restrain against cash outflows because under risk-sharing system, there would be better transformation between liabilities and assets (Mirakhor 2012; Maghrebi and Mirakhor 2015). However, Chong and Liu (2009) suggest that most of the deposits are not invested in risk-sharing financing. Instead of questioning the reasons behind this behaviour of banks, they conclude that Islamic banks should be regulated and supervised under the same regulations as conventional banks because they are offering similar products (Chong and Liu 2009). In this context, the researchers have to answer this question: If Islamic banks are offering the same products and they are being regulated in a similar manner as conventional banks, why do we need Islamic banks?

10.4 Malaysia Liquidity Regulations and the Importance of the LCR

The financial crisis of 2008 showed that liquidity is essential for the proper functioning of financial markets and the banking sector (Bonner 2014; BIS 2013). Before the crisis, thanks to a low level of monetary policy rate in developed markets, funding rate was very low, and funding liquidity was very high. After the crisis, market conditions changed very rapidly, and market liquidity and funding liquidity evaporated within days and hours. According to the BIS (2013), the primary objective of the LCR is to promote the short-term resilience of the liquidity risk profile of banks. The LCR is expected to improve the banking sector's ability to absorb shocks arising from financial and economic stress. The LCR is designed to act as a buffer against liquidity run.

The LCR was developed as a minimum level of liquidity for internationally active banks (BIS 2013). It is proposed that the LCR will contribute to banking liquidity as well as market liquidity. Banks are expected to meet this standard, but national regulatory authorities may set higher minimum levels of liquidity. Many countries including Malaysia have already started to implement the LCR since 1 January 2015 with the implementation of a minimum requirement at 60% level, which will rise in equal annual steps to reach 100% on 1 January 2019. This progressive approach was recommended by the Basel Committee though many countries are already applying a higher level of LCR. According to IFSB (2015a), all supervisory authorities should put into effect the LCR requirement for Islamic banks starting from 2015 with the minimum level of 60%. The IFSB regulation requires an Islamic bank to find enough stock of unencumbered high-quality liquid assets that can be liquefied easily with no loss, or slightly acceptable loss. In this sense, when an asset is sold in the market, 10% of loss is accepted as a threshold for treating these assets as liquid assets. According to IFSB (2015a), the LCR would be composed of stock of *Shari'ah*-compliant HQLA and total net cash outflows calculated for the next 30 calendar days. Total net cash outflows are calculated as total gross expected cash outflows minus lesser of total expected cash inflows or 75% of the total expected cash outflows.

IFSB (2015b) sets the LCR based on a scenario in which there are both idiosyncratic and market-wide shocks. According to the IFSB (2015b), the HQLA are divided into two broad categories, or levels, almost the same as the Basel LCR standards: Level 1 and Level 2. Level 1 assets can constitute an unlimited share of the pool and are not typically subject to a haircut under the LCR. Level 1 assets cover coins, banknotes, central bank reserves, *Sukuk*, and other high-quality securities such as those of the International Islamic Liquidity Management Corporation (IILM) which are assigned a 0% risk-weight under IFSB-15. Level 2 assets compromise Level 2A and Level 2B assets as permitted by the supervisory authorities. Level 2A assets are subject to a 15% haircut applied to the current market value of each asset and limited to the *Shari'ah*-compliant marketable securities/*Sukuk* issued or guaranteed by sovereigns, central banks, Public Sector

Enterprises (PSEs), Multilateral Development Banks (MDBs), or relevant international organizations. The Level 2B assets are subject to a 25% haircut. However, *Sukuk* and other *Shari'ah*-compliant securities that meet all of the requirements stated by the IFSB (2015b) may be included in Level 2B, subject to a 50% haircut.

As another option, Islamic banks may use Alternative Liquidity Approach (ALA) treatments only when there is evidence of a genuine shortfall in the HQLA in the domestic currency after being decided by the regulatory authority. In these case, banks have three options. The first choice is to use contractually committed liquidity facilities from the relevant central bank with a fee. This facility can be used under *Wakalah*, *Mudarabah*, or Commodity *Murabahah* contracts. There are certain *Shari'ah*-related issues in this matter that should be handled very carefully. The second option is to use foreign currency denominated HQLA to cover domestic currency liquidity needs. In this option, Islamic Development Bank (IDB) *Sukuk* or the IILM *Sukuk* can be used. The last option is to use additional level 2 assets with a higher haircut decided by the regulatory bodies. Fuhrer et al. (2017) share that Swiss banks are permitted to use either option two or three to fulfil their requirements even if the approach was not expected to be used by advanced economies. Unfortunately, many Islamic banks are not permitted to use such options.

There are many tools developed by BNM for liquidity management of Islamic banks in interbank market, including central bank *Wadi'ah Acceptance,* Bank Negara Monetary Notes-i (BNMN-i), *Mudarabah* Interbank Investment (MII) and sale and buyback agreements etc.

New issuances of BNMN-i may be issued either on a discounted or a coupon-bearing basis depending on investors' demand. *Mudarabah* Interbank Investment (MII) is the main instrument used in interbank market. The operational mechanism of this product is simple; a liquidity deficit bank obtains fund from the bank having excess liquidity on a *Mudarabah* pro rata profit sharing basis. Though, this product was originated especially for overnight borrowing, it is not possible for bank to use this money for investment for overnight basis. Therefore, banks use their long-term profits as a benchmark for calculating profit rate for overnight transactions. Malaysian *Shari'ah* scholars accept these transactions as *Shari'ah*-compliant transactions (Obiyathulla 2008).

BNM developed "liquefiable assets" concept, wherein certain qualifying characteristics have been identified. These assets should be easily convertible to cash and should have low counterparty risks and have sufficient demand in secondary markets. Many Islamic financial instruments in Malaysia can easily be converted to cash, but having deep secondary markets is a big concern for many Islamic securities. Some Islamic securities and *Sukuk* are specifically classified in BNM regulations. For example, Cagamas *Sukuk*[4] is accepted as Class-1 liquefiable assets. Recently, IILM *Sukuk* has been defined as Level 1 high-quality liquid asset under Basel III

[4] Cagamas *Sukuk* are issued by the National Mortgage Corporation of Malaysia (Cagamas) to fund the purchase of Islamic home financing from the financial system. https://www.cagamas.com.my/cagamas-debt-securities/sukuk.

accord. Islamic corporate bonds and papers that have AAA credit rating are accepted as Class-2 liquefiable assets but are applied relevant haircut.

Applying certain discount to the securities is understood as reasonable under conventional practices. However, in Islamic markets, different classes of products affect the demand for these products. This can result in legislative arbitrage for different products. Risk-based approach is causing goods to be priced differently before they go to market. According to Islamic principles, there should be no barriers to entry or exist of goods and products to and from the market. Risk-based approach prevents the market from functioning effectively and properly because this approach builds legal barriers against market demand and supply of liquid instruments and harms price determinants of products. This increases leakages and vulnerabilities in the market. As a result of these leakages, banks are investing liquid assets or hoarding cash instead of circulating in the market. The volatility in the market liquidity cannot be handled differently from these arrangements.

10.5 Theory and Measurement of Liquidity Risk

10.5.1 Methodology and Data

In this study, we assess the factors affecting the liquidity risk management of Islamic banks of Malaysia for the period between April 2007 and August 2015 based on cumulative data, for the reason that Malaysia is one of the leaders of Islamic finance and has very resilient and developed liquidity management framework for Islamic banks. We develop a model in which liquidity risk is used as a dependent variable and calculated according to BIS standards. Hence, liquidity risk is used as a dependent variable in many studies on Islamic banks or conventional banks or on both types of banks (Mohamad et al. 2013; Roman and Sargu 2015; Ogilo and Mugenyah 2015; Amin 2016; Bonner 2014; Banerjee and Mio 2014; Aldasoro and Faia 2016; Wagner 2007; Krasicka and Nowak 2012; Ahmed et al. 2011; Vodova 2013; Mongid 2015 and Ariffin 2012; Cuccinelli 2013; Leykun 2016; Laštůvková 2016; Distinguin et al. 2013; Hong et al. 2014). However, there are different applications on the usage of liquidity risk metrics in banking literature.

Prior to the introduction of LCR framework, most empirical studies employ accounting-based measures of liquidity risk, among which include loans to total assets ratio (Roman and Sargu 2015), total deposits to total assets ratio (Mohamad et al. 2013) and loans to total assets ratio (Amin 2016). While these measures are easily computed from banks' balance sheets, they contain two main weaknesses. First, they do not capture different implications of liquid assets, degree of liquidity treatment of liquid assets, and impacts of cash inflows and cash outflows on liquidity risk. Second, as argued by Poorman and Blake (2005) and Distinguin et al. (2013), using such metrics for liquidity could be inaccurate under several conditions. Subsequently, new metrics of liquidity risk based on high-quality liquid assets, cash inflows, and cash outflows are developed by the Basel Committee (BIS 2013). Numerous new metrics of liquidity risk are adopted in the conventional banking literature. Bonner (2014) uses liquidity ratio as a dependent variable defined by Dutch Central Bank (DLCR- Dutch Liquidity Coverage Ratio) according to Basel requirements. Moreover, Banerjee and Mio (2014) employ the share of HQLA to total assets as a dependent variable to analyse the behavioural reaction of banks to a tightening of liquidity regulation.

Aldasoro and Faia (2016) use liquidity coverage ratio, while Wagner (2007) adopts liquid asset ratio as a measure of liquidity. Cucinelli (2013) uses both liquidity coverage ratio and the net stable funding ratio for measuring the liquidity risk. Leykun (2016) estimates liquidity risk by calculating the liquid assets to total deposit ratio. Distinguin et al. (2013) use a liquidity creation indicator computed as weighted sums of assets and liabilities, where weights are assigned according to their liquidity levels, and divided by total assets. Laštůvková (2016) defines liquidity as positive flows (cash inflows), the negative flow (outflows) and the net change, in which four methods were used to calculate this dependent variable. About Islamic banks, Krasicka and Nowak (2012) and Ahmed et al. (2011) use liquid assets to total assets as a measure of liquidity. Liquid assets to total funding (Mongid 2015) and the total liquid assets of liabilities (Ariffin 2012) are other proxies used for liquidity risk for Indonesian Islamic rural banks and Malaysian Islamic banks respectively. To the best of the researcher's knowledge; no study has specifically investigated the effects of liquidity requirement ratio or liquidity coverage ratio in a dual banking system, where Islamic banks and conventional banks coexist. The present paper measures liquidity risk by calculating the liquid assets to total net cash outflows ratio.

The paper adopts time series econometric modelling empirical approaches to examine the determinants of liquidity risk in the Malaysian Islamic banking system (Gujurati 2011). The time series econometric modelling is to uncover especially short-run relations among the variables under study. Banking data are mainly collected from publicly available data supported by the Bank Negara Malaysia (BNM), Bankscope, and SNL web pages. Macroeconomic variables (credit default swap (CDS) rate, government bond rate, and interbank rate) are extracted from Bloomberg Terminal.[5] The inflation rate of Malaysia was derived from the Department of Statistics Malaysian, Official Portal. Several statistical programmes are used.[6]

[5]The Bloomberg Professional service (Bloomberg Terminal) is a software solution and flexible platform for financial professionals, academicians, and public authorities who need real-time data, news, and information. For more information, please see http://www.bloomberg.com.

[6]We used EV (which is a statistical, forecasting, and modelling tool with a simple object-oriented interface) and Stata 14 statistical package (Stata is a general-purpose data analysis and statistical software package used by researchers and professionals. It is a complete, integrated statistics package that provides a broad range of statistical analyses, plus data management, graphics, simulations, and custom programming. For more information, please see http://www.stata.com).

10.5.2 Empirical Model

There are several studies on liquidity of Malaysian banks, especially Islamic banks. Mohamad et al. (2013) study the liquidity of Malaysian Islamic banks by using dynamic panel data estimation for 17 banks and find an evidence of influence of macroeconomic control variables on the behaviour of these banks in managing their liquidity. It is also evidenced that total asset size is negatively related to liquidity. However, Krasicka and Nowak (2012) claim that Malaysian Islamic banks have responded to economic and financial shocks in the same way as Malaysian conventional banks. Also, Khediri et al. (2015) find that Islamic banks are, on average, more liquid and profitable than conventional banks, but using parametric and non-parametric classification models.

The model used in this chapter covers the model based on cumulative data of Malaysian Islamic banks (16 Islamic banks). There are many similar models used in the previous literature as we have referred in previous chapters (Bonner 2014; Akhtar et al. 2011; Mohamad et al. 2013; Boudt et al. 2017; Ergeç and Aslan 2013):

$$\begin{aligned} \mathrm{LCRY} = \alpha_i &+ \beta_{1it} * RR + \beta_{2it} * \mathrm{CAR} + \beta_{3it} * \mathrm{LINF} \\ &\beta_{4it} * CDS + \beta_{5it} * \mathrm{INTER} + \beta_{6it} * \mathrm{BOND} \\ &+ \beta_{7it} * \mathrm{LCRE} + \beta_{8it} * \mathrm{LDEP} + \beta_{9it} * \mathrm{SUKUK} + \beta_{10it} \\ &* LAS + \varepsilon_{it} \qquad i = 1,2,3,4,5 \text{ and } t = 1,2,3\ldots 101 \end{aligned} \tag{10.1}$$

where, L is the natural logarithm of a variable. ε_{it} is the common error term and α is the bank-specific effect. We include the logarithm of total assets (las), the logarithm of credit (lcre), the logarithm of deposits (ldep) and the logarithm of inflation (linf) with lag to alleviate the endogeneity problem. Liquidity, the dependent variable, is measured as the liquidity ratio as defined and formulated by Bank Negara Malaysia and it is providing this ratio and also it provides LCR ratio defined by the BIS (2013) after June 2015. However, it is possible to calculate the liquidity ratio based on banks' assets especially liquid assets with very low error margin even if the supervisory authority does not provide. Bank's liquidity is expected to be dependent on individual behaviour of banks, market, macroeconomic environment, and structural factors (exchange rate regime, regulations, etc.). Net profit is very important for understanding the relations of liquidity and efficiency of these banks. Unfortunately, we could not find net profit for Islamic banks of Malaysia. There are other variables used for time series analysis (Table 10.1). These are *Sukuk* stocks, logarithm of total credits (CRE), logarithm of total deposits (DEP), the statutory reserve requirement (SRR), logarithm of inflation rate, CDS rate of Malaysia, 3-month treasury bills rate (BOND) and 3-month London Inter-Bank Offered Rate (LIBOR) rate (INTER), and capital adequacy ratio (CAR) (Akhtar et al. 2011; Demirguc-Kunt et al. 2004; Yaacob et al. 2016; Praet and Herzberg 2008; Bonner 2014; Mohamad et al. 2013; Arif and Anees 2012) (Table 10.1).

Table 10.1 List of variables

Variable (short form)	Variable	Description
LLCR	Logarithm of liquidity coverage ratio	High-quality liquid assets/net cash outflows
SRR	Statutory reserve requirement	Required reserves of banks
CAR	Capital adequacy ratio	Tier 1 capital + tier 2 capital/ risk-weighted assets
LINF	Logarithm of inflation ratio	Consumer price index
CDS	Credit default swap	CDS rate of the country
INTER	Interbank	Interbank money market rate
BOND	Treasury bonds	3-month treasury bond return
LCRE	Logarithm of total credits	Total financing
SUKUK	*Sukuk*	Lease certificates and *Sukuk*
LDEP	Logarithm of deposits	Total deposits
LAS	Total assets	Total assets
E		Error term
A		Constant

Table 10.2 Summary of descriptive statistics

Variable	Mean	Std. dev.	Min	Max
LLR	4,54	0,11	4,32	4,78
CAR	15,27	0,85	13,72	17,97
SUKUK	40.872.602	17.789.904	9.873.601	64.515.391
LSRR	95,16	10,81	75,56	119,34
LCRE	18,85	0,63	17,41	19,72
LAS	19,36	0,53	18,13	20,06
LDEP	19,16	0,52	17,94	19,87
CDS	135,92	52,62	20,20	288,82
INF	1.75	0.490	0.86	2.60
INTER	3.19	0.49	2.11	3.86
BOND	2.93	0.43	1.82	3.58

10.5.3 Descriptive Statistics

Malaysian banks descriptive statistics can be seen in Table 10.2. Descriptive statistics for these banks show that all variables in the model have statistically significant relations. We have 101 observations for 10 variables, which are generally accepted as sufficient for such panel data analysis.

We checked heteroscedasticity and autocorrelation. For heteroscedasticity, Breusch-Pagan-Godfrey test was used, which results show that heteroscedasticity hypothesis was rejected. Then we tested Breusch-Godfrey serial correlation LM test, in which lag was specified as 4. The results show that there is no serial correlation. Correlation coefficients can be seen from Table 10.3.

Table 10.3 Correlation coefficients

	LLR	LAS	LCRE	LDEP	LINF	CDS	LSRR	SUKUK	BOND
LLR	1.000	−0.2631	−0.1838	−0.3382	0.0516	−0.0070	0.8948	0.5239	0.0059
LAS	−0.2631	1.0000	0.8099	0.9294	0.0815	0.2849	−0.2524	0.0843	−0.0274
LCRE	−0.1838	0.8099	1.0000	0.7749	0.0601	0.2735	−0.1730	0.0014	−0.0029
LDEP	−0.3382	0.9294	0.7749	1.0000	0.0086	0.2435	−0.3255	0.0996	0.0108
LINF	0.0516	0.0815	0.0601	0.0086	1.0000	0.1887	0.0435	−0.0451	0.0682
CDS	−0.0070	0.2849	0.2735	0.2435	0.1887	1.0000	−0.0111	−0.0600	0.1197
LSRR	0.8948	−0.2524	−0.1730	−0.3255	0.0435	−0.0110	1.0000	0.5484	−0.0049
SUKUK	0.5239	0.0843	0.0014	0.0996	−0.0451	−0.0600	0.5484	1.0000	0.2331
BOND	0.0059	−0.0274	−0.0029	0.0108	0.0682	0.1197	−0.0049	0.2331	1.0000
CAR	0.0049	0.0136	0.0611	−0.0062	0.0234	−0.1313	−0.0031	−0.0993	−0.1577
INTER	0.0306	0.0554	0.0456	0.0256	−0.1161	−0.2101	0.0275	0.0403	0.5652

10.6 Results

10.6.1 ARDL Approach for Liquidity Time Series Model of Malaysian Islamic Banks

We apply the same ARDL approach to cointegration (see Pesaran et al. 2001) for Malaysian Islamic banks. In this test the liquidity ratio is dependent variable, and we run ten independent variables. We used bounds test for the presence of a long-run relationship using two separate statistics, mainly an *F*-test and a t-test on the lagged level dependent variable. The statistics have a non-standard distribution and depend on whether the variables are individually *I*(0) or *I*(1). In this test, the maximum dependent lags were specified as 4 (Table 10.4).

We used Akaike information criterion (AIC) for model selection. All variables' lag form was used, and there are 97 observations after making certain adjustments. The numbers of models evaluated are 39.062.500. According to our test results, *F*-statistics was found as 5.160305, which is above critical bound at 1% critical value. This means that our model has cointegration and all variables can be accepted as *I*(0). Selected ARDL model is ARDL (1,3,2,1,4,2,2,2,4,4,2). The ARDL cointegration test shows that there are significant relations between liquidity and total assets, credits, deposits, CDS, inflation, statutory reserves, *Sukuk* stocks, interbank interest rate, government bond rate, and capital adequacy ratio. Among these variables, total assets, deposits, inflation, government bonds, capital adequacy and interbank interest rate show positive significant relations with the liquidity. The relation of inflation with liquidity is positive and in line with the evidence of

Table 10.4 ARDL cointegration tests (Malaysian Islamic Banks)

Variable	Lag	Coefficient	*t*-statistic
LLR	1	0.5905	5.5494***
DLAS	3	0.2825	2.5725**
DCRE	2	−0.5811	−3.4094 ***
DDEP	1	0.6953	2.4910 **
CDS	4	−0.0004	−3.3044 **
INF	2	0.3194	1.6766*
SRR	2	−1.2608	−1.7421*
DSUK	2	−5.2909	−2.6563**
BOND	4	0.0706	2.5664**
CAR	4	0.0179	2.0185**
INTER	2	0.1035	1.8685*
C		0.7880	03200

Notes: The upper limit of the critical value for the *F*-test (all *I*(0) variables) is 1.98 (5%) and 2.41 (1%) and for the *t*-test, 4.280632 (1%); critical values obtained from Pesaran et al. (2001); *, **, and *** indicate, respectively, 10%, 5%, and 1% significance level

Mohamad et al. (2013)'s study on Malaysian Islamic banks. Although Mohamad et al. (2013) find negative relationship between asset size and liquidity, we evidence positive and significant impact of asset size on liquidity. However, CDS rate of the country, statutory reserves, and *Sukuk* stocks show negative significant relations with the liquidity. Consistent with the finding of Mohamad et al. (2013), credit has negative and significant relationship with the liquidity. On the other hand, there is not any variable that showed insignificant relations with the liquidity of the Islamic banks.

10.6.2 Long-Run Relations of Malaysian Islamic Banks

The sign of CointEq(-1) is negative, and coefficient is −0.409, and it is significant at 1% significance level, which shows that we have one cointegration. This shows that we have a meaningful long-run cointegration. Long-run cointegration is found as the below equation:

$$\begin{aligned} LR = {} & 3.291 * LAS - 1.937 * \mathrm{LCRE} - 1.206 * \mathrm{LDEP} - 0.004 * CDS \\ & - 0.270 * \mathrm{LINF} - 0.00003 * SRR + 0.0000\mathrm{SUKUK} - 0.372 * \mathrm{BOND} \\ & - 0.056 * \mathrm{CAR} + 0.450 * \mathrm{INTER} + 1.925 \end{aligned} \tag{10.2}$$

Table 10.5 shows that there is a positive statistically significant long-run relation between *Sukuk* and interbank interest rate and liquidity ratio of Malaysian Islamic banks. However, negative but significant long-run relations were found between liquidity and credits, deposits, required reserves, government bond rate, and capital adequacy ratio. Although CDS and inflation rate showed significant relations in the

Table 10.5 Long-run coefficients

Variable	Coefficient	*t*-statistic
LAS	3.2912	3.8605***
LCRE	−1.9372	−2.6103**
LDEP	−1.2060	−1.8878*
CDS	−0.0003	−0.7014
LINF	−0.2702	−0.6119
SRR	−0.0000	−3.1826***
SUKUK	0.0000	2.525**
BOND	−0.3719	−1.9292*
CAR	−0.0559	−2.1673**
INTER	0.4501	2.3751**
C	1.9247	0.3349

Note: *, **, and *** indicate, respectively, 10%, 5%, and 1% significance level

short-run, these relations become insignificant in the long-run. These results are partly consistent with other findings in the literature.

10.6.3 Granger Results for Malaysian Islamic Banks

After finding the correlation, which does not necessarily imply causation, we need to find causation among variables. For this purpose, we apply Granger causality/Block Exogeneity Wald tests to measure precedence and information content. Granger (1969) approaches the question of whether X causes Y equivalent to asking how much of the current value of Y can be explained by past values of X and then to see whether adding lagged values of X can improve the explanation. If X helps in the estimation of Y, or equivalently if the coefficients on the lagged X's are statistically significant, Y is said to be Granger-caused by X.

Table 10.6 shows the results of Granger causality tests. According to the results, Malaysian Islamic banks' liquidity is related to interbank rate at 10% significance level. This means the change in government bond rate has causal effect on liquidity of Islamic banks. On the other hand, total assets are related to liquidity at 1% significance level and to deposits at 5% level, CDS at 5% level, required reserves at 5% level and capital adequacy at 1% level. As well as total assets, liquidity has causal effect on credit at 5% level, deposit at 1% level, CDS at 10% level, and interbank rate at 10% level.

10.6.4 Impulse Response Test Results for Malaysian Islamic Banks

After conducting Granger causality/Block Exogeneity Wald tests for Malaysian Islamic banks, we use impulse response test to capture direct influences of a variable on another variable as well as indirect influences that are propagated through other variables. Since impulse response analysis gives the graphical results of Vector Decomposition (VDC) test,[7] we discuss only impulse responses here to complement the Granger analysis in order to obtain the magnitudes and signs of a variable's responses to impulses in other variables. The Y-axis of Fig. 10.1 shows the shock given to the LR and the X-axis shows the response of a variable within 10 periods (months).

According to Fig. 10.1, when a shock is given to the liquidity for Malaysian Islamic banks, all variables especially logarithm of the credit, total assets, and deposits respond starting from second month and continue to respond till the end of 10 months. At the end of 10 months, CDS rate of the country, logarithm of deposits,

[7] Vector Decomposition (VDC) test results for liquidity of Malaysian Islamic banks are shared at Appendix 13.

Table 10.6 VECM-based Granger results (Malaysian Islamic banks)

Dependent variable	Independent variable										
	Statistics of lagged 2nd differenced term (*p*-value)										
	LR	AS	CRE	DEP	INF	CDS	SRR	SUKUK	BOND	CAR	INTER
LR		2.7025 (0.2589)	26,211 (0.2697)	3.4532 (0.1779)	3.2280 (0.1991)	3.5656 (0.1682)	4.1507 (0.1255)	3.3320 (0.1890)	5.4224 (0.0066)*	3.0191 (0.2210)	2.0343 (0.3616)
AS***	21.2510 *** (0.000)		0.5051 (0.7389)	7.887** (0.0194)	2.708 (0.2581)	7.9517** (0.0188)	18.20*** (0.001)	2.2644 (0.3223)	3.6498 (0.1612)	14.555*** (0.0007)	0.7550 (0.6856)
CRE***	7.1099** (0.0286)	0.4860 (0.7843)		1.9938 (0.3690)	1 1911 (0.5513)	2.6460 (0.2663)	5.7490* (0.0564)	0.8034 (0.6692)	2.8745 (0.2376)	14.009*** (0.0009)	0.1376 (0.9335)
DEP***	16.2148*** (0.0003)	0.1855 (0.9114)	0.5818 (0.7476)		1 6237 (0.4440)	8.1647** (0.0169)	12.5925***(0.0018)	2.4077 (0.300)	3.6107 (0.1644)	9.6722*** (0.0079)	1.3305 (0.5141)
INF**	0.2537 (0.8808)	1.9108 (0.3846)	2.2425 (0.3259)	0.8813 (0.6436)		1.3571 (0.5073)	0.2197 (0.8960)	1.1185 (0.5716)	7.3836** (0.0249)	4.0314 (0.1332)	3.2538 (0.1965)
CDS**	4.7970* (0.0909)	0.4468 (0.7998)	1.5158 (0.4686)	0.1889 (0.9099)	1.4338 (0.4882)		3.6403 (0.1620)	1.4448 (0.4856)	1.8754 (0.3915)	1.1836 (0.5533)	3.8471 (0.1461)
SRR	3.8868 (0.1432)	2.9509 (0.2237)	1.7600 (0.4148)	3.8897 (0.1430)	2 5413 (0.2806)	3.6336 (0.1625)		3.0177 (0.2212)	5.1426* (0.0764)	2.5356 (0.2814)	2.1439 (0.3423)
SUKUK	0.6473 (0.7235)	2.3528 (0.3084)	0.1977 (0.9059)	4.4075 (0.1104)	0 8363 (0.6583)	6.1146** (0.0470)	0.5444 (0.7617)		1.9856 (0.3705)	2.1936 (0.3339)	1.6457 (0.4392)
BOND***	2.7369 (0.2545)	0.9363 (0.6261)	0.5851 (0.7463)	0.6957 (0.7062)	5 2534* (0.0723)	3.1978 (0.2021)	3.5160 (0.1724)	4.0259 (0.1336)		10.6745*** (0.0048)	9.5435*** (0.0085)
CAR	2.3450 (0.3096)	1.5226 (0.4671)	1.0653 (0.5870)	3.6035 (0.1650)	0 8349 (0.6587)	1.4782 (0.4775)	2.5609 (0.2779)	3.6404 (0.1620)	0.2455 (0.8845)		1.2842 (0.5262)
INTER***	5.0638* (0.0795)	1.9842 (0.3708)	0.4903 (0.7826)	2.9308 (0.2310)	10.0931*** (0.0064)	9.189** (0.0101)	4.7046* (0.0951)	1.8088 (0.4048)	2.9053 (0.2339)	10.1510*** (0.0062)	

Note: Granger causality/Block Exogeneity Wald tests. *, **, and *** indicate, respectively, 10%, 5%, and 1% significance level

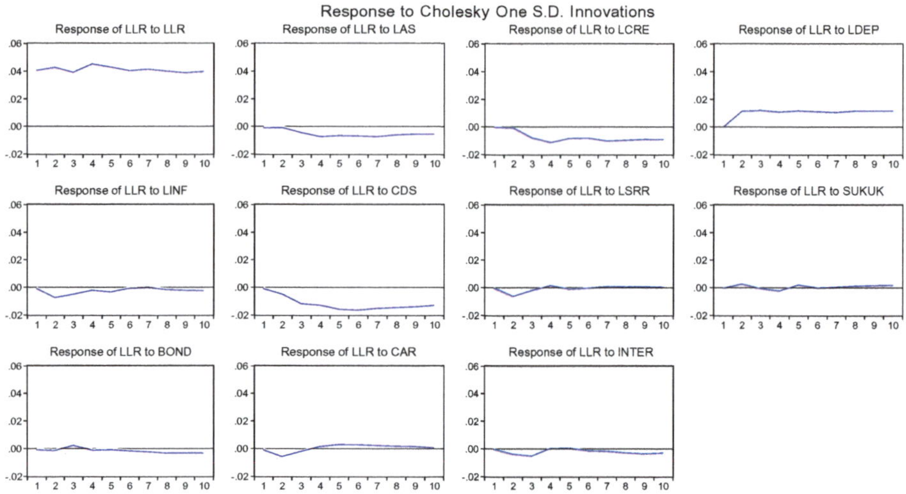

Fig. 10.1 Impulse response results. (Source: Author's own calculation)

logarithm of assets, and logarithm of credit respond more than 1%. This means that these four variables have causal relations with liquidity at 10 periods. In 10 periods, CDS, deposits, credit, and inflation respond to the liquidity chocks. Credit and deposits show causal relations both in 3 months and 10 months, but inflation decreases its responses in 10 months. This is because inflation is effective on short-run and its effects decreases within the time period.

10.7 Conclusion

This chapter critically investigates the factors that affect liquidity risk management of Islamic banks in Malaysia. The specific risk profile of an Islamic bank requires developing a new and more efficient and resilient regulatory framework. The Islamic banking system relies on risk sharing and needs to maintain symmetric information among parties. Moreover, the Basel standards and the IFSB standards are not providing the appropriate playing field required for Islamic banks. Indeed, these standards mimic those of the conventional system. For example, the LCR of the IFSB is almost similar to the Basel LCR (2013), except the former gives a higher treatment of several *Sukuk*. However, it needs to be noted that liquidity risk management of Islamic banks has become highly crucial after the introduction of the LCR standards. The new liquidity framework entails the necessity to have enough eligible liquid assets, *Shari'ah*-compliant secondary markets for these instruments, and functional interbank short-term markets that have *Shari'ah*-compliant instruments.

In this chapter, the short-term and long-term determinants of these banks' liquidity holdings are examined using monthly data over the period of 2007–2015 using liquidity model that incorporates *Sukuk*, interbank market rate, required reserves, inflation rate, and credit default swap rate, and these factors are compared with conventional banks' liquidity. A time series-based liquidity model assessed liquidity management of banks in Malaysia based on the ARDL test and long-run and short-run analyses. Since the LCR was formulated for the short-run, greater importance was given to short-run relations.

The conducted ARDL cointegration test finds that there are statistically significant relations between liquidity and total assets, credits, deposits, CDS, inflation, statutory reserves, *Sukuk* stocks, interbank interest rate, government bond rate, and capital adequacy ratio. Among these variables, total assets, deposits, inflation, government bonds, capital adequacy, and interbank interest rate display statistically positive significant relations with the liquidity. However, CDS rate of the country, statutory reserves, *Sukuk* stocks show negative significant relations with the liquidity. These results are consistent with previous studies' findings.

After conducting the Granger causality tests, we find that Malaysian Islamic banks' liquidity is related to interbank rate at 10% significance level. This means the change in government bond rate has causal effect on liquidity of Islamic banks. On the other hand, total assets are related to liquidity at 1% significance level and to deposits at 5% level, CDS at 5% level, required reserves at 5% level, and capital adequacy at 1% level. As well as total assets, liquidity has causal effect on credit at 5% level, deposit at 1% level, CDS at 10% level, and interbank rate at 10% level. The main result is that market liquidity influences banks' liquidity, and banks' liquidity responds to the profitability of Islamic banks.

As for policy implications, international liquidity management initiatives, enhancing cooperation, trust, and communication, are vigorous for controlling vulnerabilities, mitigating risks and curtailing regulatory arbitrage. Moreover, both macro-level and micro-level mitigating mechanisms should be designed. Since Islamic banks are exposed to market liquidity and funding liquidity risks, more liquid instruments within a tailored regulatory framework are required for the safety and profitability of these banks.

References

AbdulGaniyy, A., Ogunbado, A. F., & Ahmad, N. H. (2017). Islamic perspectives on liquidity risk management practices of Islamic banks in Malaysia and Bahrain. *Asian Journal of Multidisciplinary Studies.*, *5*(1), 100–108.

Ahmed, N., Ahmed, Z., & Naqvi, I. H. (2011). Liquidity risk and islamic banks: Evidence from Pakistan. *Interdisciplinary Journal of Research in Business, 1*(9), 99–102.

Akhtar, S. (2007). *Building an effective Islamic financial system.* Global Islamic Financial Forum Governor's: Financial Regulators Forum in Islamic Finance, Kuala Lumpur, Malaysia.

Akhtar, M. F., Ali, K., & Sadaqat, S. (2011). Factors influencing the profitability of Islamic banks of Pakistan. *International Research Journal of Finance and Economics.*, *66*, 117–124.

Alam, N. (2013). Impact of banking regulation on risk and efficiency in Islamic banking. *Journal of Financial Reporting and Accounting, 11*(1), 29–50.

Aldasoro, I., & Faia, E. (2016). Systemic loops and liquidity regulation. *Journal of Financial Stability, 27*, 1–16.

Amin, S. I. M. (2016). *Liquidity risk determinants: Are islamic banks different from conventional banks? Dissertation*. Petaling Jaya: INCEIF.

Arif, A., & Anees, A. N. (2012). Liquidity risk and performance of banking system. *Journal of Financial Regulation and Compliance, 20*(2), 182–195.

Ariffin, N. M. (2012). Liquidity risk management and financial performance in Malaysia: Empirical evidence from Islamic banks. *Aceh International Journal of Social Sciences, 1*(2), 77–84.

Banerjee, R. N., & Mio, H. (2014). The impact of liquidity regulation on banks. In *BIS Working Papers No. 470*. Basel: Bank of International Settlement.

BIS, (Basel Committee on Banking Supervision-BCBS) (2013. Basel III: The liquidity coverage ratio and liquidity risk monitoring tools.

Bonner, C. (2014). In Center for Economic Research (Ed.), *Liquidity regulation and bank behaviour*. Tilburg: CentER.

Boudt, K., Paulus, E. C. S., & Rosenthal, D. W. R. (2017). Funding liquidity, market liquidity and TED spread: A two-regime model. *Journal of Empirical Finance, 43*, 143–158.

Chong, B. S., & Liu, M. L. (2009). Islamic banking: Interest-free or interest-based? *Pacific-Basin Finance Journal, 17*, 125–144.

Cucinelli, D. (2013). The relationship between liquidity risk and probability of default: Evidence from the Euro area. *Risk Governance and Control: Financial Markets and Institutions, 3*(1), 42–50.

Distinguin, I., Roulet, C., & Tarazi, A. (2013). Bank regulatory capital and liquidity: Evidence from US and European publicly traded banks. *Journal of Banking & Finance, 37*(9), 3295–3317.

Demirguc-Kunt, A., Laeven, L., & Levine, R. (2004). Regulations, Market Structure, Institutions, and the Cost of Financial Intermediation, Journal of Money, Credit, and Banking, 36(3), 593–622.

Ergec, E. H., & Aslan, B. G. (2013). Impact of Interest Rates on Islamic and Conventional Banks: The Case of Turkey. *Applied Economics*, 45(17), 2381–2388.

Fuhrer, L. M., Müller, B., & Steiner, L. (2017). The liquidity coverage ratio and security prices. *Journal of Banking and Finance, 75*, 292–311.

Granger, C. W. J. (1969). Investigating causal relations by econometric models and cross-spectral methods. *Econometrica, 37*(3), 424–438.

Gujarati, D. N. (2011). *Basic Econometrics, Fifth Edition*. The McGraw-Hill Companies.

Haan, L. D., & End, J. W. (2013). Bank liquidity, the maturity ladder, and regulation. *Journal of Banking and Finance, 37*(10), 3930–3950.

Hesse, H., Andreas, A. J., & Sole, J. (2008). Trend and changes in Islamic finance. *World Economics, 9*(2), 175–193.

Hong, H., Huang, J. Z., & Wu, D. (2014). The information content of Basel III liquidity risk measures. *Journal of Financial Stability, 15*, 91–111.

IFSB. (2015a). *Islamic financial services industry stability report 2015*. Kuala Lumpur: Islamic Financial Services Board.

IFSB. (2015b). *Guidance note on quantitative measures for liquidity risk management in institutions offering Islamic financial services*. Kuala Lumpur: Islamic Financial Services Board-15.

IFSB. (2017). *Islamic financial services industry stability report 2017*. Kuala Lumpur: Islamic Financial Services Board.

Ismal, R. (2010). Assessing the demand and supply of liquidity in Islamic banking (the case of Indonesia). *ISRA International Journal of Islamic Finance, 2*(1), 85–110.

Khediri, K. B., Charfeddined, L., & Youssef, S. B. (2015). Islamic versus conventional banks in the GCC countries: A comparative study using classification techniques. *Research in International Business and Finance., 33*, 75–98.

Krasicka, O., & Nowak, S. (2012). What's in it for me? A primer on differences between Islamic and conventional finance in Malaysia. In *IMF Working Paper, WP/12/151*. Washington DC: International Monetary Fund.

Kumar, T. V. (2008). *Why liquidity is important for banks*. GT News Global Treasury Intelligence, London: The Global Treasurer.

Laštůvková, J. (2016). Liquidity determinants of the selected banking sectors and their size groups. *Acta Universitatis Agriculturae et Silviculturae Mendelianae Brunensis, 64*(3), 972–978.

Leykun, F. (2016). Determinants of commercial banks' liquidity risk: Evidence from Ethiopia. *Research Journal of Finance and Accounting, 7*(15), 47–61.

Maghrebi, N., & Mirakhor, A. (2015). Risk sharing and shared prosperity in Islamic finance. *Islamic Economic Studies, 23*(2), 85–115.

Mirakhor, A. (2012). Islamic finance, risk sharing and macroeconomic policies. *MPRA Paper No., 56338*, 1–42.

Mohamad, A. A. S., Mohamad, M. T., & Samsudin, M. L. (2013). How Islamic banks of Malaysia managing liquidity? An emphasis on confronting economic cycles. *International Journal of Business and Social Science, 4*(7), 253–263.

Mohammad, S. (2015). Liquidity risk Management in Islamic Banks: A survey. *Afro Eurasian Studies, 1*(2), 215–230.

Mongid, A. (2015). Liquidity risk Management in the Islamic Rural Banking: Evidence from Indonesia. *Banks and Bank Systems, 10*(3), 61–67.

Obiyathulla, I. P. (2008). The Islamic inter bank money market and a dual banking system: The Malaysian experience. *International Journal of Islamic and Middle Eastern Finance and Management, 1*(3), 210–226.

Ogilo, F., & Mugenyah, L. O. (2015). Determinants of liquidity risk of commercial banks in Kenya. *The International Journal of Business and Management, 3*(9), 256–265.

Poorman, F., & Blake, J. (2005). *Measuring and modelling liquidity risk: New ideas and metrics. FMS White Paper*. Chicago: Financial Managers Society Inc.

Praet, P., & Herzberg, V. (2008). In Financial Stability Review Banque de France (Ed.), *Market liquidity and banking liquidity: Linkages, vulnerabilities and the role of disclosure* (Vol. 11, pp. 95–109).

Pesaran, M. H., Shin, Y., & Smith, R. J. (2001). Bounds Testing Approaches to The Analysis of Level Relationships, *Journal of Applied Econometrics*, 16(3), 289–326.

Rashid, A., & Jabeen, S. (2016). Analysing performance determinants: Conventional versus islamic banks in Pakistan. *Borsa Istanbul Review., 16*(2), 92–107.

Roman, A., & Sargu, A. C. (2015). The impact of bank-specific factors on the commercial banks liquidity: Empirical evidence from CEE countries. *Procedia Economics and Finance, 20*(15), 571–579.

Saeed, M., & Izzeldin, M. (2014). Examining the relationship between default risk and efficiency in Islamic and conventional banks. *Journal of Economic Behavior and Organization, 132*. (Supplement, 127–154.

Verhoef, B., Azahaf, S., & Bijkerk, W. (2008). Islamic finance and supervision: An exploratory analysis. In *DNB Occasional Studies 6(3)*. Amsterdam: de Netherlandsche Bank.

Vodova, P. (2013). Determinants of commercial bank liquidity in Hungary. *Financial Internet Quarterly, e-Finanse, 9*(3), 64–71.

Wagner, W. (2007). The liquidity of bank assets and banking stability. *Journal of Banking & Finance, 31(1*, 121–139.

Yaacob, S. F., Abdul Rahman, A., & Abdul Karim, Z. (2016). The determinants of liquidity risk: A panel study of Islamic banks in Malaysia. *Journal of Contemporary Issues and Thought, 6*, 73–82.

Chapter 11
Fintech-Enabled Islamic Financial System and Financial Stability

Etsuaki Yoshida

11.1 Introduction

This chapter picks up recent trends of Islamic Fintech, and sheds light on its potential effects on the stability of a financial system. While growth of Islamic finance was evident not just in its market volume but in product development as well, the industry has often been criticized by academic scholars that the current practice of Islamic finance is not in the direction of pursuing its objective of the religion, or *Maqasid al-Shari'ah.* The industry offers Islamic derivatives, Islamic project finance, and Islamic asset management services using financial engineering technique, to name just a few, but those scholars are not satisfied with their functions and outcomes, as discussed later.

Meanwhile, a wave of development in information and communication technology (ICT) has completely reached the huge continent of the financial industry, and financial services highly enhanced by ICT are recently called "Fintech". Originally, money is conceptual existence, and theoretically, notes and coins contain no value by themselves under the current fiat money standard. Due to these natures, financial services are well-harmonized with ICT which deals with data processing, and we can expect infinite varieties of forms of financial services even in the near future.

Under these circumstances, preceding studies on the theme of Islamic Fintech are very limited, and the Google Scholar came up with only one result by the search of "Islamic Fintech". Rather, a section in the Islamic Financial Services Industry Stability Report 2017 (IFSB 2017) provides a comprehensive landscape of Islamic Fintech. It appears as one of emerging issues in Islamic finance, and wraps up *Shari'ah* compliance and regulatory aspects of Islamic Fintech.

E. Yoshida (✉)
Kyoto University, Kyoto, Japan

M. Zulkhibri et al. (eds.), *Islamic Monetary Economics and Institutions*,
https://doi.org/10.1007/978-3-030-24005-9_11

This chapter intends to identify how Islamic Fintech will best contribute to the industry in terms of *Maqasid al-Shari'ah*, as well as its potential effects on financial stability brought by the pursuit of the religious objective in its product development.

11.2 Fintech and Islamic Financial Products

11.2.1 Recent Trends

Fintech recently enjoys growing interests in the financial industry all over the world. The word itself did not even exist 10 years ago, but we are sure that it will give a huge impact on shapes of financial business in coming 10 years, or even shorter.

Islamic finance also enjoys benefit of this growing Fintech. Just a quick look at several stories depicts how Islamic Fintech is recently seen as a significant element that will make a big change in contents of Islamic financial services. The 22nd World Islamic Banking Conference held in 2015 in Bahrain picked up Fintech as one of the sessions of this prestigious industry event with the longest tradition among others. At the Global Islamic Finance Forum held in Malaysia in 2015, Governor of Bank Negara Malaysia mentioned Fintech as one of the three key issues of Islamic finance in his keynote speech.

In 2016, the Islamic Fintech Alliance was established in Malaysia by firms providing Islamic Fintech services including crowdfunding platform providers. Led by 'Ethis Ventures', other firms such as 'blossom', 'FundingLab', 'Easi', 'Narwi', 'LaunchGood', 'KapitalBoost', and 'Skolafund' joined the Alliance. RedMoney launched the "IFN Fintech" newsletter and held "IFN Fintech Forum", both in 2017. Several cities in the Middle East are making efforts to become an Islamic Fintech hub, as described in Economist (2017). Islamic Development Bank Group is now calling for business ideas of Islamic Fintech under the project called "Fintech Islamic Finance Challenge". The project is in collaboration with Spain's IE Business School and the Islamic Banker magazine.

Note that Fintech is a general and collective term and it has many varieties of financial services practiced now. A research firm called Venture Scanner categorized Fintech companies into 13 groups by their businesses: (1) lending, (2) personal finance, (3) payments, (4) equity financing, (5) remittances, (6) retail investing, (7) institutional investing, (8) security, (9) infrastructure, (10) business tools, (11) Crowdfunding, (12) online banking, and (13) research and data. This implies that we need to look at concrete forms of financial services among various types, when we talk about the actual transaction.

11.2.2 Historical Development of Islamic Financial Products

Historically, the practice of contemporary Islamic started with the establishment of Dubai Islamic Bank in 1975. The global market size is now estimated around US$ 2 trillion or more, as measured by *Shari'ah* compliant assets, showing geographical expansion of Islamic finance into more countries, not just within the Middle East and Southeast Asia, but also to emerging economies and even to Muslim-minority countries such as the United Kingdom, Singapore, Luxembourg, France, Japan, Hong Kong, and South Africa.

On the product front, it has continued to evolve, mainly in the direction of realizing the same function with conventional instruments, by skillful arrangement of financial and legal techniques. The industry has not been able to innovate and develop various types of new Islamic financial products. It is not too much to say that the product suite of Islamic finance is roughly similar to that of the conventional equivalent products. Table 11.1 shows in a chronological order the brief history of product development of Islamic finance.

11.2.3 Criticism by Academia Against the Current Practice

There is wide agreement among them that the majority of Islamic financial markets, or assets, should not be occupied by debt-based transactions, such as *Murabahah* and *Ijarah*, as it actually is today. This tendency is concisely represented by the phrase, "*Murabahah* Syndrome", a terminology by Yousef (2004). On top of that, Hasan (2010) criticizes that the industry does not care about the objective of Islamic finance, and hence, there is a mismatch between structure and objective of the religious economic behaviour. El-Gamal (2003) describes the current situation as "Islamic finance quickly turned to mimicking the interest-based conventional finance". In addition, Hamoudi (2007) calls the current situation as "Jurisprudential

Table 11.1 Chronological development of major Islamic financial products

Year	Content (main area of product development)
1950–63	Prototypes of financial institutions [South Asia, Egypt, Malaysia]
1975–79	Genuine practice of banking activity [Middle East, North Africa]
1979	*Takaful* [Sudan]
1986–93	Equity funds [US, Singapore, South Africa, etc.]
1990	*Sukuk* [Malaysia]
1994	Project finance (non- or limited-recourse financing) [Pakistan]
2005	Securitized (residential mortgage-backed) product [Malaysia]
2006	Exchange-traded fund (ETF) [Turkey]
2006	Derivatives (profit-rate swap) [UAE, Malaysia]

Source: author using various sources (for prototypes of Islamic financial institutions and Islamic banks in the industry's incipient stage, see (Wilson 1983; Lewis and Algaoud 2001) as major sources of information. Comprehensive history of Islamic finance, including financial products, is depicted in the literature of Iqbal and Molyneux (2005), including *Takaful* and *Sukuk*. For Islamic equity investment funds, Al-Rifai (1999) is of use. Dar (ed.) (2010) provides information on the first Islamic project finance, while details of Islamic RMBS is written in Leong (2014). Diaw et al. (2010) is a good reference on Islamic ETF, while Askari et al. (2010) refers to development of Islamic derivative products)

Schizophrenia" and De Lorenzo (2007) banters it as "*Shari'ah*-conversion technology". Also, Al-Zuhayli (2001) says, "The primary goal of Islamic financial institutions is not profit-making, but the endorsement of social goals of socio-economic development and the alleviation of poverty."

These opinions can be summarized as that principles of Islam prefer "equity-based" transactions to "debt-based" ones. Nagaoka (2012) calls this widespread preference among Islamic economists as "*Mudarabah* consensus". Kayed and Hassan (2010) recognize Islam as an "entrepreneurial religion", which makes equity-based financial transactions more appropriate than debt-based ones from the religious perspective. The original and major supporters of this idea were economists such as Umer Chapra, Nejatullah Siddiqi, and Osman Ahmed, who were called the "Jeddah School" by Zubair Hasan (2005).

Gainor (2000) describes this recognition in a very concise manner. "Much of the research and development that has worked its way into existing products in the marketplace has been generated from adapting conventional products. It may follow that if a product was successful in the conventional marketplace, then if successfully engineered as to not be inconsistent with Islamic *Shari'ah*, it should be successful in the Islamic marketplace." Thus, there is a cognitive dichotomy on the development of Islamic finance between practitioners and Islamic economists.

In short, the criticism by several Islamic economists mentioned earlier in this section can be categorized into two natures: One is the failure of product development in the direction of equity-based, summarized as "*Mudarabah* consensus" and "*Murabahah* syndrome" earlier. The failure of the current situation of this kind is a "Type I failure" of development of Islamic finance. The other kind of failure is that the current practice does not include enough social and religious elements, i.e. it does not contribute to poverty alleviation to increase equality in society. Let's describe this failure, hereafter, as "Type II failure" of development of Islamic finance.

11.3 How Fintech Can Respond to Criticisms Against the Current Practice

11.3.1 Against Type I Failure: More Equity-Based Transactions

As shown in the previous section, there are two kinds of failure in practical development of Islamic financial industry so far: Type I failure is the current debt-oriented practice, and Type II failure is lack of social aspects in financial transactions towards a more equal society. Fintech is considered to function as one of the solutions to these failures.

Type I failure will be mitigated by growth of Islamic equity crowdfunding, one of the forms of Fintech. From the beginning, equity transaction is more difficult to happen in the current financial system. Since the principal of a financial transaction is not protected, a provider of fund needs information on the investment target, which causes collectively higher transaction cost, and this is considered to be one of the reasons why debt-based transaction is dominant in the current financial system. A marginal solution to this issue was establishment of a fund, which is operated and managed by an investment professional with a lot of information on the investment target.

A Fintech-based economy is considered to show a different story. Figure 11.1 depicts a basic mechanism of crowdfunding. A platform on the internet provides information on each project for the sake of potential investors. If an individual decides to invest certain amount of money on the project he/she would like to support, he/she does so by clicking a relevant button on the website or the application software. The funds are provided typically in four ways; (1) donation, (2) reward (physical products such as manufactured goods), (3) loan, and (4) equity (Massolution 2015). If financial transactions are structured in the form of equity, it will be "equity crowdfunding", and if done in a *Shari'ah*-compliant manner with the evidence of *Shari'ah* screening as fatwa, it will be "Islamic equity crowdfunding".

Also, it might be much easier for a start-up company to collect US$100,000 from 1000 people (US$100 each) through crowdfunding than acquiring investment of the same amount from a private equity investment firm or an "angel". In this way, crowdfunding mechanism enabled by technology-based transmission of information will be able to enhance equity-based financial transactions, which is more desirable under the teaching of Islam.

It is not a conceptual dream and there are already several examples. An old and famous case is Shekra in Egypt. World Bank et al. (2015) describe an overview. More recently, a case in Malaysia should be regarded as a more organized framework of Islamic equity crowdfunding. It is called "Investment Account Platform", launched in 2015, which was initiated by Bank Negara Malaysia (BNM 2014). It provides an equity investment platform integrated for participating Islamic banks (see Fig. 11.2). Investors and venture companies are customers of them, and potential investors, with deposit account in any of these banks, can invest in any project

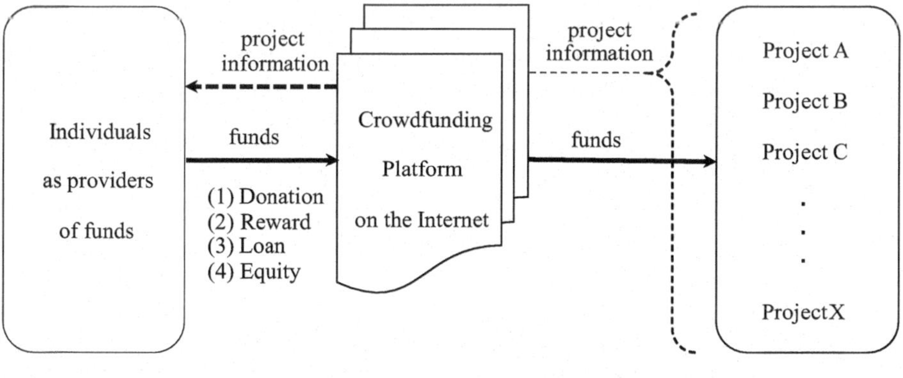

Fig. 11.1 Crowdfunding Mechanism. (Source: author's own illustration)

Fig. 11.2 Investment Account Platform. (Source: Investment Account Platform)

on the platform. The economic aim is to assist financing to SMEs and start-ups, but the qualitative aspect of this mechanism is in line with *Shari'ah* in the sense that those who have money provide funds to new businesses, in the form of equity, which has profit/loss sharing nature.

11.3.2 Against Type II Failure: Promoting Economic Fairness

For Type II failure, Fintech will be a powerful solution as well. Conceptually, use of ICT will make re-distribution of income from the rich to the lower-income group much easier. Above all, data on financial access (Fig. 11.3) shows that the ratio of the unbanked is high in the Middle East and South Asia, where there are a lot of Muslims. This fact suggests that promotion of Islamic Fintech is one of the keys to increasing financial inclusion on a global scale. Under these social and economic conditions, Islamic Fintech is going to play a bigger role. Let's see the crowdfunding-based cash *waqf* collection platform, called the *Waqf* World (Fig. 11.4). It was led by Tun Abudullah Badawi, the ex-Prime Ministry of Malaysia, and launched at the 12th World Islamic Economic Forum held in Jakarta in August 2016. The idea was reportedly first presented by Research Centre for Islamic Economics and Finance (EKONIS) of National University of Malaysia (UKM) at a forum held by IRTI in January 2016.

Fig. 11.3 Ratio of the Banked Population (%). (Source: Demirguc-Kunt et al. 2015)

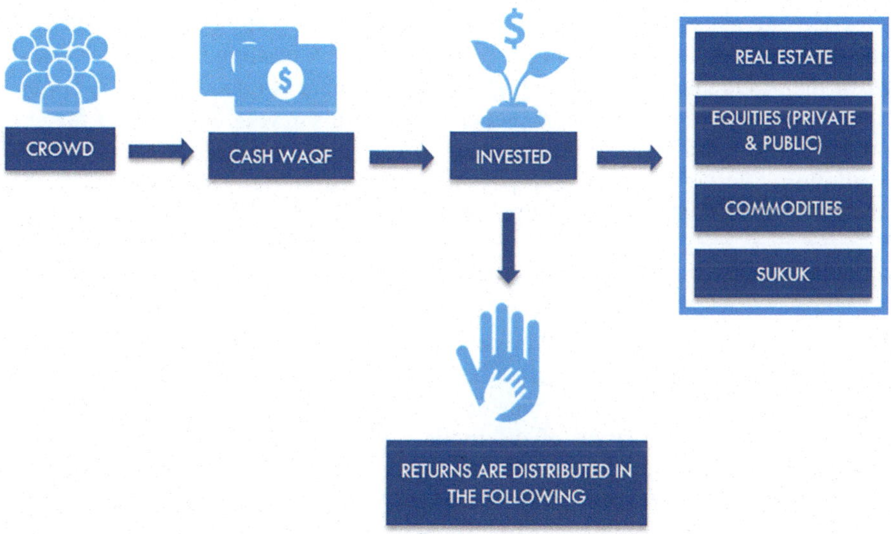

Fig. 11.4 Structure of *Waqf* World. (Source: *Waqf* World)

A potential donor (*waqif*) of cash *waqf* will go to the website of the *Waqf* World and provide details of *waqf* amount and the waqif him/herself. The collected funds will be invested into real estate, equities (private and public), commodities, and *sukuk*, to name just a few, in a *Shari'ah*-compliant manner, and the profit gained from those investments will be distributed to the people in need. Operation of this platform, including technological aspect, is carried out by Ethis Ventures, which usually offers Islamic equity crowdfunding platform.

Zakat is also recognized as income re-distribution system in Islam. The actual operations of collection and re-distribution of funds vary among countries and communities, but there are already many online *zakat* payment systems, offered by banks, payment service companies, local governments, and religious organizations. Basically, these are just simple online payment, but Fintech will be able to structure a better-organized *zakat* collection and management system.

Let's consider the following hypothetical case as an example of a Fintech-enabled *zakat* system. As an assumption, most people in a jurisdiction have smartphones, in which a comprehensive *zakat* management application is installed. The *zakat* management institution is able to provide information on the potential usage of the funds collected. Personal information (name, registration number, bank account, etc.) of each zakat payer and *nisab* (annual required amount of *zakat*) are given to the *zakat* management institution.

Figure 11.5 shows a brief structure of a Fintech-enabled *zakat* system with "usage-choice" option. During the specific payment period (within a year), the *zakat* payer will find, in the *zakat* management application in his/her smartphone, many concrete projects which require money as *zakat* receiving purposes (such as financial assistance for the low-income people, mosque and madrasa-related constructions, to name just a few). The payer will choose several projects he/she likes, and make a remittance from his/her bank account, by pushing some buttons in the *zakat* management application. The total paid amount is managed by the application. By the deadline of the payment period after finishing the selection of favoured projects, the *zakat* payer will pay the rest of *nisab* to the *zakat* management institution. Of course, he/she can pay the total *nisab* to selected projects, or even more than *nisab*, and the excess amount above the *nisab* will be considered as *Sadaqa*, or voluntary donation.

What are the strong points of this proposed system, especially in terms of the religious values? The first is the increased consciousness of *Ummah*. Under the traditional *zakat* system, the payer makes a payment with ambiguous recognition about the usage of funds. Theoretically, *zakat* is compulsory under the religion and payment itself has the religious meaning, but practically, people should be happier if they know the destination of the funds. Another strong point is transparency, which leads to decreasing *gharar*, or ambiguity. As each *zakat* payer provides funds based on all the information about the usage of funds on the platform, they can know the usage and have no concerns about unintended use of funds.

All these become possible by broader use of ICT. Of course, there is a need to prepare such application software, *Shari'ah* and legal framework, account management system and project sourcing and management structure in a *zakat* management institution, public awareness, and so forth. A Fintech-enhanced financial system that contributes to increasing economic fairness is worth considering practically for governments, financial authorities, and communities for the great public benefit. It is also a big advantage that penetration rate of mobile phones and smartphones is rather high even in lower-income countries.

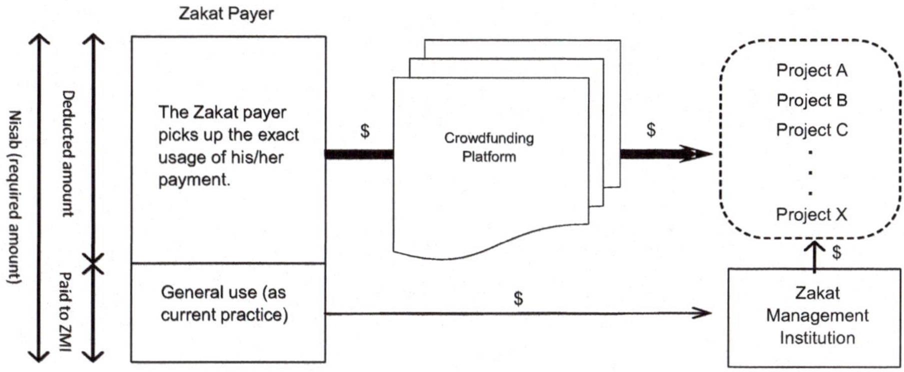

Fig. 11.5 *Zakat* System with "Usage-Choice" Option. (Source: author's own illustration)

11.4 How Islamic Fintech Contributes to Financial Stability

11.4.1 Ideal of Islamic Finance and the Dual Banking System

In this study, the story was only on Islamic finance in terms of its history and the status quo mainly focusing on Islamic Fintech. This study gives comparative positioning of Islamic finance (and Fintech) by including the existence of a conventional financial system in order to better understand the effects of growing Islamic finance on the stability of a comprehensive financial system.

Globally, Islamic finance occupies less than 1% of the financial market in terms of asset. IFSB (2017) says the world's total assets of Islamic finance amount to US$2 trillion, while IMF estimates the global financial assets around US$300 trillion. Even in many Muslim-majority countries, the share of Islamic banking over the total banking assets is not necessarily the majority, rather around 20–40% even in leading markets of Islamic finance such as Malaysia and GCC, as seen in Fig. 11.6.

This situation makes a practical approach, with the assumption of the dual banking system, more plausible than a theoretical (and ideal) approach just under *Shari'ah*. In the first place, existence of conventional financial system gives positive effects on Islamic financial system in terms of liquidity, product development, financial literacy among stakeholders, and regulatory framework among others (Zulkhibri et al. 2016). In this sense, we can recognize that there is "institutional complementarity" between a conventional financial system and Islamic equivalent. In this context, of course, an Islamic financial system depends a lot on the conventional financial system, but the opposite can also be considered and is discussed later.

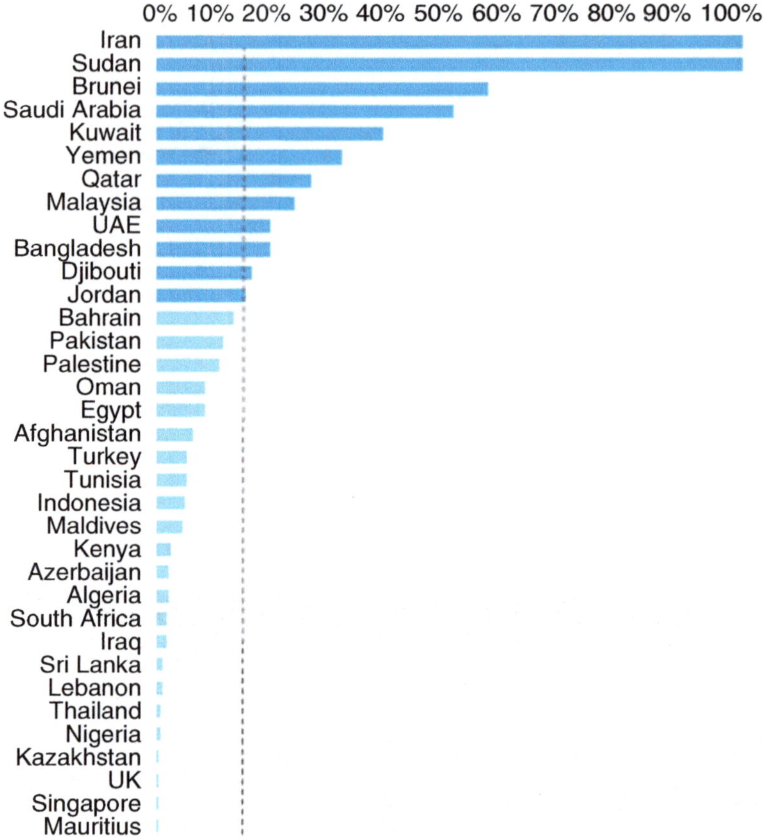

Fig. 11.6 Share of Islamic Banking. (Source: IFSB 2017)

11.4.2 Potential Positive Effects on Financial Stability

Islamic Fintech can contribute to promoting economic fairness in a society and to increase equity-based financial transactions. When it happens, financial stability is theoretically improved through the following two channels.

One is the channel of financial inclusion. If financial inclusion is achieved to some extent, it gives positive effects on economic growth, which contributes to financial stability, according to Sahay et al. (2015). Also, Islamic Financial Services Board (IFSB) is positive towards financial inclusion, by holding a seminar on the theme in Jakarta in 2015 and launching a financial inclusion task force this year. Basically, the aim of IFSB is to promote financial stability as an international standard setting body. Under the recognition that financial inclusion leads to financial stability, IFSB is expected to continue the effort on enhancing financial inclusion.

The other channel is through increasing diversity in market participants and in increasing flow of funds. Theoretically, a financial system composed of diversified elements is more stable and resilient against one external shock than a less-diversified financial system. Mr. Toshihiko Fukui, ex-Governor of Bank of Japan, once said in a seminar on Islamic Finance, "Growth of Islamic finance will increase diversity in financial markets, which is important in terms of stability of the global financial system. Higher diversity provides higher robustness in financial markets and financial system, compared to a situation with only uniformed market participants and simple transactions."

11.5 Conclusion

This chapter picks up the emerging trend of Islamic Fintech and its application to Islamic financial products, which are more Islamic, and discusses its positive potential effects on financial stability through the channels of financial inclusion and diversity of flow of funds.

Increased use of ICT in financial services is expected to create huge changes, and so is to Islamic finance as well. Fintech will reduce the cost related to supply and consumption of financial services, but there is more than that. This chapter sorted out those benefits of using Fintech by describing positive effects in terms of *Shari'ah* as increase in equity-based transactions and in social finance, *waqf* and *zakat*. This enhances financial inclusion and diversity in flow of funds, which theoretically brings about higher degree of financial stability.

The second *Caliph*, Umar, is considered to have said, if he were to live longer, he would see to it that even a shepherd on the Mount Sana'a received his share from his wealth, according to Bukhari. Under the context of Fintech, the story can be interpreted as follows: if the *Caliph* lived longer enough until the days when smartphone is available to everybody and donation is easily done on the palm, a shepherd in the Mount Sana'a could have received the donation from the *Caliph* living in Madinah.

The voyage with Fintech has just begun. It is a big challenge for the human society whether we can fully utilize the powerful tool for qualitative development of financial system in terms of *Shari'ah*, and financial stability as part of *maslahah* (public interest), or we just end with having more efficient financial transactions.

References

Al-Rifai, T. (1999). *Islamic equity funds: A brief industry analysis*. Failaka International Inc.

Al-Zuhayli D. W. (2001). *Islamic Jurisprudence and its Proofs*. (translation by El-Gamal, M.A.) Damascus: Dar al-Fikr.

Askari, H., Iqbal, Z., & Mirakhor, A. (2010). *Globalization and Islamic finance: Convergence, prospects, and challenges*. Singapore: John Wiley & Sons (Asia).

BNM. (2014). *Financial stability and payment systems report 2014*. Kuala Lumpur: Bank Negara Malaysia.

De Lorenzo, Y. T. (2007). *The Total returns swap and the Shari'ah conversion technology stratagem*. New York: Dinar Standard.

Demirgüç-Kunt, A., Klapper, L. F., Singer, D., and Van Oudheusden, P. (2015). The Global Findex Database 2014: Measuring Financial Inclusion Around the *World, World Bank Policy Research Working Paper No. 7255*. Washington, DC: World Bank.

Diaw, A., Hassan, S., & Ng, A. B. K. (2010). Performance of Islamic and conventional exchange traded funds in Malaysia. *ISRA International Journal of Islamic Finance, 2*(1), 131–149.

Economist. (2017). *The race to become Islamic banking's fintech hub.*

El-Gamal, M. A. (2003). "Interest" and the paradox of contemporary Islamic law and finance. *Fordham International Law Journal, 27*, 1.

Gainor, T. (2000). *A practical approach to product development*. A paper prepared for the fourth Harvard University Forum on Islamic Finance.

Hamoudi, H. A. (2007). Jurisprudential schizophrenia: On form and function in Islamic finance. *Chicago Journal of International Law, 7*(2), 605–622.

Hasan, Z. (2005). Islamic banking at the crossroads: Theory versus practice. In M. Iqbal & R. Wilson (Eds.), *Islamic perspectives on wealth creation* (pp. 11–25). Edinburgh: Edinburgh University Press.

Hasan, Z. (2010). *Islamic finance: Structure-objective mismatch and its consequences*. A paper presented at the workshop on Islamic finance at the business school Strasbourg University, France, on March 17, 2010.

IFSB. (2017). *Islamic financial services industry stability report 2017*. Kuala Lumpur: Islamic Financial Services Board.

Iqbal, M., & Molyneux, P. (2005). *Thirty years of Islamic banking: History, performance and prospects*. New York: Palgrave Macmillan.

Kayed, R. N. and Hassan, M. K. (2010). *Islamic entrepreneurship*. Durham Modern Middle East and Islamic World. New York: Routledge.

Leong, C. C. (2014). *Development of securitisation in Malaysia – Cagamas experience*. A presentation made at the Indonesia International Conference on Islamic Finance Surabaya, Indonesia, 3–4 November 2014.

Lewis, M. K., & Algaoud, L. M. (2001). *Islamic banking*. Cheltenham: Edward Elgar.

Massolution. (2015). *2015CF: The crowdfunding industry report*. Toronto: The National Crowdfunding Association of Canada.

Nagaoka, S. (2012). Critical overview of the history of Islamic economics: Formation, transformation, and new horizons. *Asian and African Area Studies, 11*(2), 114–336.

Sahay, R., Cihak, M., N'Diaye, P., Barajas, A., Mitra, S., Kyobe, A., Mooi, Y. N., & Yousefi, S. R. (2015). Financial inclusion: Can it meet multiple macroeconomic goals? In *IMF staff discussion note SDN/15/17*. Washington DC: International Monetary Fund.

Wilson, R. (1983). *Banking and finance in the Arab Middle East*. London: Macmillan.

World Bank. (2015). Islamic Development Bank, and Islamic Research and Training Institute. In *Leveraging Islamic Finance for Small and Medium Enterprises (SMEs), Joint WB-IDB Policy report*. Washington DC: World Bank.

Yousef, T. M. (2004). The *Murabaha* syndrome in Islamic finance: Laws, institutions and politics. In C. M. Henry & R. Wilson (Eds.), *The politics of Islamic finance* (pp. 63–80). Edinburgh: Edinburgh University Press.

Zulkhibri, M., Ismail, A. G., & Hidayat, S. E. (Eds.). (2016). *Macroprudential regulation and policy for the Islamic financial industry: Theory and applications*. New York: Springer.

Glossary of Arabic Terms

Transliterated from original arabic word	English meanings
'adl	Justice, equity, fairness
'āmil ('ummāl)	Worker(s), manager(s), entrepreneur(s)
'aqār ('aqārāt)	Immovable property(ies), building(s)
'aqd ('uqūd)	Contract(s), agreement(s), bond(s)
'arbun/'urbūn	Down payment
'īnah	Debt buying and selling
'iwaḍ	Compensation
'urf	Custom, usage, common practice
al-ghunm bi alghurm	Earning profit is legitimized by risk taking. Earning is subject to taking risk
al-kharāj bi aldamān	Revenue is subject to liability
al-mujāzafah	Speculation
amānah	Trust, honesty, trustworthiness
bay'al-murābaḥah	Mark-up sale
bay'(buyū')	Sale(s)
bay'al-'urbūn	Sale with down payment
bay'al-dayn	Sale of debt
bay'al-kālī' bi-alkālī'	A sale in which both the delivery of the object of sale and the payment of its price are delayed. It is similar to a modern forward sale contract
bay'al-salam	Sale in which payment is made in advance by the buyer and the delivery of goods is deferred by the seller
bay'al-wafa'	Buyback sale, sale and repurchase
bay'bi al-taqsīt	Sale at instalments
bay'bi al-thaman al-ājil	Credit sale or sale at deferred payment
bay'mu'ajjal	Credit sale or sale at deferred payment

(continued)

M. Zulkhibri et al. (eds.), *Islamic Monetary Economics and Institutions*,
https://doi.org/10.1007/978-3-030-24005-9

Transliterated from original arabic word	English meanings
bay'-al-'inah	Buying an object for cash and then selling it to the same party for a higher price whose payment is deferred so that the purchase and sale of the object serve as a ruse for lending on interest
bayt al-māl	Treasury
dalīl	Proof, evidence, reason
ḍamān	Guarantee
ḍarar	Harm
ḍarūrah	Necessity
ḍarūrīyāt	Basic needs
dayn (duyūn)	Debt(s)
dhimmah (dhimam)	Liability(ies), responsibility(ies)
dīnār	Dinar (currency)
dirham	Dirham (currency)
fā'id (fawa'id)	Surplus(ses), excess(es)
fadl	Excess, additional, surplus
faqīh (fuqaha')	Jurist(s)
faqir (fuqara')	Poor person(s)
fatwa (fatāwá)	Religious verdict(s) made by a *faqih*-competent *Shari'ah* scholar
fiqh	Islamic jurisprudence
fiqh al-mu'āmalāt	Jurisprudence of transactions
fiqhī	Juristic
ghabn/ghubn	Misappropriation or defrauding others in respect of specifications of the goods and their prices
ghanīmah (ghana'im)	Spoils of war, booty(ies)
gharar	Excessive risk and uncertainty, ambiguity
gharar fāḥish	Excessive risk
gharar yasīr	Minor risk
ghārim (ghārimīn)	Indebted, bankrupt
ḥādīth (aḥādīth)	Sayings of the Prophet Mohammed. Plural of *Hadith*
hadiyyah (hadāya)	Gift(s), donation(s)
ḥalāl	Permissible, lawful, allowed
ḥarām	Not permissible, unlawful, not allowed
ḥawālah	Bill of exchange, promissory note, cheque, draft
hibah (hibat)	Donation(s), gift(s)
ḥīlah (ḥiyal)	Trick(s), ploy(s), ruse(s)
ḥisbah	Ombudsman, regulation
ḥukm (aḥkām)	Ruling, decision
iḥsān	Benevolence, compassion, kindness
ijāb	Offer (in contract)
ijārah	Leasing, rent

Transliterated from original arabic word	English meanings
ijārah muntahia-bitamlīk	Hire purchase
ijārah wa-iqtina'	Hire purchase
islām	Submission, peace
istiṣnā'	Manufacturing contract whereby a manufacturer agrees to produce (build) and deliver a well-described good (or premise) at a given price on a given date in the future
istithmār	Investment
ju'ālah	Commission, fee, wage
kafālah	Guarantee
kafīl	Guarantor
khamr (khumur)	Intoxicant(s)
kharāj	A levy on land use, revenue
khayr	Good, beneficial
khiyār	Choice, option
khiyār al-shart	Optional condition
khiyār al-wasf	Optional specifications
khums	One fifth
khusrān	Loss, failure
madhhab (madhāhib)	School(s) of Islamic jurisprudence, regime(s), system(s)
mafsadah (mafāsid)	Spoiler(s)
māl (amwāl)	Capital, money, property, wealth
manfa'ah (manāfi')	Benefit(s), utility(ies), usufruct(s)
maqsad (maqāṣid al-sharī'ah)	Objectives of Islamic law
maṣlaḥah (maṣāliḥ) mursalah	General benefits, public interest(s)
mawqūf	Suspended
maysir	Gambling
mithlī	Similar
mu'āmalah (mu'āmalāt)	Transactions
mubāḥ	Permissible
muḍārabah	A partnership whereby one party the capital owner provides capital to an entrepreneur to undertake a business activity. Profits are shared between them as agreed, but any financial loss is borne only by the capital owner as his loss is his unrewarded efforts put into the business activity
muḍārib	The partner in *Mudarabah* contract providing work, entrepreneurship, and management
mufti	Jurist who provides legal *Shari'ah* opinions

(continued)

Transliterated from original arabic word	English meanings
mughārassah	Share-cropping between two parties, whereby one provides land, equipment, and shoots of trees and the other agrees to plant the trees and take care of them in return for a share in the harvest or the profit
mujtahid	Legal expert or a jurist who exerts great effort in deriving a legal opinion
muqāraḍah	Same meaning like *Mudarabah*
muqāyadah	Barter
murābaḥah	Mark-up sale, sale at a margin
musāqāh	A sharecropping contract whereby the owner of a garden/orchard shares the produce with a worker in return for his services in irrigating the garden/orchard
musāwamah	Bargaining on price, haggling
mushārakah	Partnership whereby all the partners contribute capital for a business venture. The partners share profits on a pre-agreed ratio, while losses are shared according to each partner's capital contribution
mushārakah mutanāqiṣah	Diminishing partnership
mushtarik	Participant
mustahab	Meritorious
mutawallī	Manager, director
muzāra'ah	A sharecropping contract whereby one party agrees to provide land, seeds, and equipment and the other do the work needed in return for a part of the produce of the land
qāḍi	Judge
qarḍ (qurūḍ)	Loan(s)
qarḍ ḥasan	Interest-free loan
qīmah (qiyam)	Value(s)
qimār	Gambling
Qur'ān	The sacred book of Islam
qurūḍ	Loans
ra's al-māl ru'ūs al-amwāl	Capital(s)
rabb al-māl arbāb al-māl	Capital owner(s)
rahn	Collateral, pledge, guarantee
ribā	Usury, interest
ribā al-buyū'	Usury of trade. Another name for *Riba al-fadl*
ribā al-duyūn	Interest/usury of debt. Another name for *Riba al-nasi'ah*
ribā al-faḍl	Difference in exchanging two similar commodities
ribā al-nasī'ah/ alnasa'	Interest-based lending for the delay in repayment
ribā al-qurūḍ	Interest on loans
ribḥ (arbāḥ)	Profit(s)
ṣadaqah jāriyah	Perpetual charity
ṣadaqāt	Charity(ies)

Transliterated from original arabic word	English meanings
sadd al-dharī'ah	Prohibition of a deed which, if permitted, may lead to another prohibited deed
ṣakk (ṣukūk)	Asset based or asset backed financial certificate(s)
salaf	Loan. Another name for Salam
salam	Forward sale where the price of a specific good is paid in advance for its delivery at a specified time in the future
sanad (sanadāt)	Bond(s)
ṣarf	Currency exchange
sharākah	Partnership
shari'ah	Islamic law
sharikah (sharikāt)	Company(ies), enterprise(s), partnership(s)
sharikat 'uqūd	Contractual partnership
sharikat abdān	A partnership company based on the skills of professionals working together and sharing the proceeds
sharikat amwāl	Financial partnership
sharikat 'inān	Limited liability partnership
sharikat milk	Joint property partnership
sharikat mufawadah	Unlimited liability partnership
sharikat sanāi'	A partnership company based on the skills of professionals working together and sharing the proceed. Same as *sharikat abdān*
sharikat wujūh	A partnership company based on the credibility and creditworthiness of the partners
sharṭ	Condition
sukūk	Equity-based certificates of investment
ta'āwun	Cooperation
tabarru' (tabarru'āt)	Donation(s), gift(s), charity(ies)
tadāwul	Circulation, dealing
taḥawwuṭ	Hedging
takāful	Solidarity, mutual support
takaful ta'awuni	Cooperative risk-sharing and mutual insurance
tawakkul	Trust in God
tawarruq	The process of buying a commodity at a deferred price, in order to sell it in cash at a lower price. Usually, the sale is to a third party, with the aim to obtain cash. This is the classical form *Tawarruq* that is permissible. Organized *Tawarruq* where the bank plays both the roles of the seller and buyer is not permissible according to the majority of contemporary *fuqaha'* (jurists, scholars)
tijārah	Business, commerce, trade
ujrah	Allowance, commission, fee, salary, wage
uṣūl al-fiqh	Islamic legal bases
wa'd (wu'ūd)	Promise(s), undertaking(s)

(continued)

Transliterated from original arabic word	English meanings
wadī'ah (wadā'i')	Deposit(s)
Wakālah (wakālat)	Agency is a contract whereby one party appoints another party to perform a certain task on its behalf, usually for payment of a fee or a commission
wakil (wukalā')	Representative(s), agent(s)
wali	Guardian
waqf (awqāf)	Endowment(s), foundation(s), trust(s)
zakāh, zakāt	Obligatory contribution or poor due payable by all Muslims having wealth above *nisab* (threshold or exemption limit)
zakāt al-fiṭr	Poll tax payable on every Muslim at the end of Ramadan (the month of fasting)
zakāt al-māl	An annual levy on the wealth of a Muslim (above a certain level). The rate paid differs according to the type of property owned
zakāt al-rikāz	Levy on treasure trove
zakāt al-tijārah	Levy on business
ẓulm	Injustice, oppression, and exploitation

Source: IRTI

Index

M. Zulkhibri et al. (eds.), *Islamic Monetary Economics and Institutions*,
https://doi.org/10.1007/978-3-030-24005-9

Printed by Printforce, the Netherlands